Living on Wilderness Time

LIVING ON
Wilderness
Time

Melissa Walker

To Bonnie,
With loving memories
of living on our own
sweet time!
Merry christmas, 2004
Love. Syl

UNIVERSITY OF VIRGINIA PRESS
CHARLOTTESVILLE AND LONDON

University of Virginia Press
© 2002 by Melissa Walker
Printed in the United States of America on acid-free paper

First published 2002
First paperback edition published 2003
ISBN 0-8139-2110-4 (paper)

9 8 7 6 5 4 3 2 1

The Library of Congress has cataloged the hardcover edition as follows:

LIBRARY OF CONGRESS CATALOGING-IN-PUBLICATION DATA
Walker, Melissa.
  Living on wilderness time / Melissa Walker.
      p.   cm.
  ISBN 0-8139-2109-0 (cloth : alk. paper)
  1. Wilderness areas—West (U.S.) 2. Walker, Melissa—Journeys—West (U.S.)
I. Title.
  QH76.5.W34 W36 2002
  333.78′2′0978—dc21

                                                          2001008483

*The paper used in this publication is New Age TCF, produced without chlorine
compounds and blended with acid-free pulps from non-old-growth forests.*

Contents

Preface

WILD NATURE was once my playground. Throughout childhood I lived with my parents and sister in the last house on the edge of a small town in the coastal plains of southeast Georgia. My wilderness started across the road in the woods on the other side of cotton fields. Summer days were spent mostly out-of-doors. My father passed on to me a love of forests, swamps, freshwater springs, and the Oconee River, where we often ended our frequent family outings sitting on the bank listening to crickets, frogs, and the call of owls preparing for the hunt. My mother taught me to pay attention to birds, to notice their colors and songs and the trees and bushes where they nested and found food. She seemed to know almost to the day when the cedar waxwings were due to descend on the holly tree and eat every berry.

No one seemed to object when as a seven-year-old I set up a tent in the backyard and spent the night out alone. Nor did my aging parents blink when at the age of fifty-one I announced that I was leaving home for a while to go to the wilderness. I explained that the trip I was planning was the beginning of a new writing project. At that time—1993—I believed that I would have one more chance to make a major shift in my life's work, and I wanted a task that was big enough and important enough to hold my interest and consume my energy. After spending over a year completing a textbook about the growing number of threats to the environment, I was ready to take action and to choose one battle as my own. The possibilities were endless: global warming, toxic waste, urban sprawl, rain-forest destruction, declining atmospheric ozone, species loss, soil depletion, water and air pollution, diminishing wildlife habitat, and on and on. Of all the possible ways of joining forces with the millions of Americans concerned about the environment, I was most of all attracted to the preservation of wild places. The magic word for me was *wilderness*. I began to think of wilderness protection as a personal cause, but before I could really be effective, I had some learning to do about our National Wilderness Preservation System and about the Wilderness Act of 1964.

I clearly had two interrelated yet at times seemingly incompatible goals: I was looking for the contentment, peace, and solitude that I expected to find in remote parts of the natural world; at the same time I wanted to meet people who would teach me about wilderness and the ways that nature and culture intersect, who earn their living in nature, and who in various ways have escaped the pressures of urban living. Other than setting up a trip into the wilderness with a guide who would teach me some of the skills I would need, I had no plans. I would let chance and inclination determine what happened.

As I focused my energy in this way I had a growing desire for adventure, for new insights, for knowledge of wild places and natural processes that were unfamiliar to me. I was determined to turn a corner in my life, and I believed that time in the wilderness would make it possible, forcing me to slow down and simplify. The time for change had come.

The way I ordinarily lived my life, I often fell short of my intentions. I was chronically late, and my house was anything but immaculate. Once I arrived my usual seven minutes late for an eight o'clock class, only to find the academic dean standing at the door of my classroom. A few days after this embarrassment, I was kneeling on the floor in the bathroom to clean the tub before the arrival of houseguests. Pushing the shower curtain aside, I exposed a perfect mushroom growing in the grout beside the tub. Wildness was taking over.

Why did I take on more than I could handle? Probably for the same reasons that motivated millions of other American women who came of age in the sixties. Driving us were the expectations of family, workplace, and society, but most of all we drove ourselves. There was a part of me—and of most women I knew—that enjoyed being in charge of things, at home and at work. What I lacked was any understanding of where to draw the line.

My interest in wild lands, which would become a passion, provided a convenient justification for doing what I sensed was necessary for me to put my life in reasonable and sustainable balance. As it turned out, my instincts were right. No one tried to argue with me when I announced that I intended to go on the road for an indefinite period of time to learn about American wilderness and to write about it. Several friends and acquaintances asked if they could join me, but I declined, explaining that what I was up to required solitude. The one exception was my friend Marjorie. We agreed that she would join me for a few days when she had a break in her treatment for breast cancer.

The prospect of disconnecting from all social responsibilities was immensely appealing, and once I began to imagine what such freedom might be like, I decided to liberate myself. I did have some practice in detaching myself from my daily life. Writing articles and books had required that I hide away now and then, but except for three weeks on Ossabaw Island at a retreat for writers and artists, the most time I'd had away for writing was four or five days. Secluded in a friend's mountain cabin, I would work all day and into the night, sleep a good eight hours, and wake to do it all over again. I did not take the time for reflection or exploring the natural world outside the cabin door.

When I left home this time, I thought of wilderness as the location for the fieldwork I needed to do to learn more about the natural world and what threatens it, and also as a laboratory for my own growth and the changes I wanted to make. For once my personal desires and public aspirations were one. I wanted to be away from the city. I wanted to be alone with nothing in particular that had to be done. I wanted to learn firsthand about our National Wilderness Preservation System, and I wanted to write about it. I was brimming with excitement and newfound energy as I prepared to enter unknown territory.

In 1993 I took off from home on the first of three solitary trips extending over a fifteen-month period and totaling more than two hundred days. *Living on Wilderness Time* grew out of events during this time. The process and way of life that began for me then continues to this day, and I expect it will shape the rest of my life. My destination was Wilderness with a capital *W,* the kind that I assumed could only be found west of the Mississippi somewhere beyond the Great Plains.

The story begins with an account of two trial runs—one in late March in the Sky Islands of southern Arizona, the other in late June and early July in and near wilderness in Yosemite National Park. I wanted to find out what it would be like to camp alone in remote places. Could I sleep on the ground night after night? Could I tolerate the absence of nearby showers? Would I be afraid? The answer to all these questions turned out to be "yes." Sleep had never been so profound; showers could be bought or begged.

Fear was another matter. On the road and in the wild, fear had to be reckoned with, and I learned to pay attention when body sensations alerted me to danger. Any number of situations could trigger a sudden chill to the bone—the rooting of bears outside my tent; a trail that without warning turned into a narrow ledge on the edge of a precipice; flashes of lightning instantaneously followed by deafening thunder and hailstones the size of golf balls; the sound of gunshots or the growl of a menacing canine; an icy road and blinding snow; and the suspicious behavior of other human beings. To my surprise I found the sensations of fright would dissipate when I thought that I'd done all I could to protect myself. Having hurried down the side of a mountain away from towering trees, I sat out a thunderstorm in relative calm, transfixed by lightning bolts striking the mesa above. As it turned out, the hazards of wild weather were far more threatening than wild animals. Yet fear was only an occasional visitor. Most of the time I felt comfortable, safe, and at peace. Morning after morning I awoke eager for what the day would bring, and night after night I quickly drifted into a deep, undisturbed sleep.

The excitement of those first two forays into the wild was all it took for me to make a commitment to set out on my own in earnest. The first leg of what I thought of as the real journey began a month after I returned from Yosemite when I headed west from Atlanta on a scorching August afternoon, and it ended ninety days later when I pulled into the lane in front of my house on a crisp fall morning in November. On the first night out I drove across the Mississippi and found a campsite in the woods north of Little Rock. I crossed Texas in a day, took my time traveling through eastern New Mexico, and spent two nights in a forest next to Rocky Mountain National Park. Swinging north and coming into Wyoming, I was surrounded by those wide-open spaces I'd dreamed about. Nearby were some of the most remote wildernesses in the Lower 48. Less than a week after leaving home, I set up camp on the banks of the Popo Agie River on the edge of Lander, Wyoming. There I reflected on the meaning of the trek I was undertaking. In those first days I learned about feedlots, grazing rights, and ranching as well as wildlife and wilderness survival; I enjoyed the benefits of solitude and the delights of meeting people whose lives were very different from mine. I was sometimes frightened and always thrilled by close—and not so close—encounters with wild animals. By the time I emerged from the wilds of the Wind River Range in Wyoming, I'd been broken in, my city habits replaced by ways more appropriate to the remote country of the West. I was ready to be taught by the people I would meet and the places I would enter.

The northwest corner of Wyoming, dominated by Yellowstone and Grand Teton National Parks, has millions of visitors a year, and no part of their combined two and a half million acres is designated wilderness. Maps of our National Wilderness System give no indication of the extensive backcountry in these parks, but the Park Service is under a legal mandate to manage it as if it were designated wilderness. That story is being played out in Glacier, the Grand Canyon, the Smoky Mountains, and elsewhere throughout the park system, but I knew nothing about all this on the August evening when I entered Yellowstone for the first time.

I was thrilled to be in grizzly territory, to encounter a herd of buffalo beside the road, to come close to a huge moose, and to hike down the trail wondering what was beyond the bend. From there I traveled through the greater Yellowstone ecosystem toward Glacier National Park in northern Montana, where once again I was in the land of large predators. Warnings about grizzlies and mountain lions in campgrounds and on trails kept me feeling alert and very much alive.

By early September I was in the temperate rain forest of the Olympic National Park, and from there I traveled to the Glacier Peak Wilderness, which lies less than two hundred miles away as the crow and raven fly. Lacking wings, I had to travel back to Seattle and then work my way north and east to the foot of Lake Chelan, where I parked my van, took a ferry up the lake, and then traveled fifteen miles inland by bus to Holden, Washington, an old mining village at the edge of the wilderness. Some effects of mining on the natural world, such as mountainsides covered with ugly and toxic tailings, were obvious; others—hollowed out mountains, streams with no sign of life, mornings without birdsong—were obscured by surface beauty. Heading for the backcountry, much of which is protected, I suppressed memories of the harsh reality of mining and lost myself on the trails and beside the lakes and streams of the North Cascades.

After two weeks in Holden I was back on the road traveling south and west to Oregon. In the Mount Hood Wilderness I encountered the kind of wildness associated with people who use firearms, not just to kill animals but also to intimidate those who might interfere with their activities in the more than two million acres of designated wilderness in Oregon that stretch south from Mount Hood to California. Yet to come were surprising adventures in the canyon lands of southern Utah, the Grand Canyon, the Navajo Nation, and on both the Mexican and American sides of the Rio Grande.

Back in Atlanta in early November, I tried to sort out what I'd experienced and to consider the significance of what I'd learned. Having set myself the task of understanding our National Wilderness Preservation System and wrapping that undertaking into a personal adventure, I was acutely aware of how many questions remained unanswered. By late January of 1994 I was preparing for the second and shortest leg of my journey, this time to the Everglades and other parts of wild Florida. (At almost a million and a half acres, Florida has approximately the same amount of federally designated wilderness as the other states east of the Mississippi combined, most of it in the Everglades.) Then in early August I said goodbye to family and friends once more and set out on the third leg of the journey I'd started a year before. Again I left home without a specific destination, and again luck was with me.

For the next three months, I visited radically different human communities, all close to wilderness. Among them was Sturgis, South Dakota, where hundreds of thousands of motorcyclists convene every August; the isolated village of Haines in southeast Alaska, where people share their backyards with moose and grizzly bear; and Paradise, Montana, a small logging town where residents gather in the summer for an annual grave-digging party. The wildernesses I visited are equally diverse. Among them are the tall-grass prairie of the Sage Creek in the Badlands in South Dakota; the rugged, sharp summits and more benign valleys of the Cloud Peak in eastern Wyoming; the rock, ice, and calving glaciers in the Mount Baker Wilderness; the island wildernesses of southeast Alaska; and the vast Gila of southern New Mexico.

Even those who travel constantly can see only a small fraction of the 106 million acres of the National Wilderness Preservation System. After the first two hundred days I spent exploring wild places, I knew why wilderness is important, and I also knew something about mining, logging, prospecting for oil, development, grazing, agriculture, and the other human activities that threaten it. I was no expert, but I had learned enough to want to know more.

My last sustained stay on the third leg of my journey was in the Gila Wilderness in southern New Mexico. The first night there I huddled in my tent trying to keep warm as winter blew in and temperatures dropped below twenty degrees, but day broke with a warming sun, inviting me to come out and explore. It seemed appropriate to end my journey in the Gila, the first designated wilderness in the world. After years of dedicated effort, Aldo Leopold succeeded in bringing about the protection of 574,000 acres of this wild land in 1924, some forty years before the passage of the Wilderness Act in 1964. Without Leopold, there might not be a National Wilderness Preservation System.

In this historic place I looked back on my journey and tried to remember all that I had seen. The feelings associated with the memories varied from serenity to terror. The common thread was the growing awareness that in the wild I could not call the shots in anything but the smallest matters. I could decide what to eat, when to sleep, how to protect myself against the weather, whether to climb a mountain or start down a trail, and when to break camp. But I could have no predictable effect on the behavior of bears rooting around my tent in the Popo Agie Wilderness, a bighorn sheep approaching me on a narrow trail in the Grand Canyon, a mountain lion announcing its desires with a screeching growl in the rain forest of the Olympic Peninsula, or the destination of a lightning bolt in the wilds of New Mexico.

It was in the wilderness that I began to understand that efforts to influence the behavior of people I know were as futile as trying to change the habits of animals in the wild. At the beginning of the journey I didn't know that the peace and calm I found sitting by a wild river waiting for dark would be available to me at home once I'd learned to choose my responsibilities with care, respecting the choices of others the way I respected grizzly bears and other wild creatures. There was a time in my life when I was driven by ego and the assumption that success in life was achieved by individual effort. This way of thinking gradually dissolved during my time in the wilderness, as day after day I confronted the hidden structures that bind life to life. Each part of nature is directly or indirectly connected to every other part of the natural world. Humans are no exception.

My desires had shifted from an urgent yearning to accomplish something substantial on my own to wanting to play a part in an enduring communal undertaking. Working to preserve the last wild places in America is a slow and arduous process, but the rewards far outweigh the cost. What continually motivates wilderness advocates is the pleasure of working with kindred spirits, the intensely interesting topics that the work addresses, and the personal renewal that springs from signing on to a project valuing all life-forms, including human life.

The story that follows was first recorded as notes I kept during my travels; in the years following I shaped it into a narrative, and as I write these words in the summer of the year 2001, I am looking back at the first two hundred days I spent in wild places. Since then I have returned again and again to the vast wildernesses of the West and to the smaller wilds of the Southeast, my own part of the country. The original story has not changed, but my understanding of the significance of what I experienced expands and deepens every time I return to the wild.

I know much now that I didn't know when I began, and from time to time insights I have had about wilderness, the natural world, and myself are woven into the narrative. Readers of this book who spend considerable time in wild places may take pleasure in revisiting familiar territory, and those who love being in the natural world and long to spend more time there may be moved to venture out more often. Perhaps others, who have lived mostly in urban settings, may discover that they too would like to leave the city to experience places where humans are visitors who do not remain. For a multitude of reasons, some readers may never undertake a wilderness adventure but nevertheless will gain fulfillment in wildness found close to home, in forests, parks, backyards, or even between the covers of books. All, I hope, will be left with the conviction that wilderness and the vitally connected life-forms within it are irreplaceable.

BEGINNINGS

Hurry Sickness

≈≈≈≈ ONE NIGHT early in the spring of 1993, I had a dream. I was in an airport, rushing to make a plane. I'd lost my ticket, and I was searching frantically to find it. I tried desperately to get to the departure gate, but I could only walk in slow motion. Time was running out, and I couldn't find my way. Then came an announcement on the loudspeaker.

"Attention, Melissa Walker. Come to the Delta information desk for a message." There a faceless woman handed me a piece of paper with the words "Hurry up and die" scrawled across it in longhand.

I woke in an anxious sweat. It was 6:00 A.M. The alarm would go off in another fifteen minutes. My husband, Jerome, would get up, jog, shower, eat breakfast at the kitchen counter, and head off to work a little after 7:30. I would walk my dog, Hugo, make a pot of coffee, and sit in the garden to read the *New York Times* before going up to my study and sitting down in front of the computer. By 8:00 A.M. I would be at work.

Usually when I had an upsetting dream, I told Jerome about it immediately, but I put off telling him about this one. Unable to write, I made another cup of coffee and went out into the garden. I stared at a cherry tree as a light breeze loosened the blossoms and sent them fluttering to the ground. The more I hurried, the closer I came to—what? Death? I took a deep breath. I'd been in a hurry all my life. And if hurry wasn't killing my body, it surely was killing my spirit.

For twenty years I'd taught full time in colleges and universities. I'd always rushed from one thing to another—from teaching a class to lunch with a friend, from my son Richard's soccer game to my daughter Laura's swim match, and from research in the library to dinner and a movie with Jerome. I traveled several times a year to professional meetings around the country, but it had been years since I'd had a vacation unrelated to work. In fact, I couldn't remember spending even a whole weekend just hanging out. On the surface my life had become less hectic in the five years since the children had left home. Laura and Richard had both graduated from college. She was living in California; in less than a month he and Monica would be married. I'd given up full-time teaching in order to spend more time writing. But even when no one was setting deadlines for me, I set them for myself, and I was always in a hurry.

All my life I had packed as much into a day as possible. I timed myself as I rushed though household chores and expressway traffic: five minutes to blow-dry my hair, fifteen minutes to walk the dog, twenty minutes to water the garden, thirty for dinner preparations, and two hours and ten minutes to drive the hundred and fifty miles to my parents' home. Beating the clock had been a lifetime game for me, and I almost always lost. I rushed and rushed and still kept people waiting. I was chronically late—not thirty minutes, but five or ten for almost everything I did.

After an hour or so, I recovered from the nightmare enough to put the final touches on the environmental textbook I'd been working on for the last year. When I finished, I looked up from the computer and saw an open road. When Jerome came home that night, I explained that I wanted to educate myself about designated wilderness areas, to go out west and do what I thought of as my fieldwork, and—if I could see my way—to write a book about what I learned. At first uncomfortable, Jerome eventually went along with the idea of a trial run. We decided that I would see what it would be like to be on my own in wild places. A few days later I flew to Phoenix, rented a car, and headed south. It was almost dark when I set up my tent in a driving rain in Madera Canyon in the Coronado National Forest. By the time I crawled into my sleeping bag, lightning was flashing and thunder roared down the canyon.

During the night the rain turned to sleet, then hail, and finally snow. I had only a light sleeping bag, good down to thirty-two degrees, and by dawn the temperature had dropped to eighteen, with a wind chill of God-knows-what. There were times when I thought the wind would carry the tent away with me in it. Before I could fall asleep, I'd had to put on gloves, a hat, and all my clothes—thermal underwear, a sweater, a down vest, and a Gore-Tex jacket. Around 3:00 A.M. I crawled from the tent to use the pit toilet some fifty yards away. The storm was over, the sky clear, and the stars more numerous and bright than I had ever seen them. I'd left home expecting to find warm days, cool nights, and a desert in bloom. Instead I found this last blast of winter, a snow-covered landscape with a view of the universe so clear that it was difficult to turn my eyes away from the sky. I breathed deeply and felt the cold, starlit space rush in. To my amazement, from that moment and for several days to come I became increasingly energized, happier, full of life.

The next several days I spent exploring southeastern Arizona, the peaks around Madera Canyon, the Patagonia Sanctuary, parts of the Sonoran Desert, and the Chiricahua Mountains. Pictures I'd seen of the gigantic and surreal hoodoo rock formations of the Chiricahuas had drawn me to the area. One of Arizona's island ranges, the Chiricahua Mountains rise almost ten thousand feet out of the surrounding sea of desert and grasslands. Because of the storm, I had them to myself, or so it seemed.

Heading north early one morning on Highway 80 from the border town of Douglas, Arizona, where I bought a wool blanket and gloves, I drove some fifty miles and passed only seven vehicles, six of them pickup trucks. As I gained altitude the light rain turned to sleet, and at Rodeo, New Mexico, I stopped for a cup of coffee and cinnamon buns at a restaurant/gas station/general store, one of the town's few business establishments. From there I turned west and passed by the town of Portal, Arizona, home to about eighty inhabitants. Greater Portal—population 300, I later learned at the town's only store—includes the town of Paradise and surrounding isolated homesteads. From Portal I entered the eastern side of the Coronado National Forest and located a campground. There I put up the tent some distance from the only other occupied campsite, and I didn't see another human being until the next day when I set out on a hike down Cave Creek Canyon and passed a couple of bird-watchers on the lookout for the elegant trogon that nests in the canyon. I listened for its raucous call and looked for the flash of red and emerald green to no avail. Too early, I thought. The few trogons who cross the border to breed in these canyons were probably still in Mexico waiting for spring. It's just as well. The unexpected winter storm might have been more than the tropical creatures could endure, and my first sighting of these rare birds was yet to come. The Chiricahuas are known for birds. Among others rarely seen elsewhere are the Mexican chickadee; the Montezuma quail; and hummingbirds — the violet-crowned, broad-billed, blue-throated, magnificent, and Lucifer.

Two days later, I moved my camp to the western side of the Chiricahua range in plenty of time to set up camp and take a long hike in a lightly blowing snow through the Chiricahua National Monument, much of which is designated wilderness, though at the time I didn't know that. Walking along the slippery, snow-covered trail, I frequently stopped to test my footing and gaze at the huge shapes that surrounded the path. I stared—actually gawked—at these gigantic monoliths and rocks intricately carved by nature's artisans—wind, water, gravity. As I remember those strange geological forms, I'm tempted to use the adjectives that editors and English teachers are continually striking from overwritten prose—*spectacular, fantastic, awesome, amazing.* Instead I'll just say that they were one of those sights that remind us nature can always outdo humans when it comes to creation.

That night I again put on all my clothing before settling into my summer sleeping bag and covering up with the wool blanket. The temperature was in the low twenties, but somehow I managed to sleep soundly. I woke to the dawning of another clear day and a feeling of extreme well-being. I felt rested, full of energy, ready for wilderness.

As I hiked through landscapes that offered up biological as well as geological wonders, my feelings ranged from near euphoria to a deepening calm and peace. Passing through groves of Apache pine and Gambel oak, I saw for the first time a sign that has since become familiar: YOU ARE NOW ENTERING A DESIGNATED WILDERNESS AREA. I paused, took a deep breath, and registered the moment. This was the first time I had entered a wilderness designated by the Wilderness Act of 1964.

Walking through that serene forest, I was aware of feathery shadows flitting from tree to tree. Finally one, a few feet above my head, caught my attention and held it. Its plumage was the reddest red I could imagine, and when the sun penetrating the trees spotlighted those feathers, I felt that I had entered another world of color. No paint, no fabric, no gem could compete with the brightness and intensity of this red. It was a male vermilion flycatcher, the first I'd seen. The northern cardinals that frequented my bird feeder at home were dull in comparison.

When I emerged from the wilderness, I found a pay phone at the visitors' center and called Jerome to tell him that I thought my search had ended. For months we had been talking about what I would do when the environmental book was finished. I knew I didn't want to teach, except occasionally when an invitation to teach a course meshed with other things I wanted to do. I knew I wanted to do something that would help me learn more about the environment—about wild places and what was necessary to preserve them. And to tell the truth, I wanted adventure.

"Wilderness," I told Jerome.

He wasn't surprised. As a child I was always outdoors, aimlessly exploring the woods, the fields, the creeks and ponds, collecting insects, crayfish, rocks, and seeds. I wanted to do that again but on a larger scale: to learn about landscapes and the plants and animals they sustained; streams and rivers and their watersheds; mountains, canyons, glaciers.

A few weeks later I made what I thought of as one more trial run. Jerome had a meeting in San Francisco, and I joined him for a couple of days in the city before renting a car and driving to the Stanislaus National Forest just west of Yosemite. Traveling on Highway 120, I passed through Chinese Camp, Big Oak Flat, Groveland, and Buck Meadows. Evergreen Road took me into the Stanislaus National Forest, where I found an idyllic campsite on the bank of the Middle Fork of the Tuolumne River just outside the park. Before I turned off the road into the camping area, a lone coyote stepped into the road, stopped and stared at me, and bounded into the bush. As I made the turn, the first thing I saw was a warning sign: "BEAR HABITAT." I pitched my tent in a grove of ponderosa pines and incense cedars, far from other campers. The site sloped gradually toward the rushing river full with runoff from the still-melting snow high above. I moved my few belongings into the tent: a sleeping bag, an air mattress, a lantern, wool clothing, a down vest, my journal, and a copy of John Muir's *Yosemite*. This time I had Jerome's winter sleeping bag, wool socks, and a small stove for boiling water. Bears in this part of California are notorious for breaking into tents and cars if they can see or even smell food, so I carefully stashed all my food in the trunk of the car, where the bears would not be able to see it.

Now what? I could do whatever I chose. I could take a nap, read, go on a hike, climb a mountain, dangle my feet in the river, explore the Hetch Hetchy Reservoir area, or climb one of the domes in the high country of Yosemite and wait for the moon to rise and the sun to set. Or I could get a wilderness permit and pack into the backcountry and spend the night alone. For the moment I found my journal and sat propped against a tree, facing the river. I stared at the river and listened to the Steller's jays fussing above. I was both alone and not alone. In the late afternoon I hiked upstream until I found a large, flat rock in the river, perfect for solitary contemplation. I must have sat there for an hour or more as the sound of the icy river washed my inner landscape clean. I made it back to camp in time to make supper before dark.

The next day I drove up Evergreen Road to hike around the Hetch Hetchy Reservoir. Once a valley that rivaled Yosemite Valley, Hetch Hetchy was turned over to the city of San Francisco in

1913. The Tuolumne River, which runs through the valley, was dammed to provide the city with water. In the spring and early summer in years when there has been heavy snow, the reservoir is full, and for those who don't know about the giant trees, meadows of wild flowers, and rich wildlife that once lived below, it seems a pretty enough scene. But in times of drought and late in the season, the partially filled basin is a scar on the landscape.

When I arrived back at the trailhead from an all-day hike, I noticed a telephone by the side of the road. Except for an apparently empty Nissan pickup truck parked by the roadside, there were no signs of people. I had not spoken to my friend Marjorie since I left home eight days before. An anthropologist with a love of adventure, Marjorie had encouraged me to strike out on my own. We must have talked on the phone thirty minutes, and during that time no cars passed. The sun was dropping lower behind the mountains, and I probably had little more than an hour of light. Toward the end of our conversation, Marjorie asked how I felt about being alone.

"Well, let me ask you," I replied. "When you are in the bush in Africa, do you ever wonder what the hell you're doing there? Why you're not home with your family enjoying a warm meal and watching a video movie? Here I am in this incredibly beautiful place. The weather is perfect. It's late afternoon and the sun is about to set. And I'm all by myself. Why am I doing this?"

"You'll find out. Remember, don't have any particular expectations. Be open to possibilities and do what you want to do."

"Say more about that."

"Well, if you want to sit by the river and write, do that. If you want to read in your tent, do that. Take a nap, climb a mountain, or sit and stare at the wildflowers. Do what you want to do. Go where you feel drawn to go."

When I hung up the phone, I was very aware that I was alone and it would soon be dark. I turned and saw a man coming down the hill out of the forest behind me. He walked toward the white truck, and I walked toward my car. Only slightly uneasy, I turned to look at him before opening the car door.

"Is that a photojournalist vest you have on?"

When I answered "yes," he explained that he was a photographer. For the next hour Gary and I sat at a nearby picnic table —one I had not even noticed before—and talked.

I knew what I wanted to do, but until I met Gary, it didn't seem possible. I wanted to pack into the backcountry of Yosemite and spend the night alone. Gary told me that in the summer he works as a guide leading backpacking trips into wilderness areas, and he had just returned from a three-day trip with eight women. At the end of our talk Gary and I struck a deal. The next day he would introduce me to map and compass work and take me to several places off the Tioga Road. We would hike in and he would leave me for short periods of time. Then at night we would backpack in to a forested area where I'd put up a tent, and he'd leave me there to enjoy the night, the moon, the owls, and perhaps the bears. He agreed to camp far enough away so that I would be truly alone.

We met early the next morning for breakfast and then headed for the West Gate of Yosemite and to the wilderness permit office. Then we wound our way up the Tioga Road. Leaving the truck by the side of the road, we hiked into areas with no trails or roads. For short periods of time Gary left me with map and compass to explore alone. In the afternoon we headed into the wilderness. There was still some snow on the ground and there was no visible trail, but I followed Gary's footsteps until the full moon was high in the sky. When we came to a clearing surrounded by large pines, I told him I was ready to stop. As promised, he left me alone to set up camp in the moonlight.

When he climbed up a hill silhouetted in the moonlight, I called up to him.

"I'll yell if the bears come."

"Remember, I won't be able to hear you," he said before disappearing over the other side.

It must have been close to midnight when I zipped up my tiny backpacking tent and climbed into my sleeping bag. Using a flashlight, I pulled a copy of Gary Snyder's *The Practice of the Wild* out of my pack and began what I thought of as a mandatory read-down. Turning pages in search of a topic that would carry me into a deep sleep, I came to a list of definitions for wilderness—"A place of danger and difficulty: where you take your own chances, depend on your own skills, and do not count on rescue." Though I was alone in a designated wilderness high in the Sierras where mountain lion and black bear hunt and forage, I did not feel the presence of danger the way I sometimes do on a city street. The terrain Gary and I had walked through was not difficult, and I was confident that I could use a compass and walk back to a road in less than half a day if for some reason he didn't come back. The biggest chance I'd taken was in trusting Gary, but trust him I did, and I did not expect to need a rescue.

This is not to say I wasn't afraid. The night was anything but silent. There were rustlings and scurryings and squawkings that I could imagine were made by harmless creatures. But there was something else that chilled my blood—a noise more like a splat, as if someone had thrown a ball of mud against the towering pine near my tent. The first time I heard the noise, I sat up waiting in terror for something to happen. Nothing. The next time I mustered the courage to unzip the door of the tent and peek out. All I could see was a moonlit clearing bordered with towering trees and patches of luminous snow. Whatever was making the strange noise must not have been interested in me. After that, I slept soundly until dawn.

Gary had given me careful instructions: "Dig a hole at least six inches deep and cover it carefully." I crawled from my tent, wide awake. Armed with a garden trowel, I went in search of the perfect spot. In a matter of minutes I was scattering pine bark over the carefully covered hole. The deed was done, and I'd left not a trace. No newly trained two-year-old could possibly have felt as proud.

Gary had promised to retrieve me around noon. I had hours to explore. The tent was pitched in a flat clearing near a giant Jeffrey pine. The ground in the clearing was covered with wildflowers, mostly miniature blue lupine. The land sloped gradually to the south toward a dense forest of red fir—large conical-shaped trees with reddish brown bark. To the north were hills of granite dotted with huge boulders. Gary had advised me to pay close attention to the landscape to determine what part called to me. Was it the deep woods below or the boulder-strewn ridge above? Did I want to scramble up to higher, sunny ground for a larger perspective, or was I called to go down to the shadows and chill of the forest?

I took a day pack with nothing but water and a first-aid kit. After taking a bearing with my compass on the giant pine at 340 degrees, I turned around headed in the opposite direction, almost due south across a forest floor half covered with thick patches of hard-packed, dirty snow. Along the way I noticed deer tracks, a large pile of dry bear scat, and small footprints—raccoon, rabbit, marmot. Except for a doe and fawn and one unidentified fleeing creature—a coyote, perhaps—I saw no other animals. I felt their presence, though, just as I felt the life force of the giant trees I walked through. Whatever had gone splat in the night must be nearby. I hiked as far as I dared before turning back. The giant pine was long out of sight. Using the compass, I turned 180 degrees and carefully retraced my steps until the tree appeared. When I broke into the clearing, Gary was standing on the ridge above waving his arms. My time of solitude in the wilderness was at an end.

He and I spent much of the rest of the day together, hiking off Tioga Road and taking pictures. In the afternoon we separated again. He left me in Tuolumne Meadows, where I walked over the river and again into the wilderness. I hiked until I came to a rushing river spanned by a wobbly log. I stopped, thought about the cold water, and decided the risk was not worth the payoff. I'd have to turn around soon anyway in order to meet Gary before dark.

As we drove back down Tioga Road to camp, I sat riveted by the moonlit landscape of Yosemite, listening as Gary talked about his hopes and dreams for the future. For once I had nothing to say about myself. I did, however, manage to ask about the strange noises I'd heard in the night.

"Flying squirrels," Gary answered with confidence.

Back at base camp, I headed for my tent, Gary for his truck. So how did I know that Gary was not the only serial killer in Yosemite? Don't they always seem especially nice? Wouldn't a serial killer be lurking around a pay phone in a remote part of the park in hopes of finding a woman alone looking for help? Wouldn't he cook up a story about having just completed an official three-day backpacking trip for the Yosemite Association? I didn't think Gary was such a man, but then there was no way I could be certain. Let's say I was lucky. Gary had been the perfect guide—competent, patient, reassuring, and kind. Nature had been at her most benign. I had spent a night in the backcountry, and even now I was camped on the banks of a wild river that made enough noise to drown out my cries if man or beast had come after me. Yet I felt more at ease than I did walking to my car in the parking lot of a shopping mall at night. I smiled at the idea that a gun would have been useful and slept soundly without waking until an hour after dawn.

I spent the days after Gary left exploring some of the trails off Tioga Road, but every night I would come back to the trees, the birds, the butterflies, and the rushing water of the middle fork of the Tuolumne River. I woke early on the morning of the Fourth of July to the sound of croaking ravens, fussing Steller's jays, and the roar of the river. I broke camp and then drove into Yosemite Park for one last hike across Tuolumne Meadows. While I was sure the Yosemite Valley was overrun with people that day, as it is every day of the season, I sat alone in the early morning light in one of the most beautiful spots in America. A doe and fawn were browsing nearby. There was no other human in sight.

As I was leaving Yosemite from the western gate, I looked up at the flag and felt a surge of pride that this country has set aside such places for everybody to enjoy. Feeling a warm glow of patriotism, I waved good-bye to the rangers. Little did I know then how threatened our public lands are and how much will be required to preserve the wild in wilderness.

Home

~~~~~~ ALMOST EVERYTHING I remember about childhood took place in a small town in south Georgia. Much of what I remember happening inside houses is tinged with anxiety or boredom, but as soon as I place myself in the outdoors—climbing a mimosa or a chinaberry tree, camping out in the backyard in a war-surplus pup tent, clinging to a runaway pony, setting off alone for a trek through the woods, catching crawfish and picking scuppernongs—the emotional climate of memory changes. Only in the outdoors do I remember feeling lighthearted and carefree. Inside closed rooms I felt—and sometimes still feel—oppressed and stifled and sad. My child spirit flourished best outdoors in the heat and humidity of a south Georgia summer day.

Although the winter months in Georgia are mild and almost every month of the year will have at least a few warm days, I remember suffocating in closed-off, overheated living rooms; shivering in ice-cold bathrooms; and suffering the application of a mustard plaster intended to clear the congestion that had settled in my chest after a winter cold. There may have been fewer than ninety days of what southerners call cold weather, but winter seemed endless and wearisome. Warm weather came in fits and starts. Daffodils and forsythia bloomed in February; cherry, pear, and peach trees in March; by the first of April dogwood and azalea were in full bloom and the air was full of pollen. On the first day of May, my mother always allowed me to shed my shoes after school and go barefoot. Real summer began a month later, and days tended to blur one into the other. Most of my memories of those days are laid down in broad strokes. I see myself climbing trees; wading in creeks; swimming in cold water springs; tromping through the woods with Rip, my cocker spaniel.

My favorite chore was emptying the garbage. I remember my mother handing me a paper bag full of the day's trash. I would take it from her, walk out to the edge of our yard, and deposit it in the old dented metal can, dutifully returning the top of the can to discourage dogs and raccoons.

The edge of my yard was also the edge of town, my house the last one on the street. I would often stand there in the evening when the sun was setting and look out at a landscape that has gained intensity in my memory with the passing years: first the cotton fields, stretching for acres and acres; beyond that meadows and brush and then the woods of old oaks and hickories and pine trees. Beyond it all was the intense fiery red of the southern sunset. When I recall that scene today, it's sometimes autumn, the cotton bursting open, glowing in the fire of the sunset, the dark woods periodically illuminated with the brilliant gold of a hickory or the deep red of an oak. But more often it's summer, with green, green, green both near and far.

Even as a small child I was allowed to roam the fields and woods. The ditch on the other side of the garbage can was the boundary between home and yonder, between comfort and the unknown, tame and wild. My favorite toys were creatures—crawfish, tadpoles, doodle bugs, June bugs, and lightning bugs. My mother helped me hand-feed baby birds that had fallen from the nest, and around the time her father—my beloved grandfather—died, I came home with a baby flying squirrel. We called him Sad Sad and raised him to adulthood. One day my mother and I released him to the wild. For a long time I waited for Sad Sad to return, and I looked for him as I roamed the woods alone.

Along one edge of the yard was a bamboo hedge where my friends and I built secret hiding places connected with narrow passageways that we cut through the bamboo. It was in one of these secret rooms that I kept my treasures. I can still close my eyes and see six-year-old hands opening a cigar box and taking out those precious objects: the rattles from large rattlesnakes that my father brought me from his own adventures in the woods; buckeyes—large seeds that were supposed to bring good luck; the prized Indian arrowheads that we found in the nearby cotton fields; and large slices of sparkling mica from the north Georgia mountains.

When I took off across the fields toward the woods, I always imagined that some great adventure was about to take place. Maybe someday I would find a small village of Creek Indians who had been living in secret. I combed the woods for signs of the people who once lived there; though I occasionally found arrowheads, I never found bones or pottery shards, let alone the live Indians of my mind's eye. With long braids, sun-bronzed skin, and a headdress my mother made from hawk feathers I found in the fields, I thought of myself as an Indian girl.

From an early age I lived in two worlds: the rough-and-tumble world of the outdoors and the ladylike world of dress up and tea parties. Although I wore patent-leather shoes, organdy dresses, and white gloves to Sunday school and fancy birthday parties, I have practically no memories of those events. I do remember catching and cooking crawfish and bringing home a leathery egg I'd found in the bushes by the house.

"Snake egg," my mother said, and together we sliced into the egg and poured out a blue snake shape swimming in what looked like the white of a chicken egg. With my mother's blessing, I buried the remains in the pet cemetery in the backyard. For my mother all life was sacred. For my father a snake was a snake, as my growing collection of rattles proved. Once I stuck my head inside the hollow of a large tree and saw what appeared to be dozens of rattlesnakes all coiled up together in a large pile. There may have been only a few, four or five or so, but the sight of those snakes is one of my strongest and scariest memories.

It was my mother who taught me to pay attention to birds. I must have been a toddler when she first pointed out the common backyard birds: blue jays, cardinals, brown thrashers, and mockingbirds. Then came bluebirds, woodpeckers, vultures, and hawks. Walking across the field toward the woods, I would look to the sky for a red-tailed hawk or a turkey buzzard. Soon I learned to recognize the little birds—titmice, nuthatches, and chickadees. The arrival of cedar waxwings or a flock of goldfinch was a celebratory event that Mother announced to the family and neighbors. She had a knack for finding birds on nests, and when she did she would tell me where they were, swearing me to secrecy. On summer evenings we would watch robins and house wrens tending their broods. When a neighborhood cat nailed a fledgling, I felt the terror of predation as only a small child can.

Birds for my father were another matter. Quails, doves, ducks, wild turkeys, and geese were prized prey, and when on a crisp fall day my father came home with the pockets of his hunting jacket full of dove or quail, I joined in the ritual of plucking feathers and removing the entrails of what would be the best part of a celebratory meal. While I hated what seemed to be the cat's senseless wasting of a newly fledged wren, I wasn't troubled that my father killed, my mother cooked, and we all ate birds. Yet I learned to whistle at an early age, and I loved to mimic the bobwhite's call and to listen for a response.

I wouldn't say I was a tomboy, though I walked the thin line between doing what is required of a southern lady and following the dictates of nature. My maternal grandmother taught me how. She loved the woods and swamps of rural Georgia. At Thanksgiving she would gather family and friends for an elaborate campout at the mouth of Turkey Creek, and each June everybody would go to the Ogeechee River Swamp for serious fishing. Whenever the fishing was really good, however, she would take off alone or with a friend, pushing off in a rowboat into Flanders Lake, Rocky Creek, or one of several small ponds in the area. Often on a weekday, with no one else around, she would spend hours fishing, and usually she caught a nice string of trout, bream, or redbreast, which she would then bring home for supper. Once when I was with her, our boat was suddenly surrounded by several large, hideous water moccasins attempting to feed on the string of fish we were trailing. When I cried out to my grandmother that the snakes were after us, she snapped at me, insisting that they wouldn't hurt me.

My grandmother was a true southern lady. She had graduated from college, read George Eliot, played a mean game of bridge, raised roses, secured her silk dresses at the throat with a diamond bar pin, and coiled her long braids queenlike on the top of her head. But she was happiest camping out at the mouth of Turkey Creek or paddling out to the other side of an isolated pond early in the morning, or whenever the fish were biting. Never mind that she couldn't swim. She taught me that to do what you want to do requires taking risks. I can still imagine her voice when I get in a tight spot.

"Those snakes aren't interested in you, and we're not going to turn this boat over. So calm down and start paddling."

To most southerners, home is the place where they were born and grew up. Like many people my age in the South, I lived in one place until I left to go to college, and that place is the center of a larger geographical area extending from the Georgia Sea Islands and the Okefenokee Swamp in the south to the Appalachian Mountains in the north. Even though I have lived in the same house in Atlanta with Jerome and our children for more than a quarter of a century, our house there is only one of many linked elements that all together comprise home.

Home is the sun setting behind a cotton field, a cold-water spring bubbling out of the ground and flowing into a river swamp, a small pond surrounded with cypress, and a red clay road winding through acres and acres of pines. Home is a stand of blooming peach trees in the spring and a pecan orchard raining nuts all over the ground in the fall. It's a towering oak tree I planted as a seedling and the antique rose that's the last remnant of my grandmother's once carefully tended garden. Home is the way the trees grow, the land lays, and the scent of a skunk or honeysuckle lingers in still air. Home is the past, memory, a time gone by. Home is more than the sum of its parts, more than a house, a river, cotton fields, red clay, a wild rose, or fat little pecans hiding in wet leaves.

Before I went away for the first time, I would have said that Jerome and I have stayed in the South out of a sense of obligation

BEGINNINGS

to be near our parents. Now it seems that we stayed in Georgia because we felt pulled to be there; we *wanted* to be there. When people I met asked where my home was, I simply said "Georgia," and I said it with feeling. It would be a long time before I'd learn that it's possible to hold that intense attachment to one place in tension with a passion for other places and other ways of life.

Rock Springs

〰〰〰 As LONG AS I can remember and until less than a year
before he died, my father found his greatest pleasure in tromping
through the forests he thought of as his own. His passion was the
outdoors; his greatest gift to his family was sharing that love. He
found it difficult to be inside, and on long summer afternoons he
would pull into the driveway after work, blow the horn to announce his arrival, and command my mother, my sister, and me
to join him for what he called a "daunty." Though no one else
seemed to use this word—I never could find it in a dictionary—I
knew exactly what it meant. A daunty is an outing in the country, one with no planned itinerary but one intended to take advantage of serendipity and to welcome the unexpected—a rattlesnake stretched out in the sun, a tree laden with ripe plums, a
hedge of blackberries.

When she heard the familiar horn, Mother would quickly assemble a picnic from leftovers, and away we'd go. This often repeated ritual continued throughout my parents' long lives, and
long after we'd left home my sister and I were expected to go
along for the ride whenever we visited. Some weeks after my father died and a few months before her own death, I suggested a
daunty to my grieving mother, who couldn't quite bring herself
to admit that Daddy was gone. As we drove down a familiar red
clay road and stopped on the banks of the Oconee River, tears
rolled down her cheeks.

"Mama, you're thinking about Daddy," I observed, taking her hand.

"I've been pretending he's not dead, but it's not working anymore."

The river, the wind in the pines, the red clay road seemed to release my mother from the denial that had gripped her since his death. The sadness of her ravaged face released a flood of memories for me.

A typical daunty on a hot summer day of my childhood began with a ride through the country with a stop by the property my father called the Burney Farm to see how the trees were growing. On the property is a natural stand of mature longleaf pines, rare survivors of the ninety million acres that once extended across the coastal plain and piedmont of the Southeast. My mother, my sister, and I dutifully waited in the car while Daddy strode across the land, lingering in the longleaf, deep in thoughts that I could never penetrate. Toward the end of his life, I walked the land with him, listening as he talked about board feet, pine beetles, wire grass, fire, and the endangered red-cockaded woodpecker.

On hot summer days the daunty often ended at a literal watering hole, a cold-as-ice spring that bubbled from deep in the ground into a basin some fifty feet across. On such an afternoon, he loved to surprise us by opening the trunk and lifting out a watermelon, which he would then with much fanfare lower into the clear, cold water of Rock Springs to cool. We always swam before eating. Diving down into the boil, we imagined seeing monsters of the deep. We dug spiral mollusks from the sand and searched the outlet stream for crawfish and minnows. When I close my eyes, I see water oaks, yards of Spanish moss, and cypress knees pushing through the sand. After we played for an hour or so in the water, our lips were blue and our skinny bodies were chilled to the bone. We welcomed the heavy, warm air as we settled down on the sand to feast on fried chicken, cold biscuits, and watermelon. As dusk settled we returned to the water to recapture the chill that would keep us comfortable through the hot summer night.

Just as abruptly as he announced our outing, Daddy would order us into the sensible Chevrolet sedan he always drove. On such nights Mother reminded him that what she wanted more than anything was a convertible with red leather seats. Years after I first heard her half-joking request, he surprised her with just such a car—a new 1960 silver Chevy Impala convertible with white top and, yes, red leather seats.

While we enjoyed the honeysuckle-scented air blowing through the car and watched the sheet lightning on the horizon, Mother and Daddy sang romantic songs, many featuring the moon:

"It's not the pale moon that excites me, that thrills and delights me . . ."

"Moonlight becomes you, it goes with your hair . . ."

"Carolina moon, keep shining . . ."

"Shine on, shine on harvest moon, up in the sky . . ."

"In the cool, cool, cool of the evening . . ."

They seemed to know all the lyrics, and to this day, on warm moonlit nights, I can join my voice to the memory of theirs.

After driving the thirteen miles from Rocks Springs to town, we always stopped by the post office to check the mail. I wondered what my father did for so long in the P.O. He must have read his mail and left it in the box, because when he came back to the car he never brought anything addressed to him. Occasionally there was a letter for my mother, or the *Saturday Evening Post;* always there were the candy bars we had grown to expect. I don't think I ever believed that he found the candy in the P.O., but I never let on that I knew he slipped out the side door and crossed the street to a service station to chat with the attendant and make his purchases—Hershey Bars for me and my sister, an Almond Joy for Mother, and Lucky Strikes for himself.

By the time we pulled into the driveway, the sky was full of stars and the heat of the day had diminished if not broken. Crawling into the twin beds in the room we shared, my sister and I must have talked, though maybe not. I remember only the night sounds—owl, cricket, tree frog, and sometimes rain. Thanks to my mother's love of storms, I was happiest when rain was accompanied by sound and light. The closer the lightning, the louder the thunder, the more I enjoyed the spectacle. To this day I feel a surge of excitement when I see lightning strike on the horizon and hear the roar of thunder.

Like many who weathered the Depression as young people, my father never had any confidence in the stock market. Whenever he had money to invest, he would buy what he called a "piece of land," fifty, seventy-five, a hundred acres of timberland in the coastal plains of southeast Georgia. Most of the land he leased to a large corporation, thinking that the annual lease money, combined with his Social Security, would provide for a comfortable old age for him and Mother. He was right, and now my sister and I enjoy that income.

When I was asked to record my father's occupation on forms for school, I never knew what to write. *Realtor* seemed my only choice, but it didn't really describe what he did. Rather than houses and office buildings, he sold farms, timberland, even swamps. My father provided for his family with money earned from the land, and he made what he called "a good living." More important to this story, however, is the profound attachment he felt for the land. A regular walk in the woods was essential to his physical and mental well-being. When he was knocked down by some ailment or injury, he would badger the doctors until they assured him that he would indeed be able to walk the woods again.

I truly believe that my father loved trees in the way that some people love birds, roses, or waterfalls. He would point out a particularly beautiful stand of longleaf pine in a reverent tone of voice, and—truth to tell—he never wanted to cut a tree. On the few pieces of land he retained for himself, he delayed harvesting the trees as long as he could, sometimes until pine beetles or drought threatened them. In the battle between the monetary value of timber and the connection he felt to the forest, I can't say that either won out. He seemed to live with the tension created by conflicting values: trees for money, the woods for feeling alive. I grew up in this tension, and I live there still.

Guns, Bears, and
Jumper Cables

~~~~~ BACK IN Atlanta, I had a lot to do before I could leave home—the garden to care for, my parents to visit, Jerome to bring around. When I first began talking about an extended trip, he urged me to wait until the next spring. That way I'd have plenty of time to oversee the house renovations we had scheduled for the fall, complete a writing project I'd promised, and get ready to go. But next spring was nearly a year away, house renovations were the last thing I wanted to supervise, and I knew I could get ready to go. Besides, I didn't know what would be happening in the spring. Someone I cared about might be sick or dying. The door was open now, and I was determined to go.

Jerome was not altogether happy about my being away for three months, but when we agreed that he should me join first for a week in the Olympic Peninsula in Washington State, then for another week a month later in Utah, he became enthusiastic about my project. Our best car was a 1982 Volvo station wagon. There was no question that we needed a new vehicle for travel, and we both agreed that a new minivan would be perfect for me to take on the road. I spent the better part of a week finding what I wanted—a fuel-efficient four-cylinder, five-on-the-floor Dodge Caravan with no bells and whistles. According to the salesman, the one I bought was the only one in all of Georgia. No one, it seems, wants manual windows, seats, and mirrors. I spent another couple of days having the backseats removed and a platform with six compartments built to hold my belongings—one for clothes; another for cooking equipment and food; a large one for camping equipment; the others for cameras, tapes, books, maps, and miscellaneous supplies.

We spent a weekend selecting camping gear, including a new sleeping bag and a small tent. Jerome focused on the little things that can make all the difference on a backpacking trip—a lightweight stove and a filter for purifying water from streams. He also bought a cumbersome contraption called a bear can especially designed to keep food safe from bears, and I ended up with five flashlights, ranging from one the size of a lipstick to a two-foot Maglite heavy enough to bludgeon someone to death.

Jerome knew better than to insist that I arm myself with guns or knives, but he urged me to have some kind of alarm system for the van. I didn't want the embarrassment of an alarm going off accidentally in a campground, but even so, he bought an expensive portable alarm from Sharper Image, one small enough to hold in my hand. One squeeze and it would send off a sirenlike sound loud enough to wake the dead. To please him, I took the alarm along on my key chain, only to have it go off without any provocation four times in the first three days, once in a truck stop in Arkansas, the last time in a restaurant in Estes Park, Colorado. Later it fell out of my shirt pocket into a toilet. After that the eighty-dollar gadget was silent.

Friends as well as near strangers repeatedly asked me how my husband felt about my being gone so long and how he could get along without me. Some could not resist the innuendo that I was putting my marriage at risk or that the trip was really the first step in a separation.

"Excuse me for asking, but is Jerome okay about this?"

"Most men don't like being left alone, you know."

"Aren't you afraid things will change while you're gone?"

"I would never leave my husband for three months."

"How's he going to manage without you?"

I told them it had crossed my mind that Jerome might take up with someone else while I was gone, but I wasn't really worried. Besides, I wasn't willing to box myself in out of the fear that something bad might happen. I told them that he was quite capable of managing on his own and I was much more afraid that things would not change than that they would. Change, after all, was what I was after.

When I told my friends and family about my plans, I explained that I was going to learn firsthand about wilderness. To my surprise, everyone seemed to understand when I told them that I wanted to take on a project I cared deeply about, one that might see me out. There were those, of course, who couldn't imagine themselves choosing to be alone away from home in places that seemed frightening, but most of my friends and even my aging parents understood that for me the choice seemed right.

Jerome was not the only one to get involved with the preparations for my departure. I also received advice from family members, friends, and the odd stranger. The two recurring subjects in their many warnings were guns and bears. Before taking off, I arranged for Ken Clanton, a climbing buddy of our good friend Ernest Fokes, to teach me some basic wilderness skills. Ken had been one of the top instructors at the National Outdoor Leadership School in Lander, Wyoming, and Ernie asked him to help me out.

Just before I left home, Ken called to make plans. "Melissa, Ken Clanton here. Ernie tells me you're coming to Lander." We talked for a while about what he might teach me. I explained that I wasn't interested in technical climbing and that I mainly wanted to learn more about how to use a topo map and compass and how to get around in the backcountry. Ken seemed skeptical and told me a string of horror stories.

"You know there are only so many cards in a deck. People get nailed out here by lightning all the time. I get to hang out of helicopters and bring them back in body bags. Remember, your body is mostly water, and that's a pretty good conductor of electricity."

"How about bears?" I asked.

"I know more about bears than I want to know. We only have black bears here. They're bad enough, but the real worry is a grizzly. When one of them turns bad up in Yellowstone, the rangers shoot him up with drugs and bring him to the north part of the Wind River Range. Don't worry, though, we won't go up there."

I wondered how the bears knew where the north Winds ended and the south Winds began, since there was really just one continuous range of mountains.

"Why don't they wander south?" I asked.

"Well, you never know what a bear is going to do. So far nobody has seen one down here. But who knows? People can't do 'bear think.' You probably won't have to worry about grizzlies if you stay out of the backcountry of Yellowstone and Glacier."

"Do you go in the backcountry there?"

"Of course I do, but I go prepared. It's illegal to have firearms in Yellowstone or any national park for that matter, even in the backcountry. But I carry a gun. I'd rather go to jail than meet a situation I couldn't handle. You might want to think about that."

"I won't be carrying a gun, Ken."

"Well, just keep in mind, all the bears in the north Winds are bad bears."

In the days before I left, friends continued to offer advice, suggesting that I take along firearms, knives, mace, a guard dog.

My friend Sue: "You're taking a gun, aren't you? I'm thinking about bears."

My mother-in-law: "You mustn't go in the woods alone. There're bears out there." Rendered in her soft southern drawl, her warnings seemed less threatening than those I heard from Ken Clanton, whose warnings came from years of exposure to the indifference of the wild.

My father had a novel solution to whatever worried him about my adventure. "Look here, sugar girl, you make sure you take yourself some jumper cables," he advised. "They can get you out of some bad fixes."

My friend Marilyn, who has been on many serious outdoor expeditions with her husband, Ernest Fokes, ranging from climbing Mount Rainier to trekking in Nepal, sent practical advice in the form of "M's Hard-earned Tips for Packing in the Back Country":

1. Take baby wipes. Any "moist towelette" should do, but something designed for babies would surely be all right for any part of the body.

2. Take two Ziploc baggies, one for clean tissue paper, one for dirty.
3. Put on a fresh panty liner every morning and remove it in the evening. Place in zip lock baggy with dirty tissue paper.
4. Don't wear cotton T-shirts. They can be dangerous in cold, wet weather.
5. Leave behind all perfumed cosmetics or toiletries. Bears are attracted to fragrances.
6. Take a Polartec jacket and ball it up for a pillow at night.
7. Treat all stream or lake water with iodine crystals before drinking and add powdered lemonade to make it more palatable.
8. Freshen hair by scrubbing it with dry oatmeal.

I rejected all offers for guns, knives, and mace, but I took most of M's tips seriously. And yes, I took along jumper cables.

After I left home I discovered that wilderness has lessons to teach that I could never have imagined. To climb up a boulder field or ford a rushing stream safely requires adjusting to the slope of the land or the force of the water. Time as I had known it disappeared as I gradually discovered "wilderness time," which is not measured by minutes and hours but by the position of the sun, the strength of the wind, the temperature of the air. Bedtime comes when it's too cool or wet or dark to sit outside the tent comfortably, lunch hour is dictated by hunger, rest by fatigue, work by the requirements of place.

In the wilderness I focused mainly on what was in front of me. I wanted to minimize danger, so I paid close attention to the clouds, the lay of the land, the tracks of animals, the presence of humans. Whenever possible, I merged my own actions with the rhythms of nature. I found that living on wilderness time usually required focusing on the task at hand rather than the time required to complete it. There are times, however, when a leisurely pace may be deadly. Protecting oneself in an electrical storm, fire, or cold; eluding threatening people; acting on feelings of fore-boding, getting out of the way of dangerous animals—these actions are best taken with instinctive alacrity. Many everyday tasks —eating, reading, sleeping, walking, bathing—are generally best done without regard to the clock. During the time I spent living mainly outdoors I occasionally acted as quickly as possible to escape real or perceived danger, but most of the time I did not. In the evenings I typically sat quietly at my campsite as darkness fell. Not once did I feel any urgency about the matter or wish to hurry the setting sun.

Altogether I spent more than seven months on the road and in remote and wild places—from August 9 until November 6, 1993; the month of February, 1994; and from August 4 to November 5, 1994. On wheels I covered some thirty thousand miles, on foot a few hundred. I spent an average of about twenty-five dollars a day, including gas, food, and occasional camping fees. When I rolled into Atlanta that last time in the fall of 1994, I'd driven more than nine hundred miles in one day. I'd called ahead and told Jerome not to wait up for me. The house was quiet. Our dog, Hugo, was sleeping on the porch. I opened a beer, ran a hot bath, and soaked off some of the road fatigue. About 2:00 A.M. I crawled into the bed next to Jerome and fell instantly asleep.

AUGUST 1993

FROM HOME TO WILDERNESS

Alone in the Dark

~~~~ GETTING OUT of town wasn't easy. My plan was to leave by 6:00 A.M., but I had gone to bed at midnight the night before with piles of unanswered correspondence and unpaid bills still stacked on the kitchen table. No way I could handle all that before noon. Up at dawn, I made endless phone calls, whittled the stack of papers down to the few that could wait three months, and put a cooler of food and other last-minute supplies in the van. The temperature in Atlanta was ninety-five degrees, the humidity ninety percent. I showered for the second time that day and dressed in what would become my uniform—hiking pants, a long-sleeved shirt, and a khaki travel vest.

I called Jerome for one last good-bye, took Hugo for one last walk, and headed out of town at 1:30 P.M. to a tape of K. T. Oslin singing, "I'll Always Come Back, Baby, to You." In less than fifteen minutes I was zooming along Interstate 20 feeling happy, free, even young again. I was on the road, heading for wild places; I had no idea how this adventure would play out.

I passed through Anniston, Birmingham, and Tupelo in daylight, but by the time I crossed the Mississippi at Memphis the sun had set and I could barely see that mighty river pouring under the bridge at full flood. Around midnight, I was driving down a country road following signs to a campground in a wooded area north of Little Rock. The camp host showed me to a site and scolded me. When I pointed out that the sign read "OPEN

6:00 A.M. 'til midnight," she responded rather tartly, "Yeah, but no one ever comes in this late."

I set up the tent in the dark, inflated a Thermarest pad, and unrolled my sleeping bag. The air was close and sticky, but I was too tired to be bothered by the heat. I stretched out on top of the bag and within minutes fell into a deep sleep. An hour or so later I was wakened by the sound of owls calling out to each other across the forest. The familiar hoots (generally translated as "who cooks for you") were interspersed with frantic barking sounds. Satisfied that on my first night out I had settled down in a forest inhabited by large raptors, I drifted back to sleep.

By dawn the heat had broken. I crawled from my tent and headed for the bathhouse. On the way back a forty-something man emerged from a tiny tent pitched by the side of a very large Harley.

"Mornin'," he said in a friendly tone. "My name's Charlie."

"Hi," I said, without offering my name.

"You know what kind of birds made all that racket last night?"

"I'm sure they were barred owls," I answered, remembering hearing the same call in the trees around my house in Atlanta.

"Where you heading?" he persisted.

"I'm just heading west. The only thing I know for sure is that I'll be in Lander, Wyoming, at the end of the week."

"I'm going to Sturgis, South Dakota. You could do worse than come to Sturgis," he said with what I thought was an insinuating smile. "I'll be there alone if you want some adventure."

"I don't think so," I said dismissively, resisting the temptation to put him down for asking.

It didn't take me long to learn how to avoid unwanted attention from men in campgrounds. I quickly made a few rules that worked. Never smile or look men in the eye. Walk briskly with an aloof, purposeful air. Never initiate a conversation. If a lone camper seemed threatening or harassed me in any way, I usually went up to a couple or a family with children and explained that I might need their help. I never did.

I heard the Harley roar off into the distance as I set out on a jog down a dirt road through an Arkansas pine forest, feeling happier and more energetic than I'd been in years. In spite of the occasional beer can and McDonald's sack, that lonely dirt road through the woods was beautiful to me, and for a moment I remembered my child self running barefoot through the pines of south Georgia.

Back at the campsite I made tea and instant oatmeal. Then I got out my calendar and counted days. If I returned on Saturday, November 6, I would have ninety days. That seemed about right. Ninety days to explore wilderness areas on my own schedule. But I didn't make any promises. "Sometime before Thanksgiving" had been my answer to anyone who asked when I would come home.

By 9:00 A.M. I was breezing along Interstate 40. Singing along with Reba McEntire, I left Oklahoma behind me by early afternoon; with George Strait I got through much of Texas and passed Amarillo around dusk; and round about dark I turned to Willie Nelson to smooth the way along Texas Highway 287 toward Dalhart, where I pitched a tent under a cottonwood tree in a campground on the edge of town.

The next morning I woke at 6:00 A.M. to a pleasant chill and dry air. I pulled on my jogging shoes and ran out the back of the campground on a dirt road passing through the fields and pastures that surrounded this cow town. The drivers of the pickup trucks that periodically passed me all waved and greeted me with a friendly "Mornin', Ma'am." I felt safe and in friendly territory. Nothing wild here. Even the many large dogs I met seemed amiable. Most did their territorial duty by barking loudly, but they reassured me with wagging tails.

Before hitting the road again I took advantage of the warm shower included in the six-dollar camping fee. Using an electrical outlet provided at the campsite, I dried my hair and watched the owner methodically spraying Roundup on the few blades of grass trying to assert themselves in otherwise barren ground. Why he would prefer tiny brown rocks to a grassy ground cover, I couldn't imagine, but when I asked him, he politely but firmly answered, "I think it's better not to have any grass. But of course, that's just my opinion. It's the third time I've sprayed the durn stuff, and it just keeps coming back. Maybe somebody's trying to tell me something."

I was tempted to stay in Dalhart for a while, to go to the local diner and talk to folks about ranching and oil drilling and such. But I had made a commitment to learn about wilderness, and this seemed about as tame a place as I could find, so at 10:00 A.M. I pulled out of town, heading northwest on Highway 87. I soon learned, though, that wilderness is all mixed up with the nearby communities it surrounds. There is no way to understand what threatens it without knowing about the people who use it or live close by. Shortly after entering New Mexico, I spotted what I assumed was a feedlot—thousands of cows crammed into corrals barely large enough for them to stand. Fascinated with the scene, I pulled into the entrance and parked the van. For a while I wandered around looking for someone to talk to. Eventually, a man on horseback appeared from behind what seemed to be an office.

"Who are you?" he asked in a friendly tone of voice.

I looked up at a large, dark man sitting on an even larger horse. He was smiling at me in a benevolent way. His question, delivered in English with a distinct Spanish accent, had seemed one of bemused curiosity, not challenge. I told him my name, that I was from Georgia, and that I wanted to learn all about the West.

"I'm José Antonio Vital, and I'm a cowboy," he said, reaching down and shaking my hand.

"Mucho gusto, señor," I responded.

"Ah, you speak Spanish," he noted with pleasure, and for the next few minutes we chatted about how he came to this country twenty years ago, how his wife is a hairdresser in a nearby town, and how I learned Spanish at the University of Mexico when I was eighteen years old.

This rather worn, middle-aged Mexican man was obviously pleased to be thought of as a cowboy, and it was with a sense of pride that he explained how he and five other cowboys managed thousands of head of cattle, separated into many small groups in an extensive series of corrals. Everywhere I looked, almost as far as I could see, were animals packed closely together, standing in several inches of mud and manure. Many had mucus flowing from their mouths and nostrils.

"Now we don't have so many, only about 13,000, but I've had

FROM HOME TO WILDERNESS

many more. Not so long ago we had 26,000. The lots will hold 30,000. But so many together, they get sick. Now you will see many that are sick, so we give them shots. All of them get penicillin and tetracycline. I give them shots now."

I asked José if I could watch, and he welcomed me into the inner sanctum of the feedlot. In less than twenty minutes I watched as some 150 animals received two shots each. One cowboy herded them into a passageway and another pushed them five or six at a time into a chute, forcing them to go single file into an enclosed area so small they couldn't move. There two other men administered the shots, apparently with the same needles.

When I told José that I wanted to walk around by myself, he gave me an approving nod. As I wandered down one of the many alleys that separated one block of feedlots from another, the cows would pause in their continuous feeding and gaze at me, sometimes 30 or 40 at a time. One bull caught my attention. I looked at the mucus streaming from his nostrils and mouth and wondered if the antibiotics could possibly handle such disease. A wave of nausea hit me as I thought about beef laced not only with the fat created by constant feeding but with antibiotics as well.

I could only eat half of the huge plate of green-chile enchiladas that I ordered at what was billed as the most authentic Mexican restaurant in Raton, New Mexico. After lunch I merged with the traffic on Interstate 25, where I spent the next few hours breathing the dirty air and looking forward to the mountains ahead. I hit the outskirts of Denver during the late afternoon traffic and emerged on the other side with a couple of hours of daylight to go. When I turned north onto Highway 36, I decided to go all the way to the mountains before stopping for the night. It was just after dark when I pulled into a campground set in the woods just northwest of Estes Park on the edge of the Rocky Mountain National Park.

Returning to this place was a little like going home. I had spent the summer of 1961 working in the YMCA adjacent to the park. I was nineteen years old, and I had just ended a relationship with the man I'd met the summer before in Mexico. He was from a wealthy Texas oil family. Charming. Handsome. Smart. Dazzled me. Drank too much. Tried to dominate me. Wanted more than I would give.

Life at the "Y" camp was the opposite of the student life I'd enjoyed the summer before in Mexico City. I worked six days a week in the kitchen, and after work and on my one day off I headed for the peaks. In a matter of weeks I fell in love with the high country—with the mountaintops, the interglacial meadows, the see-forever-on-a-clear-day views that were still possible in those days before air pollution. I also fell in love with the simple life: sleeping in a small cell-like room with just enough space for books and a few other belongings and wearing nothing but jeans and sweatshirts.

As I settled into my tent as darkness fell, my thoughts swept back to those days more than thirty years before when I explored these mountains with the kind of energy and abandon I longed to have again. The friends I made that summer were ambitious, idealistic, and determined to make a difference in the world. In late-night sessions we talked endlessly about John Kennedy, the civil-rights movement, and the crisis in Berlin. There was no television available, but we read newspapers to keep up with Castro's fortunes in Cuba, the war in Vietnam, and freedom riders and civil-rights demonstrations in the South. In spite of increasing violence and growing tensions around the globe, we believed that the world was getting better and that we would play a part in making it so. Racism would end, America would win in space, and our bright young president would help bring about world peace and ease international tensions. It seemed that we had all the time in the world for our personal lives and for changing the world. Somehow that summer we had time to work eight hours a day, read three or four books a week, engage in harmless flirtations, and regularly climb to the tops of twelve-, thirteen-, and even fourteen-thousand-foot mountains.

Thinking about the sense of infinite possibility we had in those days, I felt with painful intensity how much more difficult social change seemed to me at the end of the twentieth century than it had then. In the early sixties and for years to come, I assumed that I could make a significant contribution to society. I expected my life to count for something beyond personal accomplishments. So did we all. Most of the young people I worked with that summer of 1961 believed as I did, that we were destined to do something BIG with our lives and that doing something big would result in public recognition if not minor fame.

Lying alone in the dark, I longed to go back to that time when anything seemed possible and few doors had been closed, a time when we worried about nuclear war but believed we could prevent it, a time when no one had heard of global warming, terrorism, or AIDS. I lingered there for two days, hiking in the Rocky Mountain National Park and contemplating from afar the same peaks that had beckoned to me so long before. Revisiting that place, I summoned up the innocent girl I'd once been, and I left with a new feeling of compassion for the multitudes who had once believed that they lived in a world of infinite possibility.

On the third day I packed up the van and headed for Wyoming. On the way I stopped in Estes Park for breakfast. Outside my window table I watched elk grazing in a meadow below, separated from what was once their territory by roads, buildings, and fences. They seemed out of place in this world of condominiums, fast-food restaurants, and gift shops. I looked forward to seeing animals in their natural habitat. As it turned out, I didn't have long to wait.

Cows in the Wilderness

～～～ OUT OF NOWHERE, a coyote crossed the road and disappeared into sagebrush and grass. I was traveling north and west on Highway 287 on the way to Lander, Wyoming. The sight of this wild canine on the side of the road is common in the West, but the only other one I had seen was watching me as I turned toward my campsite in the Stanislaus National Forest near Yosemite. Now as then, my body responded with chill bumps and a jolt of pleasure as the animal stopped to stare at me.

I stopped the van, got out, and looked all around me, stunned by the silence and the absence of human activity. I had arrived where I wanted to be. After some time, I got back in the van and continued on my way. Soon I would pull on hiking boots and head into the wilderness.

I drove into Lander in the early afternoon and wandered around until I found a bookstore where I collected information about the town and its people and about the vast wilderness area that begins just a few miles to the west. Studying a map that showed all the designated wildernesses of Wyoming, I saw that I was beginning my adventure on the southeastern end of a cluster of wildernesses—the Popo Agie, Bridger, Fitzpatrick, and Gros Ventre in west-central Wyoming; and the Washakie, Teton, North Absaroka, and Absaroka-Beartooth in the northwest corner of the state. Combined with the de facto wildernesses within Yellowstone and Teton National Parks, these wildlands are known as the Greater Yellowstone Ecosystem. Later I would learn that these corridors of wildlands are essential to the survival of much wildlife, especially large predators such as the grizzly.

The proprietor of the bookstore suggested I camp in a public campground just outside of town along the banks of the Popo Agie—pronounced *popozha*—River. When I arrived, there was no one else in the park. Behind the grassy expanse where I set up my tent was a grove of quaking aspen; in front, along the riverbank, was a line of broad-leaf and narrow-leaf cottonwoods. I sat alone by the river, listening to the water, the birds chattering above and horses neighing in the distance.

I luxuriated in the knowledge that there was nothing I needed, no one I wanted to see, nothing I had to do. I had come to Lander to meet Ken Clanton, who had agreed to be my wilderness guide and teacher for a few days, but I could call and tell him I'd be a day or two late. I could even tell him to forget the whole thing. Then I could settle into this spot, hike down the path that began on the other side of the river, walk into town for a hearty breakfast, and give up the idea of pulling on a backpack and going into the wilderness with this strange man.

I thought back to my experience in Yosemite and wondered how Ken would compare to Gary. The Popo Agie Wilderness was far more remote and far less visited than the parts of Yosemite where I had hiked and camped. Full of bear, moose, elk, and deer, it was a hunter's paradise. Hunting season, however, didn't start for several weeks, and the weather report was for near-perfect days. There might never be a better time for an introduction to the Wind River Range. Besides, Ken was expecting me.

When I arrived at Ken's place, his two dogs, Melissa and Tessabelle, met me at the curb, checked me out, and then ran back to the house to let Ken know I'd come. What to say about Ken Clanton? First of all, he was not like anyone I'd ever met. He was macho without having a macho act; he was generous and kind without being patronizing; sexy without being seductive. In his mid-forties, he still had the playfulness of a much younger man. His temperament in animal terms was somewhere between bear and puppy. Shortly after I arrived, he showed me a picture of his beautiful young girlfriend. Lest there be any misunderstanding.

Would I have trusted him the way I did Gary if I'd met him on a lonely road at dusk? Probably not, but he had the advantage of a rave recommendation from a good friend.

In the time we spent together, Ken never once seemed to be in a hurry. He was the first person I'd ever met who seemed to live on wilderness time all the time. Whatever he had to do, he took the time to do it well. He never seemed to let thoughts about what came next spoil the pleasure of the moment. He was also reserved, and if he had anxieties, he kept them to himself.

His passion was wilderness, and shortly after we met, we were sitting at his kitchen table looking at topo maps and planning our trip into the Wind River Range the next day. Ken told me about fishing trips, hunting adventures, and climbing expeditions. He told me about nearly dying of exposure and warned me that if I fell into the Popo Agie River I could die from hypothermia. Ken's near-death stories, however, always focused on survival: Don't fall in icy water, and if you do, know how to build a fire to warm yourself, even in a driving rain.

The park was still deserted when I returned to my campsite at dusk. After eating a cold supper of yogurt, fruit, and cookies, I lay on the grass outside the tent and watched the stars appear one at a time in a moonless sky until it was awash with starlight. I fell asleep almost as soon as I zipped up my sleeping bag.

The next morning, I noticed that campers had come in during the night and set up camp at the opposite end of the campground. There were three small tents and four large Harley-Davidson bikes. A weathered, middle-aged woman approached the bathroom as I was leaving. She looked me in the eye and smiled.

"Looks like we got another good day," she said.

We chatted for a while. She told me that every year she and her friends join many thousands of bikers in Sturgis, South Dakota, for the annual rally and races. I felt a little envious as she talked about the fun they had meeting with old friends and riding crazy fast through the Black Hills without helmets. While I had no desire to risk my life on a motorcycle, I did long for the freedom and exhilaration that bikers seem to experience when they take off across the country.

"You ought to go to Sturgis someday," she said.

"Maybe I will," I replied, surprised that in less than a week I'd had the same advice from two different strangers.

Sipping a cup of tea, I strolled along the banks of the river waiting for birds to present themselves. My experience with birds in the East was limited to those that were easy to see, and my habit, whether at home or in the woods, was to sit still or walk slowly, waiting for a bird appear or to announce itself with a familiar song or call. That first morning in Wyoming, I was accompanied by a flock of black-capped chickadees and an unmistakable male western tanager, the first I'd ever seen.

A couple of hours later, Ken and I left Lander in his truck and drove up a narrow dirt road miles from nowhere. We arrived at the Forest Service campground at Fiddler's Lake in the late afternoon, built a fire, made dinner, and talked about the day ahead. The spot where I camped seemed wild to me, but it didn't qualify as federal wilderness because of the road that made it accessible to vehicles. Designated wilderness, established by the Wilderness Act of 1964, is roadless and off-limits to any motorized or mechanical transport or tool—no chain saws, no helicopters, no ATVs, no mountain bikes.

I was setting up my tent when a woman and her husband, the only other campers, came over to warn us about bears. A large, aggressive sow and her cub had been spotted in the campground.

"We're sleeping in our truck," she said. "You may want to do the same."

I knew I wouldn't be sleeping in the truck with Ken, and he didn't suggest it. Instead, he reassured me that the dogs would not tolerate bears. I climbed into my tent feeling only a little uneasy. The dogs slept with Ken in his truck not far away. During the night I woke to the unmistakable sound of bears rooting around my tent, sounding like large dogs with very bad colds. I called out for help and the bears scurried away. I called again. No answer. Ken never heard me call, and the dogs never barked. I knew that bears in this part of the Winds are black bears and that they are less likely than grizzlies to attack people, but there was no way I could sleep until I thought the bears were gone. The woman had said that the sow she'd seen weighed about four hundred pounds. I lay frozen in my sleeping bag, and in a matter of minutes the bears came back, snuffling and grumbling around the edges of my tent. Again I shouted for help, and again the bears were quiet. For a long time I lay there listening to sounds of the night. Eventually I drifted off to sleep, and if the bears came back for the third time, I never knew it.

The next morning I was awakened by a loud bellowing. Excited by the prospect of seeing what I imagined were elk, I scrambled into my clothes and rushed out to encounter a herd of cattle wandering through the forest. I had thought that grazing rights on federal lands were limited to the open range administered by the Bureau of Land Management. Not so, Ken told me. Many ranchers hold permits to graze cattle in national forests and even designated wilderness areas. In addition to destroying vegetation, cattle also degrade riparian areas by congregating along stream banks and creating erosion. As plants and trees die, leaving a barren, muddy mess, fish and other aquatic creatures lose the shady habitats and clean water they require.

Later I learned that cows in wilderness areas are rarely monitored. If they are watched over at all, it is often by Peruvian or Basque herders who speak little or no English. Problems caused by grazing in the wilderness, I was later told by Forest Service officers, aren't being addressed because Forest Service personnel generally don't enforce the guidelines.

It was afternoon before we began the slow five-mile climb from Fiddler's Lake to Upper Silas Lake. At the trailhead, I stopped and read this sign:

HAZARDS ARE NOT LIMITED TO, BUT INCLUDE:
CHANGING WEATHER CONDITIONS
SNOW, AVALANCHES, AND LANDSLIDES
FALLING TREES OR LIMBS
HIGH OR RUSHING WATER
WILD ANIMALS

BECOMING LOST
HYPOTHERMIA, OVER-EXERTION, DEHYDRATION
UNREASONABLE ACTS OF OTHERS
THE FOREST SERVICE DOES NOT MANAGE OR CONTROL
ALL OF THESE OCCURRENCES.

After contemplating the sign for a moment, I wondered if the Forest Service could actually manage or control *any* of the events on this daunting list.

Ken's large external-frame pack was loaded with dog food and cooking gear as well as the usual supplies, but Ken showed no signs of stress as he kept up a steady pace. Unaccustomed to the altitude and inexperienced in carrying a forty-five-pound pack, I felt pain with almost every step—sometimes in the hip, sometimes in the knee, always in the shoulders. I carried most of the food in a twelve-by-eight-inch plastic cylinder (Jerome's bear can) strapped on top of my pack, and when I bent over to pick something up, it banged against the back of my head. Most of the time we had a clear, dry trail—except when it turned to deep, slippery mud or when it dead-ended at a rushing creek. Ken helped me across one particularly treacherous creek by carrying his pack to the other side, coming back for mine, and then talking me across the wobbly log that served as a bridge. I even had trouble boulder hopping across shallow water, but time and again Ken coached me across by reminding me never to stop in the middle but to keep up momentum until I made it across. Ken insisted that if I practiced enough, I would get over my fear. I didn't think so.

The sun was low in the sky when we finally broke out of the lodgepole and limber-pine forest into a sweeping, open meadow common to the Wind River Range at high altitudes, this one 10,160 feet above sea level. The size of three or four football fields, the meadow is bisected by Silas Creek, which flows from the lake. I slipped the pack off my back, and the pain slowly faded as I looked out at golden grasses, multicolored wildflowers, the lake, the mountains beyond, and blue sky above it all. It was 6:00 P.M. when we selected a campsite near the banks of Upper Silas Lake. Ken pitched a large tent, big enough for himself, the dogs, and considerable gear. Close by I put up my small backpacking tent. Then we set off in separate directions to explore the area. I found moose tracks, lots of deer droppings, and one pile of bear scat, but no animals.

Later, back at the campsite, we built a fire and Ken cooked our evening meal—pasta flavored with spinach soup, cheese, and sardines. Not exactly what I would choose for dinner guests, but given my appetite, the strange concoction tasted pretty good. Looking out across the lake, we saw no other signs of campfires. Ken was as pleased as I was that we seemed to be the only people in the area.

After we cleaned up from dinner, Ken taught me to how to "bear bag," that is to hang the food from a tree limb to keep bears from getting it. We hung some of the dog food and a few bulky items and put the rest of our food in the bear can, setting it some distance from our camp. Ken and the dogs crawled into their tent. For the next hour or so I sat cross-legged and alert at the edge of camp, listening and peering into the darkness. The only sounds were Ken's snoring and a steadily intensifying wind blowing through the pines.

I was almost too tired to sleep, and every muscle in my body ached. Not knowing what animals might be just beyond the campsite, I was afraid to go into the bushes. I knew that if I didn't do something about my full bladder, I'd have to get up in the middle of the night, so I crept about twenty feet away from the tent, terrified that I might bump into the moose that had made the pile of scat I'd seen down by the water.

Minutes after crawling into my sleeping bag I fell into a deep sleep and was disturbed only once by the thumping sound of what I imagined was the moose. When I woke the next morning, Ken and the dogs were still sleeping; all was quiet except for an occasional trout breaking the stillness of the water. I was glad to have time to myself. I looked around, saw fresh moose scat, then walked up into the trees and dug the requisite six-inch hole. When I looked in a mirror, I saw a face so puffy I hardly recognized it. Edema probably caused by the altitude, I thought. I looked down at my swollen hands and at my wedding ring, which was now too tight to remove. I'm a mess, I thought, as I ran a comb through my hair.

By the time Ken and the dogs emerged from what I had begun to fear was hibernation, I was starving. Ken was a slow starter, but he insisted on cooking breakfast himself. Eventually Melissa, Tessabelle, and I shared three large granola pancakes soaked in maple syrup, while Ken smoked his pipe and sipped the strong coffee he'd made in a Turkish coffeemaker. It was nearly 10:00 A.M. when we put away the cooking gear and began the day's activities.

First Ken taught me how to build a fire—how to find dry material to burn even in the rain, how to lay the most flammable material loosely on the bottom and then add increasingly large pieces of wood around that, how to leave an opening for the match, and finally, how to keep it going once it's started. After I collected and assembled the materials for a fire, Ken gave me six matches. When the last one went out, I still did not have a fire. I hadn't left an opening and was trying to ignite my wobbly structure of pine straw, bark, twigs, and rosin from the edge rather than the center. With Ken's coaching I started over, and this time I got a good fire going with the first match.

Next came map and compass lessons. Taking a bearing and traveling cross-country from one place to another was easier than building a fire. Ken and I studied the topo map and identified various features around us—lakes, peaks, meadows, and creeks. Then he told me to choose a place on the map and use the compass to get there and back to camp. I chose one of the nearby lakes, took the appropriate bearings, and lining up trees one after another, walked straight there. Still, we saw no sign of people. Ken went off with his fly rod, and I climbed up a hill and sat on a rock above the water to watch the ever-changing scene as a gusting and shifting wind played on the water and clouds.

Back in camp I prepared for the final lesson: "Surviving a Thunderstorm." Wyoming is famous for its afternoon electrical storms, and most mountaineers have a collection of near-death stories. Ken had some good advice:

1. Look around for the highest topographical formation, a mountaintop or a ridge, and quickly move to a lower position, at least half the height of the peak or ridge.
2. In such a position, you are probably safer on top of a boulder than under it, as electricity from a lightning strike travels through the ground. Never go into a cave.
3. Get rid of all metal objects: packs, keys, belt buckles, cameras, guns.
4. If you are in a grove of trees, notice the tallest tree and make sure that you are at least one half of its height away from it.
5. A group of people should spread out but stay within sight of each other.
6. Squat down, don't sit, and don't put your hands on the ground.

I tried to imagine myself shedding cameras, belt, keys, and pack while hauling full speed down a mountain. Or squatting through the storm without touching my hands to the ground. I realized that instinct would have led me to do exactly the opposite of what Ken recommended. While I knew to get off the mountaintop or ridge, I would probably grab the nearest person to huddle with me under a boulder rather than squat on top alone. I looked around for the tallest tree and tried to determine where to go to be half its height away. I wasn't sure. Of all the possible dangers in the wilderness, lightning frightened me the most.

I remembered the time on vacation several years earlier when Jerome and I had been caught in a violent thunderstorm at about thirteen thousand feet on the ridge connecting Pawnee and Toll Peaks in the Never Summer Range in Colorado. We were with a group of about eight people. None of us shed our metal belongings, but we rapidly descended together by sliding more than two thousand feet down a glacier that spilled us into a boulder-studded snowfield below. Everyone survived the glissade, but we still had to cross over a snow bridge that traversed a rushing stream. The bridge held, and once on the other side we descended still further until we were below the tree line. We were down off the ridge, and though the lightning still crashed above, we imagined that we were safe. The Never Summer Wilderness was not designated until 1980, four years after that climb.

I looked up from my reverie at Ken, who also seemed lost in some distant thunderstorm of the past.

"Think we'll have a storm today?" I asked.

"Nope," he answered, scanning the bluer-than-blue skies, marked only with rapidly moving, puffy white cumulus clouds. "Let's go fishing."

Ken was determined to add some protein to our evening meal. We hiked around the western shore of Lower Silas Lake until he found the perfect spot. Scrambling up on some rocks, he stood on a ledge and caught two cutthroat trout in only three perfect casts of the fly rod.

At Ken's instruction, I went off to find wild edibles to supplement our dinner. He suggested I look for rose crown—*Sedum rhodandthum*—a low growing plant found exclusively at the water's edge at altitudes above ten thousand feet. He told me not to pick the whole plant but to take only one or two sprigs from each. After about thirty minutes of searching, I had half filled a gallon-sized Ziploc bag. That night we had a fine dinner: a rose-crown salad, trout, and a Snickers candy bar for dessert.

Again, Ken, Melissa, and Tessabelle went to bed early while I sat cross-legged at the edge of my tent and listened to the silence for about an hour before turning in. I don't know how long I had been sleeping when I heard the commotion—scuffling, shouting, dogs barking and running. This time I had slept through the bears' arrival, and Ken had to tell me about the large bear and her two cubs that he chased away. The sow was going after the food hanging from a nearby tree; she had also knocked the bear can down and rolled it around without opening it. Even I had trouble opening the bear can, which required using a coin to turn a recessed catch and then pressing a button to spring it open. Until bears learned to carry quarters and dimes on their nocturnal raids, food in these devilish contraptions would be safe.

I woke the next morning totally uninterested in breaking camp. I longed to stay in the backcountry for at least another week, and of course I dreaded loading up and carrying my still-heavy pack. I wandered around the lake and climbed up on a large boulder. Silence. Somewhere nearby a bear and her cubs that had visited us in the night were searching for food, perhaps already feasting on berries or grubs. The moose that left the scat near my tent might be browsing in the willows by the water. I, on the other hand, had nothing whatever to do. I was at peace, satisfied, grateful, and happy. Doing nothing, I decided that day, was better than any planned activity I might devise.

The best way to talk yourself out of the backcountry is to think of the pleasures of civilization ahead. But as it turned out I could only think of two: a cold drink untainted with the iodine tablets we had used to treat the lake water we'd been drinking and a hot shower. There was no way a restaurant meal in Lander, Wyoming, could compete with cutthroat trout, rose-crown salad, or Ken's granola pancakes.

Silas Creek flows into the Little Popo Agie River, which then flows into the middle fork of the Popo Agie through Sinks Canyon. The three forks coalesce in the town of Hudson, Wyoming. From there the Popo Agie flows north through the Owl Creek Mountains. At the Wedding of the Waters it becomes the Big Horn, which flows into the Yellowstone, which flows into the Missouri and then into the Mississippi. Before we broke camp, I wandered out to the marshy area where Silas Creek exits from Upper Silas Lake. It was there that I'd gathered the rose crown for our dinner salad the night before. I watched the water flowing slowly out from the lake and I wondered how long it would be before this water would be added to the already swollen and flooded Mississippi. It had taken me only a week to get from Memphis to this spot, but I suspected that the water, which had a long, circuitous route to follow, would take much longer to pass under the Memphis bridge.

The trip back down to Fiddler's Lake was easy in comparison to the struggle up. In the three days I had adapted to the altitude, and my pack was a few pounds lighter. The log across the bridge-less river seemed wider and more stable than it had coming up, and I was a little more skilled at keeping my momentum while boulder hopping across shallow waters. On the way back to Lander we detoured to Atlantic City, a one-time mining community, where we went to the Mercantile Bar. Then we headed for town, a shower, and dinner.

That night Ken and I went to dinner at the Hitching Rack, a roadside restaurant popular with locals. We drank jug wine and put away mountains of food. Ken seemed to know most of the other patrons in the restaurant, and he introduced me to an elderly woman who negotiated the crowded room with a walker. He later explained that she had once been married to Paul Petzoldt, the founder of the National Outdoor Leadership School in Lander. Watching her deliberate and difficult progress across the room, I thought of my own mother, who at that time could still walk with a cane. I wondered how many years I would have left to lift a backpack and head into the wild and thought to myself that from then on I would do only what I really wanted to do—only what seemed worth my time.

Home on the Range

≈≈≈≈ I DROVE FOR miles on the dirt roads that cross the open range of the high country south of Lander. Ken had called his friend Bob Hellyer and asked him if he would teach me something about ranching and about the controversial issue of grazing rights. The cloud of dust I created obscured the view behind me, and I was following another dust cloud created by Bob Hellyer's four-wheel-drive Ford pickup about half a mile ahead. We had taken a number of turns down roads that blended so well with the range I might not have even noticed them if I had not been following Bob. The further we went, the rougher the roads were, and as we made the last turn Bob pulled off and motioned for me to drive on to the ranch. Bob stopped to talk to the outfitters who were taking a group of tourists through his property in covered wagons identical to those used by the pioneers who came this way on their journey west on the Oregon Trail. My van may have been the only two-wheel-drive vehicle ever to come down that increasingly rough road, and it came to an abrupt halt as the underbelly ran aground on the middle of the deeply rutted road. A couple of wranglers ran over and insisted that they would free the van and bring it to me later. Without a thought, I turned my keys over to these strangers and walked the last half a mile to the ranch.

Ahead, I could see cottonwoods and other trees—a kind of oasis. Water, I thought. Bob had warned me that there would be few amenities at what he and his wife, Martha, call the Sweetwater Ranch. The only water, I discovered, is in the Sweetwater River that runs through the property. Whenever they make a trip to town, they bring back a barrel of fresh water for cooking, drinking, and washing. The ranch house has two rooms. The large room for cooking, eating, and socializing was a Pony Express station in the late nineteenth century. A sleeping room had been added on. The outhouse was some fifty feet away.

When I arrived, Martha was busy preparing a meal for the thirty-odd folks who had paid a healthy sum to reenact the pioneer experience. There was a side of beef in the propane fueled oven. I offered to help her finish the preparations, but she had everything under control and there seemed little left to do. In no time a crowd filled the room and ate huge amounts of meat, potatoes, salad, rolls, and apple pie. They had come from England, Australia, France, Germany, New Zealand, and all over the States for the opportunity of playing pioneer. The conversation at dinner—meals they'd enjoyed, exotic places they'd visited, colleges their children attended—might have taken place at any social gathering of privileged folk. No one seemed aware of the enormous amount of work—mostly Martha's—that had preceded their feast. After dinner I dived in with the women of the family to wash dishes and clean up. In another eight hours the same ravenous crowd was back for a ranch breakfast—strong coffee, orange juice, scrambled eggs, ham, potatoes, and bread.

Martha occasionally caters for outfitters to bring in extra money, but her real work is on the range. As I helped with the breakfast cleanup, Martha talked to me about ranching. Looking straight into my eyes, she blurted out, "I love my work. And I'm afraid I won't be able to do it anymore." Then she went back to washing pots and pans. After breakfast she climbed on her horse and spent the rest of the morning moving a herd of cattle from one part of the range to another.

That morning Bob introduced me to Sam Hampton, a robust and handsome fifty-something man who owns a sheep ranch in north-central Wyoming, some thirty-two miles south of the town of Ten Sleep in northeast Wyoming. Sam's hobby is raising draft horses and restoring old covered wagons, which he uses for such happenings as this. Before I joined Bob for his morning rounds, Sam asked me to come along for a few miles on the Oregon Trail in a real nineteenth-century covered wagon pulled by two large draft horses. Plunging down the banks of the Sweetwater River with nothing to hold on to except the bottom of the wobbly bench, I looked down at the backs of the two powerful animals as they went into the water. Before I had time to be afraid, they bounded up the other side. These sleek, pedigreed animals were literally another breed and figuratively in another class from those overworked beasts that brought the original pioneers from Missouri to this spot. Careening down this riverbank, animals and people alike, must have required a level of courage that their counterparts today could not fathom.

Bob and Martha love their life, and they love talking about it. In the two days I spent with them, I got a glimpse of what it takes to run a small family ranch. Like most ranchers in Wyoming, they have a winter ranch and a summer range. At an altitude of more than seven thousand feet, Sweetwater is appropriate for grazing cattle only in the summer. Their main ranch and primary residence is just a few miles out from Lander. Year-round, they care for mother cows. There is one bull for every twenty to twenty-five cows. Most cows produce a calf every winter, and those that fail to get pregnant, or "come up open," are sold. Except for a few that are kept for breeding stock, the calves are taken to market in the fall. Bob and Martha consider their operation a "small family ranch." Together with their three children, they do all the work themselves. "Small," however, is a relative term in Wyoming, for Bob's privately owned land, combined with what he leases from the Bureau of Land Management, stretches for miles.

February and March, calving time, are particularly busy months, and it is not uncommon for someone in the family to check on first-time mothers every hour of the twenty-four-hour day. Often, it is Martha who is out in the barn assisting a cow with a difficult birth at twenty below zero at 2:00 A.M. To help a cow deliver, Martha sometimes has to reach deep into the birth canal to turn the calf around, a process that not only requires strength

z

FROM HOME TO WILDERNESS

but a willingness to endure the pain in her arm caused by the intense contractions.

Bob shares Martha's fear that they could lose their ranch. What concerns them both is that the movement to raise the grazing fee on public lands could push them and other small ranchers out of the business. At the time that I met them, they had almost given up hope of keeping grazing rights affordable. From their perspective, those who want to raise the fees have one goal: to push the ranchers off public lands. Environmentalists, they insist, are wild extremists who understand nothing about ranching. Ranchers, according to Bob, are caretakers of the land. He insists that his range is in good shape, and people outside the West don't understand that homesteaders took all the good land and that the BLM land that ranchers lease often lacks water and is inferior in other ways, requiring the ranchers themselves to make necessary improvements.

"Of course we pay more for private land. It's worth more. But we've almost given up talking to people. If grazing fees go too high, we'll lose the ranch."

In the next few weeks I'd hear lots of talk about grazing rights and the damage that cattle do not only to the open range but also to forests, streams, and the fragile vegetation in designated wilderness. More than once I would see land degraded and eroded by overgrazing, but Bob and Martha seemed to be taking care of both the land and the cows.

I spent the rest of the day with Bob on the open range. We made the rounds in his truck, while Martha rounded up a hundred or more head of cattle and moved them from one pasture to another. Stopping to check on a small windmill that brings underground water to the surface for the cows, evaluating the condition of the range, and spotting wildlife through binoculars kept us busy longer than it took Martha to finish her work on horseback.

Sagebrush never grows high enough to provide privacy. That's how I learned about one more use for a pickup truck. "Excuse me, but I'm going behind the truck for a minute," is a gentleman cowboy's way of telling a lady he's going to take a leak. After hiking out across the range to check on the condition of a stream the cattle used, I finally got up the courage to tell Bob that it was my turn to go behind the truck. But unfortunately, the ground was so dry and cracked that I created my own stream that ran lazily under the truck and beyond. There are probably unwritten rules about pissing downhill, but I thought of this too late. Bob had walked a decent distance away and pretended not to notice.

As I was driving away from the Sweetwater Ranch later that afternoon, I stopped and got out for a last look at that compelling landscape. There were no charismatic features, nothing but the warm gold desertlike soil stretching seemingly forever. Subtle shifts in the lay of the land created an illusion of contrasting colors as the lights and shadows fell at different angles on the stark terrain. There were struggling grasses, many nibbled almost to the ground, and the ever-present sagebrush. Any wildflowers that may have bloomed in the spring were long gone. Eroding washes, created by water running downhill after an uncommon downpour, cut across the land. Still, I was struck with wonder at the vast, seemingly barren world. Before driving on I slowly scanned the horizon, moving my body and my eyes counterclockwise. Then I saw a wild horse running full tilt, mane and tail streaming behind. I got back in the van and eased down the road. Going in the same direction, the horse was still running.

Sam Hampton invited me to come to his place to learn about sheep ranching. I arrived in the town of Ten Sleep, Wyoming, early afternoon the next day, phoned Mahogany Butte Ranch to make sure the Hamptons were at home, and drove the thirty-two miles south through open range and red-rock canyons. When I arrived at the ranch, Sam and his strikingly beautiful wife, Phyllis, welcomed me as if I were an old friend. We sat on a grassy lawn edged with lush flower gardens and drank a root beer; then we piled into Sam's pickup and drove out across the range. Sam, too, has his bones to pick with environmentalists, who he believes are responsible for regulations that prohibit the use of herbicides on

BLM land to kill troublesome plants like the cocklebur, which gets caught and matted in sheep's wool and reduces its value.

Many times in the coming months I would encounter folks struggling with various versions of the conflict over profit at odds with the health of the environment: mining versus clean water; logging versus bird and other wildlife habitat; ranching versus wolves, coyotes, and eagles; farming versus the Everglades. I wanted to understand Sam's point of view and appreciate his world, so I kept quiet and listened to him.

In just a couple of hours I saw more wildlife on Sam's land than I had seen in the Popo Agie Wilderness. There were antelopes running in a small herd, deer feeding alongside sheep, a pair of elks browsing in the distance, and a fox bounding across the road. Sam pointed out a golden eagle soaring above in the company of a hawk. The eagle, he explained, will occasionally take a lamb, but coyotes are more numerous and far more costly to ranchers.

"Some folks will tell you that coyotes will take a mature sheep," Sam said, "but I don't think it's true. They take lambs, rabbits, and smaller animals."

It was almost dusk when I left Mahogany Butte Ranch. I drove slowly back along the deserted road. Not one vehicle passed me for the thirty-two miles before I came to Ten Sleep. About a mile after I left the ranch behind, a pair of coyotes crossed my path. I wondered if they were joining a pack or hunting alone. Before I made it to town, three groups of mule deer crossed the road—a doe with twin fawns, two does and a fawn, and four young deer that looked like yearlings, one of them a buck. I had come to Wyoming to be in the wilderness, and I had found a strange mixture of the wild and the domestic: cows in the wilderness and wild things on the range.

Golden

A HORSE was grazing outside my tent in a commercial campground in Ten Sleep, Wyoming. In just a few days I'd had extraordinary experiences, none of which I could have predicted. I woke feeling anxious and disoriented, probably because for the first time since I'd left home I had no idea what I would do next. Three days before I'd cavalierly declared I wouldn't do anything that didn't seem important and that I didn't want to do. I had left home to go into the wilderness, to be open to whatever happened to me there, and to change what wasn't working in my life. That morning in Ten Sleep I had little confidence that I could make anything else happen, and I wondered if the experiences of the past few days had been a fluke. Maybe, I thought, I'd had my fling in the wilderness—but these thoughts didn't last long.

Over a huge rancher's breakfast at a local cafe, I got out the map of Wyoming to locate a place near the Wind River Indian Reservation that Ken had urged me to see. As I was pulling out of his driveway, he had called me back: "Before you leave Wyoming, go up to Dickinson Park. Jim Allen has a ranch and outfitting operation. And remember, lots of people know me in this part of Wyoming. Mention my name and you're golden." By the time I pulled away from Ten Sleep, the urge to go home had dissipated.

Golden was the word for everything I saw, winding up a narrow one-lane road to an altitude of 9,300 feet. Looking to the east, I saw what seemed like most of Wyoming and half of Nebraska and maybe even part of South Dakota. It was late afternoon, and the sun was already low behind the ridge I was climbing. The light glowed on the rocks and grazing lands all around me. The air was clear and clean. When I finally came to the end of miles of switchbacks, the road leveled out and I entered the Shoshone National Forest. After some miles of traveling ever deeper into the forest, I finally arrived at the edge of Dickinson Park. I learned after I arrived that the word *park* in these parts is used to refer to a large open meadow such as the one opening out from Upper Silas Lake. There was only one other group of campers: two women with their young children whose husbands were on their annual fishing trip deep in the Popo Agie Wilderness.

I pitched my tent in a secluded spot looking out on the high, rocky peaks of the Continental Divide. There was no sign of human activity. No cars, no lights, no sound. I sat down and looked out at the southern end of the Wind River Range, much of it wilderness, where I was no longer surprised to see cows grazing in the distance. I had quickly become accustomed to being alone in such places. Not so long ago when I first set up camp near Yosemite, I was a little apprehensive as darkness came on, but now I enjoyed the soft light that comes after the sun drops behind the mountains. There were threatening clouds gathering in the west, and by the time I settled in for the night, a steady rain began to fall that lasted much of the night.

The next day dawned clear and bright, so I packed a lunch and hiked out across the meadow toward the Continental Divide, at the northern end of the Popo Agie Wilderness. As I looked out at all that ice and rock, my spirits had lifted and I realized that I had set aside the debilitating emotions of the day before. I spent that entire cloudless day hiking and exploring, my inner state in perfect harmony with the clarity of the day.

From the little time I'd spent in the wilderness, I'd learned that something happens to me there that doesn't happen when I'm walking through city streets or even sitting alone in an urban garden. A few minutes to a few hours after leaving the world of parking lots and automobiles, my mind begins to clear and a lot of meaningless mental traffic dissipates. In the wilderness it's necessary to focus on survival from moment to moment, whether it's a matter of choosing the right fork in a path, finding a safe place to cross a rushing stream, taking care not to fall going down a steep hill, looking out for dangerous animals, or remembering to drink enough water. In the wilderness looking out for yourself is the first priority.

Late that same afternoon I drove two miles back up the road to Allen's Diamond Four Ranch Outfitters only to find that Ken's friends Jim and Mary Allen had gone down the mountain that afternoon and would not be back for some time. Jim was going hunting in the Yukon, Mary to buy school clothes for the children in Lander. The place was being run by a group of summer employees—young people just out of college, a forty-something professional woman from Seattle, and a part-time rancher. Still, when I mentioned Ken Clanton's name the cook invited me to take a shower and stay for dinner. There would be chili, rice, corn bread, salad, and gingerbread. Even though there was no electricity, the shower had hot water heated with a small propane heater. "Golden," I thought.

Since I'd left home two weeks before, I hadn't slept in a bed or enjoyed the benefits of electricity. I had managed to find a shower every three days or so and to keep reasonably groomed and clean in the interim, but I never dreamed I would find a hot shower in this remote place. When I opened the door of the little bathhouse on the edge of the woods, the sun was low in the sky. I lit the pilot light, checked to make sure no one was working outside the curtainless window, and reveled in the pleasure of soap and hot water.

When I returned to the common room, the place was buzzing with excitement. Geoff Tabin and George Lowe, world-class mountain climbers, had just come in from the backcountry. George Lowe's wife and baby had gone along and stayed in the base camp while the men climbed nearby. As we relaxed after dinner, the two men began to talk about other mountains they'd climbed. Geoff insisted that there is no place on the planet he loves more than the Wind River Range in Wyoming. Listening to him and George Lowe that evening, I got a sense of their commitment to living at full throttle. I looked at George's wife and baby and wondered what it must be like to love someone who takes the big risks over and over again. Geoff, who is trained as a medical doctor, made it clear that he has no intention of giving up the kind of challenges he finds in climbing the world's highest and most treacherous peaks. To do so would be to become part of what he calls "the spiritual middle class," and he wasn't willing to do that.

While I don't pretend to understand the urge that some people have to test themselves on a sheer surface of rock and ice, I was beginning to feel that confronting the fragility of life in a world where death can't be denied was necessary for me to claim my own life. Looking across the table at Geoff talking excitedly about his adventures, I felt an intense vitality coming from this man who had climbed the most challenging peaks on seven continents, had been on the team that included the first two American women to climb Mount Everest, and was committed to living every moment of his life on his own terms.

Kill You, Eat You, Too

~~~~~ As I APPROACHED the eastern gate of Yellowstone National Park just west of Cody, Wyoming, I stopped at a ranger station to find out about camping nearby in the national forest. Before opening the door to the small office staffed by only one ranger, I noticed the first of many grizzly warning signs.

"What's the story about grizzlies?" I asked the apparently sleepy ranger slouched behind the desk. "How many grizzlies have you actually seen along here?"

"Well, I've personally seen nine since April," he said, pulling himself up to a full sitting position. "I know grizzlies. Of course I can't swear I saw nine different bears, but those I saw were all grizzlies."

"How do you know it wasn't all one bear?"

"Well, let's just put it this way. One was a large six-hundred-pound male. One about a three-hundred-pound female with twin cubs. I didn't count the cubs in the nine. And another was a teenager, maybe two hundred pounds. Now wouldn't I know the difference?"

"Yeah, I guess you would. How dangerous are they?"

"Very. The problem with a grizzly is you can't predict what it's going to do, so there's no way of knowing how to behave. Whether it's best to be downwind or upwind, whether making noise frightens them away or just irritates them, whether to talk to them, back slowly away, or climb a tree. Most of the time they will turn away when they see people no matter what you do. But bears have been known to maul people using all of these tactics. And they may kill you. Eat you, too."

"Somebody told me to wear bells on my pack to scare them away. Is that a good idea?"

"Don't know. Maybe the bells just make them hungry. Some say the bears have learned to associate the bells with food."

Not at all clear that I would be able to distinguish a grizzly from a black bear, I continued to seek some reassurance.

"Is it possible to tell the difference between black-bear scat and grizzly scat?"

The ranger grinned maliciously and leaned back in his chair. "Yeah, you can. Grizzly scat has bells in it." Later I would learn that though there is no visible difference, it is possible to distinguish one from the other with a laboratory test. Grizzlies groom themselves, and some of the hair ends up in their scat. But at the time I didn't know that, and in any event it wouldn't help me know whether a grizzly was nearby in the wild.

"Are you telling me that it's stupid to hike in grizzly territory?"

"No, I'm not. In terms of the risks involved, you do more dangerous things every day of your life. But people out there are definitely bad for the bears. Chances are you won't even see one. Most people who see grizzlies don't have a problem. But if you do see one, you won't know what to do. Nobody knows what to do. The Park Service has to tell you something to protect themselves from lawsuits: 'Climb a tree or back away quietly. Play dead to convince a mother bear that you won't hurt her cubs.' Chances are that by the time you have chosen a tree to climb, if you can even find one, it'll probably be too late to do anything. But at least the Park Service can say you were warned."

"So why isn't it stupid to hike in grizzly territory?"

"Well, it's no more stupid, or risky for that matter, than driving a car on the highway. It's bad for the grizzlies, though. They need the backcountry. Every time somebody is mauled, a bear is probably going to die. And not necessarily the bear that did it."

"How about black bears?"

"Like grizzlies, black bears are unpredictable. They have different modes—a feeding mode, an aggressive mode, and a traveling mode. If you know bears, you can probably tell which mode they are in. But most people don't know bears."

I went away without getting the ranger's name, and I found myself wondering what had led him to take the bear's side in the battle of the backcountry. That night I set up camp at Madison campground, and after eating I strolled along the Madison River, the site of dramatic devastation caused by the powerful earthquake of 1959, which radically altered the geography of Yellowstone, crumbling mountains, creating lakes where none had been, and raising the temperature in the thermal springs. Near where I walked, six members of one family were swept to their deaths by the raging wind and water that accompanied the quake. More people died in a few minutes than have ever been killed by grizzlies in the park.

That night I dreamed that I was wandering through a forest looking for the ranger I'd talked to that afternoon. There was something I wanted him to tell me about bears. I finally stumbled on a boarded-up ranger station. Across the door was a large sign: CLOSED BECAUSE OF BEAR ACTIVITY. Then I wandered back into the forest. It was getting dark; the trees were gigantic. I came to the end of the trail and to another sign posted on a large tree:

CLOSED BECAUSE OF HUMAN ACTIVITY

I woke in a cold sweat, feeling closed out of both worlds.

Over morning tea, my anxiety dissipated and was replaced by excitement. For a long time I'd wanted to see Yellowstone, and at last I could take my time and explore its marvels. I could relax and join the other tourists waiting for geysers to erupt; hike along boardwalks that wandered through the thermal springs; watch elk, buffalo, and moose going about their daily routine of grazing and resting. Maybe, just maybe, I'd see a grizzly. There were no wolves, and it would be two years before they were reintroduced there.

Consulting maps had become a daily ritual: topo maps of a designated wilderness, highway maps, recreation maps, and maps of national parks. That morning I was determined not to rush my visit to Yellowstone and the nearby Tetons, and for the next few days I wandered down the geyser trails; hung out at the lodge to watch Old Faithful perform to cheering—yes, cheering—crowds; sat on the edge of the vast meadows watching deer, antelope, bison, elk, and a massive bull moose; and rafted down the Snake River, where I saw eagles, ospreys, trumpeter swans, and sandhill cranes. In the late afternoon I would sit on the edge of one of the area's many lakes, hoping and at the same time fearing I would see a grizzly come to drink or fish.

Yellowstone is a maze of dangers, and people die there every year. They scald themselves by getting too close to geysers, they burn themselves in the thermal springs, and they fall from cliffs. Some are swept away by waterfalls, struck by falling trees, gored by bison, or stomped to death by moose. Only occasionally is someone mauled or killed by a grizzly bear. Yet it is the grizzly that remains the symbol of danger, the thing to be feared. While the backcountry is grizzly habitat, bears may wander at any moment into places frequented by humans: campsites, trails, picnic areas.

"There are bears out there." How many times did I hear some version of this warning both before and after leaving home? Dozens, I'm sure. Yet no one warned me of the more evident threats to my safety. There are, after all, "cars out there," but I never took to the highway with the same jolt of adrenaline that hit me when I thought I might encounter the largest predator to roam the wilderness. All it took was a sign at the beginning of a path into the backcountry in Yellowstone or Glacier:

BEWARE: GRIZZLIES SIGHTED ON THIS TRAIL

Although fewer people are killed or mauled by black bears than by grizzlies, black bears have been known to attack, even to kill. For some reason I never worried about them, but I couldn't seem to let go of the idea that an encounter with a grizzly might be the end of me.

In spite of all the warnings and the ranger's insistence that the backcountry should be reserved for grizzlies, I was not content to limit myself to the attractions within a mile or so of the figure-eight loop tour followed by most tourists. I decided to spend a day hiking into the backcountry of Yellowstone even though I would have to go alone. At the trailhead there was a sign warning that there had recently been bears in the area and advising hikers to go in groups and to make a lot of noise. Remembering the ranger's words, I convinced myself that there was no way of knowing whether making noise would frighten or anger the bears. I decided to take my chances. When I sat down on the ground to put on my hiking boots, I noticed a woman lacing up her boots some twenty-five feet away.

"You alone?" I asked.

"Well, yes," she said, smiling since it was obvious there was no one else around.

"Shall we hike together or would you rather have some solitude?"

"No, I'd love to have some company," she said, nodding at the warning signs I'd been reading.

Patty and I took off together, and within only a few minutes we fell into an easy familiarity. She teaches in a medical school in Nevada, and when she was in college she and another woman had hiked some three hundred miles of the Pacific Crest Trail. Perhaps because we had both been alone for a while, we talked continually and told each other the major events of our lives. We talked about religion, politics, and men. She told me about her father's bypass surgery; I told her about the recent death of my editor.

Then we came to a sign warning that the trail was closed beyond that point due to bear activity. Usually "bear activity" is a euphemism for aggressive bear behavior, perhaps even a mauling— or so I thought. Regardless, neither of us had any interest in proceeding beyond that point. At the end of the trail, we exchanged addresses and said good-bye, promising to hike together again someday.

That evening as I was driving back to my campsite, I spotted several cars parked by the side of the road and a small group of people pointing out across the meadow. Before I got out of the car, I saw a huge bear on top of a hill, close enough for me to see plainly but far enough away that I felt safe. I had no problem identifying what I saw as a grizzly—dish-shaped face, muscular shoulder hump, silver-tipped fur. Its size and the absence of a cub suggested that the bear was male. For about an hour I watched him digging in the ground, foraging for roots with such rapt concentration that it was hard to imagine what it would take to distract him from his task.

Nowadays when people ask me what it is like to camp alone in wild places, I think about that bear. It's something like that. When I'm setting up a tent, walking cautiously down a trail, or preparing a meal over a camp stove, I'm usually thinking only of what I'm doing—that is, if I'm thinking at all. Sometimes for hours, even days at a time, that Woody Allen stream of consciousness that plagues me in the city is missing. That evening when I first watched a grizzly bear going about his digging, I moved into what Ken had called "bear think." I was as attentive to the foraging bear as the bear was to the foraging. Both of us were engaged in living. The bear was gathering the nutrients to build the fat that would sustain its life through the hard winter ahead; I was gathering a different kind of nourishment, what I've come to think of as the sustenance of the wild.

Watching this large predator I felt hyper-alert, intensely alive. I've learned to identify these feelings with survival instincts, with an eagerness to do what it takes to live fully and well. Ironically, such feelings come up most readily in wilderness, where I could not possibly survive for long. Left alone deep in the backcountry of Yellowstone, I would surely die in less than a month, probably of starvation, infection, or hypothermia. Yet it is there that I feel most alive.

I spent the next two nights at a campsite with a picture-postcard view of the Tetons. There I strung a clothesline and hung out my damp towels and the pair of Jerome's gaudy, flowery boxer shorts that I used to announce the imaginary presence of a man. In no time a butterfly fluttered over to the boxer shorts. His colors were the same as those in the pattern of the fabric—black, white, gold, and brown. I wondered whether this patient opening and closing of wings was a hopeless mating ritual or a fruitless effort to extract nectar from the cotton flowers.

Night after night I crawled into the tent early, intending to read and write for a couple of hours, but invariably I fell asleep after only a few minutes. I slept long and hard, and though I sometimes woke with a full bladder, I barely remembered getting up and stumbling into the bushes. What dreams I had were banished by the time I brewed my morning tea and sat contemplating the clouds, the sky, and the mountains.

On the last day I spent in the Tetons, there was frost on the ground and the temperature was twenty-six degrees. The top of Grand Teton was ringed with heavy snow clouds, but it hadn't occurred to me that I would encounter snow on the highway as I traveled north that day. Somewhere along Highway 89 south of Neihart, Montana, in the Lewis and Clark National Forest, a driving rain suddenly changed to blinding snow. Trees on the side of the road were dressed in white, and the road that just minutes before was slick from rainwater now became treacherous with ice. As I often do when I'm nervous, I started talking to myself.

"Okay, Melissa, maybe it's not going to be a grizzly that takes you out."

I had no experience driving on snow or ice. It was getting dark. I considered pulling off the side of the road and waiting, then realized that there was no side to this road, only a sheer cliff on one side and a precipitous drop-off on the other. As I crept up the icy road, I was terrified and irritated with myself for not anticipating bad weather. Scattered near the highway were a number of white crosses—grim reminders of those who had died coming this way. Far more, I thought, than had been killed by grizzlies. It's odd that we think of wild animals as so threatening when rain, ice, snow, lightning, and wind kill many times more people than all the animals put together. Before long I began to lose altitude, the snow turned back to rain, and I never went into the dreaded skid that might have taken me over the edge.

Outside Great Falls I found a commercial campground; I was grateful for the warm lights in the registration office and for hot water and showers. It was far too wet and too late to pitch a tent, so I spread out a mat in the back of the van and slipped wearily into my sleeping bag.

Lion

〜〜〜〜 I HAD ALREADY pitched my tent in a nearly deserted campground in Glacier National Park when I read the sign posted on a message board:

LARGE MOUNTAIN LION SEEN IN THIS CAMPGROUND.
CHILDREN AND SMALL ADULTS ARE PARTICULARLY VULNERABLE.
IF YOU ENCOUNTER THE ANIMAL, DO NOT RUN AWAY.
AVERT YOUR GAZE.
SPEAK STERNLY AND BACK AWAY SLOWLY.
IF ATTACKED, FIGHT BACK.

There were no other tents and no pop-up campers, only a large RV parked about a hundred feet away. I looked around and saw no sign of life. There was nothing to worry about until after dark. Mountain lions are nocturnal, and at five feet nine inches and 140 pounds I would not be mistaken for a small adult. The last thing I wanted to do was knock down the tent to go in search of another campsite. Besides, the uneasiness I felt about the lion was nothing compared to the terror I'd felt the night before while driving on icy roads in a snowstorm over the King's Hill Pass.

I set out to hike around the western side of Lake McDonald, but when I found myself alone in the fading light, my skin began to prickle and my breath grew short.

"It's not a lion," I said, trying to calm myself, but my anxiety only grew more intense. I'd begun to think of this prickly, rabbit-running-over-my-grave feeling as part of my own wildness—a survival mechanism programmed into the human species as it evolved in the wild. I never saw, heard, or smelled anything to indicate that I was in danger, but my body kept telling me I was. I'll never know if some primitive sense was picking up danger signals or if the sign warning of lions had triggered thoughts that set off the body sensations we call fear. Finally I gave in, and—suppressing the urge to run—walked slowly back to camp. It was not until after supper when I was sipping a cup of hot chocolate that I remembered I was also in grizzly country, and that I'd been hiking alone at just the hour that the big bears come out to forage for food. With that thought I emptied the tent of my sleeping gear, threw it in the back of the van, and crawled inside. Only when I slammed and locked the door did the pounding of my heart subside, but even after I fell asleep I dreamed of stalking cats.

The next morning my fear had dissipated. For the following two days I took moderate hikes through alpine meadows bordered by the massive mountains of the Northern Rockies. There were many wildflowers I'd never seen, but with the help of a field guide I identified gentian, beargrass, lupine, Indian paintbrush, and asters. When I hiked alone I made sure to take popular trails, so that if I had any trouble, someone would be along shortly and find me. And I talked to myself, clapped my hands, sang, and from time to time called out to the bears that I imagined were coming my way.

The last day in Glacier, thinking I'd had enough of hand clapping and singing to myself, I joined about ten people for a ranger-led hike. About thirty minutes after we started out, the ranger stopped to explain that just the week before two people in a group such as ours had been attacked and mauled by a grizzly right where we were standing. Their injuries were serious enough to require a helicopter evacuation. He tried to relieve our anxieties by pointing out that we were three hundred times more likely to die in a car accident on any given day in Glacier National Park than we were to be killed by a bear. If a bear should approach the group, however, we were to drop to the ground in a fetal position with face down and knees pulled to the chest to protect vital organs. We should use our arms to protect heads and necks.

To avoid injury by a mountain lion, he warned, the strategy

is very different. The ranger reiterated the advice I'd read on the message board: Never drop to the ground or run. Stand as tall as possible and face the animal while backing slowly away. Always avert the eyes, since mountain lions perceive a direct gaze as a threat or an aggressive dare. And oh, yes—speak sternly to scare the animal away. If actually attacked by a lion, we should fight back. I couldn't imagine what I'd say to a big cat except maybe "scat" or "get out of here," and I had no confidence that any words at all would come out of my mouth if I were actually looking at a mature mountain lion. Remarkably, fighting back if attacked by a bear or lion seemed possible.

Not long before I left home, I had surprised myself by doing just that. It happened on a perfect day in May. Laura and I were eating breakfast in a popular neighborhood diner, and I had parallel parked my old yellow Volvo station wagon on the street. When we emerged from the restaurant, we found that someone had parked a newish BMW right up against my front bumper. I tried backing up, but with only a foot or so between me and the car behind, there was no way to get out. I ended up with a rear wheel on the sidewalk and a small crowd gathering on the street. Then I noticed that the BMW was unlocked. With the encouragement of several bystanders, I got in the car and engaged the clutch while two men pushed from behind. Then it happened.

"Hey, you fucking bitch. Get the hell out of my car!"

I looked up just as a tall, soft young man in a three-piece business suit came charging down the sidewalk toward me. Without knowing what I was doing, I got out of the car, stood up just as he approached, and slugged him as hard as I could in the solar plexus. Looking more stunned than hurt, he just stood there as if he were waiting for something else to happen. In the background I could hear Laura shouting, "Hit him again, Mom." I looked back and saw my golden retriever jumping up and down wildly and barking in the back of the station wagon. The two men who were trying to help me move the car were all smiles.

"Now *you* can move your car," I said.

At that point a young woman I hadn't noticed before started screaming, "You can't make him move the car."

"You're right. I can't make him."

At that point they both scrambled, muttering, into the car and drove away. Now it was my turn to be stunned. What had possessed me? For one moment the wild animal that is part of all humans directed my action, as fear and anger were instantaneously transformed into an act of violence. Why did he flee? Perhaps for the same reason I hit him. He was dressed like a lawyer and we were just blocks from the courthouse. Subliminal thoughts of police reports and embarrassing publicity may have triggered his flight. Regardless, I fought and he fled.

While it's not uncommon to encounter people that seem threatening or dangerous, it's very rare indeed to meet large predators in the wild. Yet the National Park Service and Forest Service never warn us about unreasonable people. I was often in wilderness areas during hunting season, but all the warning signs referred to animals, never to a stray bullet.

Listening to the ranger talk about lions and bears, I thought back to that sunny May morning in my own neighborhood when I slugged a yuppie without having any reason to think that he wouldn't strike back. I imagined putting warning signs on Atlanta streets:

OVERWROUGHT YOUNG PROFESSIONALS SEEN ON
THESE STREETS.
TAKE CARE NOT TO GET BETWEEN THEM AND THEIR CARS.
IF THEY SHOULD MAKE AGGRESSIVE GESTURES,
AVERT YOUR GAZE.
SPEAK STERNLY AND BACK SLOWLY AWAY.
IF ATTACKED, DELIVER A SWIFT BLOW TO THE SOLAR PLEXUS.
UNDER NO CIRCUMSTANCES SHOULD YOU TOUCH
THEIR AUTOMOBILES.

I suspected that I was far more at risk of mortal injury from irate or careless urbanites in the city where I lived than I was from a hungry lion here in the wilderness.

It was late afternoon when I broke camp at Glacier National Park and headed south on Montana Highway 35 along the eastern shore of Flathead Lake. Just about dusk somewhere along that deserted stretch of road, I pulled over to consult the map. Out of nowhere an old Chevrolet pulled up beside me, barely leaving me room to get back on the highway. Two men were in the front seat, a Marilyn Monroe look-alike in the back. I rolled down the window feeling very uneasy.

The man riding shotgun glared at me and mumbled something about needing help. I was suddenly aware of sensations not unlike those I'd had in the wilderness. A pounding heart. Prickling skin. Shallow breathing. This could be a setup, I thought. Two men and a woman did not need my help, and even if they did, I had other fish to fry. Something told me it was time to avoid sounding afraid and get the hell out of there. "Sorry, I can't help you. I'm going the other way," I shouted as I pulled back onto the highway and headed north the way I'd come. After driving about ten miles I turned around and resumed my southwest journey, turning south on Highway 93 and skirting the Mission Mountain Wilderness before turning west onto Highway 200. Later, when I consulted a map, I found that I was literally surrounded by vast stretches of wilderness. To the north was the immense Bob Marshall Wilderness, sandwiched between the Great Bear and the Scapegoat; to the south, the Rattlesnake, Selway-Bitterroot, and Frank Church River of No Return.

Traveling under a full moon through the scenic Clark Fork River Valley in western Montana, I passed through the towns of Paradise, Plains, and Thompson Falls before I found a suitable campground just east of the Idaho border. The next day I would drive to Spokane, where I'd meet Jerome at the airport.

I'd been away a full three weeks before Jerome joined me for a week-long rendezvous. We spent the first night with our friends Marilyn and Ernie in Coeur d'Alene, Idaho, then the next day we drove all the way across the state of Washington to the Olympic Peninsula National Park, east of Seattle. On that drive we talked continously—I talked about lions and bears and Marilyn Monroe look-alikes, he about our dog, Hugo, his work, a robbery in our neighborhood, and house renovations going on in my absence. I told him how I loved waking up outdoors every day; he told me how he never knew how much is involved in running a house. For seven days we backpacked and camped in the wilderness areas of the park.

The good parts of having Jerome along were obvious. It was a relief to turn the driving over to him, to let him read the maps and calculate the distance from the trailhead to a designated campsite in the backcountry, and to carry the lion's share of the camping gear so that my pack weighed only about thirty pounds. I loved it when I woke in the night and felt his warm body next to mine and when he had a cup of hot tea waiting for me when I got up in the morning. It was just plain nice to have a man around the tent.

But the abrupt interruption of my journey had a cost. With Jerome along it was much harder to get into conversations with other people and to learn about what I was seeing. Before he came I'd met people on the trail, in ranger stations, and in campgrounds. People had literally come out of the woods to warn me about bears, to advise me about the weather, or just to see what I was up to. Much of what I learned in the two hundred days of my travels, I learned by serendipity as people with local knowledge voluntarily served it up. Although we talked to rangers and chatted with people on the trail or soaking in the hot baths of Sol Duc, mostly we were by ourselves. I was part of a couple rather than an independent person exploring the wilderness. And no, I didn't particularly like it. I felt somehow diminished and less sure of myself. When we were together, it was not so easy for me to walk into the offices of the Forest Service or the public-relations department of a timber company to learn about clear-cutting. Forestry is still mostly a man's world, and when I walked into an office with Jerome in tow, I was perceived as a wife and not taken seriously.

Jerome is an unusually happy person—most of the time. He loves his work, his home, the children, the dog, and me. He likes to jog, garden, hike, and canoe. He likes good music, especially jazz. He loves to dance—fox-trot, tango, waltz, and most of all swing. He always enjoyed being with my parents and insisted that my mother was so good to him that he couldn't understand

FROM HOME TO WILDERNESS

mother-in-law jokes. He takes his politics—slightly to the left of center—seriously and often fires off letters to the editor and to congressmen about the issues that concern him. He enjoys being a nice guy—generous, kind, and outgoing. People like him, maybe in part because they can count on him not to complain or sink into despair.

The downside is that he works so hard he doesn't always get to do what he enjoys. He's often so absorbed in his own thoughts that he sometimes doesn't listen to what I'm saying or even notice that I'm around. A few years after my trip into the Popo Agie Wilderness with Ken, Jerome and I went to the Wind River Range together. One afternoon after we hiked to Upper Silas, he sat at the edge of Fiddler's Lake reading Doug Peacock's *Grizzly Years.* Suddenly I heard him yell out words I seldom hear him use, and when I looked up from my own reading some distance away, a large black bear was ambling toward him. My scream and Jerome's shouts discouraged the bear long enough for us to pack up and move our camp. Sometimes I envy his ability to concentrate and ignore the outside world. But not that day, and never in the wilderness.

By now I've talked to enough women to know that there is nothing unusual about Jerome's behavior and nothing I need to do but accept it. "Men, like all humans," I tell myself and others, especially young people considering marriage, "are limited creatures." When I first shared this piece of hard-earned wisdom with my daughter, she insisted that I wasn't being fair to her father— that women, too, are limited. I reminded her that I'd said all humans are limited.

The difference is that few men expect women to create lives for them. Many women, on the other hand, expect men to do just that. Like countless women of my generation, I married with the illusion that a good man would meet all my emotional needs, maybe even provide the shape and much of the substance of my life. We believed that if a woman married a good man, she would need little more than a family and a few women friends to have a complete and satisfactory personal life. Being of the generation of women who first read Betty Friedan and signed on in various ways to the women's movement, we expected eventually to have interesting jobs and what we called "financial independence."

What we didn't expect, or even think to want, was passion and commitment in our life's work. Passion, we thought, was something husbands provided, and if husbands didn't provide it, perhaps we could find it in flirtation or even an affair. Work should be interesting but not consuming. It never occurred to us that we might have work in the world that was absorbing and compelling—work that we loved.

For years I blamed my husband for not having qualities that I now believe no man has, or at least no man grants for free. There are of course men—and women—who will provide fifty minutes of attentive listening for a hundred dollars or more, but total attentiveness and sensitivity to a woman's needs is not something that most men come equipped to give, any more than women are equipped to be eternally glamorous and sexy.

Our first day on the Olympic Peninsula, we backpacked up the Elwha Valley and camped near the banks of the Lillian River. We cooked dinner, stashed our food in the bear can, and crawled into the tent before 10:00 P.M. During the night I woke with a start to a screeching growl.

"What's that noise?" I barked, sitting upright in our tiny tent.

"I didn't hear anything," Jerome mumbled, and snuggled even deeper into our zipped-together sleeping bags. "You must be dreaming."

Okay, I'm dreaming, I told myself, sinking back into a deep sleep and not waking until dawn—but even then I knew the chilling cry was not part of a dream. The next day when we met a ranger on the trail, I reported what I'd heard during the night, adding that Jerome thought I'd been dreaming.

"Nah," he said. "That's not how dreams work. Trust your senses. You heard a lion."

"Why did it make such a noise?"

"Could be anything. It might have sensed trespassers; maybe you guys. That screeching growl might have been a warning to other predators saying, 'This is my turf.' It's even possible it was a mating cry. Warm enough out here for lions to mate year-round."

"Could it have been killing another animal?"

"Well, we don't know much about how these big cats act when they kill in the wild. I don't know anybody who's seen a kill. We do know that they stalk and sneak up on prey, so it wouldn't make a noise before an attack. After a kill, a female with young might call her cubs in to eat."

"What's your guess?" I asked.

"I have no idea. Maybe it was just crying out for the hell of it."

This ranger seemed to be an expert on mountain lions. Ready with statistics and facts galore, he began to lecture us about the big cats—how they kill large prey instantly, going for the back of the neck and severing the spinal cord; how they will fight each other, sometimes to the death; how their preferred food is deer, though they also take smaller prey such as rabbits, beavers, marmots, coyotes, and even other cougars. While visitors to wild places are frequently warned about these dangerous animals, there have been only 53 reported attacks on humans in a hundred years, only 10 of those resulting in deaths. That's a single attack every two years, a death every ten. Domestic dogs, on the other hand, attack 200,000 people a year in the United States. Approximately 20 of those die. Even deer account for the deaths of 130 people annually, most of them in automobile collisions caused by the animals trying to cross highways. As human activity continues to encroach on remaining lion habitat, there may be more attacks. There certainly will be fewer mountain lions. Before he walked on down the trail, I asked the ranger if we should be concerned about lions the way we are about bears.

"You could probably spend the rest of your life wandering around these parts and never see one. The only ones I've ever seen are young or sick or both. If you want something to worry about, try cars, or people, or even deer, but don't worry about lions. In the unlikely event that you see one, remember to stand tall, speak firmly, and back away slowly." (He forgot to say "avert your gaze" and "don't run.")

Some weeks later I met a woman in Big Bend National Park

who told me about hiking with a fellow ranger up a narrow canyon and coming around a blind corner face to face with a mountain lion. Together they began to chant the litany of rules that they'd learned to tell hikers, but when it came right down to it, they were not able to carry through. Kathy remembers saying a few stern words to the cat while trying to back down the narrow ledge out of the canyon. She also ripped up the pole like stalk of a century plant and pointed it at the lion while making a few threatening remarks. But she did not avert her gaze, and in the end she and the other ranger turned and ran as fast as they could out of the canyon. They never looked back, and apparently the lion chose not to go for the chase.

The week Jerome and I spent in the Olympic Peninsula was warm and sunny. We didn't see a drop of rain in this place where the annual rainfall is 145 inches and rain gear a must for backpackers almost every day. We spent our days exploring the coastal strip, hiking up and over headlands, and looking into tidal pools full of sea urchins, anemones, and limpets. We hiked into the Hoh Rain Forest through stands of giant Sitka spruce and Douglas fir draped with strange mosses and other epiphytes. It was a place where plants occupy every piece of earth, and some make their home on trees and other vegetation.

Having this time together made it easier for both of us to be separated for so long, and when Jerome joined me four weeks later in Utah, I was ready for another break from solitude. His visits were time-out, a vacation from the work I was doing, but by the time I took him to the Seattle airport I was eager to continue with my solitary project. At that point I had no idea how things would develop—how I would integrate a concern for wilderness into my life or how the things I was learning would lead to action.

FROM HOME TO WILDERNESS

Holden Village

~~~~~ ONCE A model mining village, now a mountain retreat owned and run by the Lutheran Church, Holden Village is deep in the Cascades. It is the most remote village of any I know in the Lower 48. Before I left home I applied to come to Holden as a paying guest, explaining that I wanted to learn about life in a village close to major wilderness and that I needed a place to write for a few days.

After I left Jerome in Seattle, I drove across Washington State to the western shore of Lake Chelan. The few people camping at the Twenty-five Mile Campground were fishermen and hunters. There were no towns, no stores; there was nothing for miles except a bait-and-tackle store that sold white bread, sausage, sardines, beer, and a few other items. The florid middle-aged man behind the counter, who had obviously had a few beers himself, was banging around impatiently, complaining that people always came in just when he was ready to close up for the night. Feeling uneasy, I half expected him to pull out a gun and order me out. I quickly paid for a can of sardines and a box of crackers and hurried down to the lake to watch the sun set. Early the next morning I drove over to Field's Point to catch the ferry that goes forty-three miles up the lake to Lucerne before continuing on to Stehekin. There was nothing at Lucerne except a boat dock, where I disembarked with a dozen other passengers to travel by bus another twelve miles up into the Cascades.

The passengers who boarded the bus with me included two young women traveling with small children; a group of geologists who were going to study the effects of mining tailings on the environment; and four hunters who had come for "high hunt," the season that allowed taking three-point bucks in the high altitudes. When we got off the bus, I looked around at snow-capped mountains facing a village that seemed more from the early nineteenth century than the late twentieth. One of the women walked over to me and said, "If there is a heaven, it must be just like this." I smiled in agreement.

For two weeks I would have the use of a single bed in a spartan room, a desk with an electrical outlet for my notebook computer, a communal shower with hot water, and a trail leading to more than half a million acres of designated wilderness. No radio, television, or telephone. Not even a daily newspaper.

Lining Holden's only street are brown, stained wooden buildings constructed in the early thirties. A large building that once housed the gymnasium and commons rooms for the miners has been converted to a sanctuary for worship and a meeting place for large gatherings. Across the street stand one of several dormitories and the building known as "the hotel," whose main floor is the dining hall. Up the hill are more dormitories, the laundry, and a few private residences occupied by permanent staff members. In one building there is a small room full of clothes left behind by previous visitors. Guests are invited to take whatever they need from this communal closet. Further down the road is the hike house, where visitors can check out water bottles, day packs, and maps of the trails into the Glacier Peak Wilderness. All the buildings have front porches with boxes and baskets of flowers, and most have porch swings and rocking chairs. Between the buildings are spacious grassy lawns.

All the village vehicles—the buses for transporting guests from the ferry to the village twice a day as well as maintenance vehicles—are brought in by boat and have no access to the outside world. Visitors only rarely hear the sound of an engine. Dogs and cats, easy prey to predators, are not allowed at Holden, but in the late afternoon a half-dozen deer commonly browse on the grass. No one feeds the animals, and they aren't tame.

Full-time staff members usually come to Holden for two-year stretches. They willingly cut themselves off from telephones, television, radio, daily newspapers, medical care, and police protection. To communicate with the outside world they rely on the sluggish U.S. mail; in an emergency they schedule a seat on the bus to the ferry landing, then ride the ferry up to Stehekin, where there is a pay phone. There is no law enforcement in Holden and no need for it. No one locks their rooms, and all the buildings are open twenty-four hours a day. The only exception is the ice-cream parlor, which was locked from the outside, while the ice-cream freezer was secured with still another lock. I never doubted that my two cameras, several lenses, and new notebook computer were safe. Ice cream was another matter.

The only store at Holden is a bookstore that also carries a small selection of candy bars and other snacks, a few T-shirts, and miscellaneous toiletries. There is no bar, no espresso shop, no grocery store, no drugstore, no beauty salon, no newsstand, no gas station, no video store. Once guests have paid for their weekly stay, money is almost irrelevant, except for the occasional ice cream, candy bar, or book.

Much of the work at Holden is done by retired couples, college students, musicians, artists, carpenters, and professional people who, for the chance to spend two weeks in this place, volunteer to cook, clean bathrooms, and compost kitchen scraps. Some come as teachers to present courses on topics ranging from "Medical Ethics" to "Right Brain Thinking."

There was no one I knew at Holden. Most of the staff and volunteers were Lutherans from Minnesota, and except for the characters on *Prairie Home Companion,* I didn't know any Lutherans or anyone from Minnesota. In the off-season when there is space, the Holden community welcomes people from different backgrounds who come as guests and pay a modest fee for food and lodging. I was lucky to be there.

On my first afternoon I went out for a walk with Carol Reed, the Holden forest ranger. We walked through the village and toward the Glacier Peak Wilderness. In less than a mile we passed a grassy spot on the right where four deer stood at attention, all intensely alert, all looking in exactly the same direction.

"Look—they know something we don't know. Probably there's a predator nearby. They either see it, smell it, or detect it with some sixth sense," Carol explained.

"What could it be?"

"Maybe a mountain lion. We walk near animals in the woods all the time and never even know they're there."

A few yards further on we came to a marten standing motionless on its back legs and looking in the same direction as the deer.

"That one knows too. Mountain lions hunt at night, but I recently saw one near here during the day."

That night at dinner I sat with the village pastor. When he asked me why I had come to Holden, I told him a bit about my journey and my interest in wilderness. Only then did I learn that the U.S. Forest Service was holding a wilderness-training conference in Holden beginning the next day. He explained that some eighty or so line officers with the Forest Service, folks responsible for designated wilderness areas in the Pacific Northwest, would be talking about wilderness values, what wilderness means to people, and how they can take care of it. He invited me to attend.

I spent the next four days listening to lectures and roundtable discussions about ways to manage wilderness that are consistent with the law. Most of the people in the audience were managers whose job is to protect wildernesses and insure that they are administered according to the Wilderness Act and subsequent legislation. I learned that managers are required to use minimum-impact tools—the double-bit ax, Pulaski, crosscut saw, brush hook, mattock, and a simple round-point shovel—for any trail maintenance and other work they do in the wilderness.

I discovered very quickly that wilderness rangers have more questions than answers about how to keep designated wildernesses wild. They acknowledge that the Wilderness Act of 1964 is full of paradox. *Wilderness* is defined by Congress as "an area where the earth and its community of life are untrammeled by man, where man himself is a visitor who does not remain." Yet hunters swarm into most designated wilderness areas of the Pacific Northwest to "harvest" deer, elks, moose, antelopes, sheep, and bears. Ranchers who held grazing rights in areas at the time that they became designated wilderness are allowed to continue grazing their animals there. While there are federal guidelines to minimize the impact of grazing, these guidelines are not usually enforced. No new mining claims have been allowed since 1984, but mining operations based on earlier permits continue.

Yet much wilderness remains in an apparently "untrammeled" state, and many questions were raised at the conference about how to keep it that way. Michael Frome, a writer who focuses on public lands, spoke of the need for professional wilderness rangers to radically change how they care for wilderness. Stewards of wilderness need to take a stand for its protection and to enforce the regulations designed to keep it wild. "Don't stay in the middle of the road," he warned. "That's where all the major accidents are." Frome also spoke of the spiritual experiences available in the wilderness and of people who go there in search of something bigger than themselves. Then he urged his audience to engage in a conversation with creation.

In subsequent sessions there was talk of grazing and mining rights; wildlife and fisheries management; air and water quality; fire management; exotic plants; and predator control. Other speakers raised questions about how wilderness can foster "personal growth" and whether wilderness experiences are useful in psychotherapy or the rehabilitation of delinquent young people.

The conference gave rangers an opportunity to talk about the values that underlie the preservation of wild places, but in their daily rounds they are less concerned with *why* than with *how*: how to repair a trail without damaging surrounding areas, how to deal with armed poachers using dogs, how to monitor grazing in the wilderness, and in general, how to limit the damage done by the increasing numbers of people hell-bent on having a wilderness experience with a capital *W*. People like me, I thought.

On the third day of the conference, participants went in small groups out into the adjoining Glacier Peak Wilderness. I hiked eleven miles to Hart Lake and back with eight rangers. Michael Frome joined our group. From time to time we stopped along the way to discuss problems that called for management solutions. What to do when a bridge washes away? Build it back? Replace it with a log? Cut a tree for the log or drag one that has fallen nearby? We came to a stream where a bridge had been washed away during the spring thaw and were able to boulder hop across it. Michael Frome seemed to convince the group that bridging this stream would be contrary to the "primeval character" mandated by the Wilderness Act, but he later told me that wilderness managers are constantly making decisions based on convenience rather than the Act.

Later, beyond Hart Lake, we gathered in a grove of old-growth cottonwoods, Douglas fir, and ponderosa pines to consider how to restore this area that had been severely damaged by backpackers who prefer to pitch tents in the protective grove of trees rather than in the more open surrounding areas. The soil was compacted, the ground vegetation was decimated, and several areas were rendered lifeless by campfires. There seemed to be no solution other than banning all camping from the area until it could regenerate.

Trails were another concern. Should they be maintained, and if so, what would be the minimum tool for doing so? Could the vegetation growing over a trail be trimmed, gravel be used to dam a wash, or chain saws be brought in to clean up after an avalanche? The answers—yes but, no, and no again—raised still more questions. The general consensus there on the ground in the Glacier Peak Wilderness was that wilderness values rather than the convenience of those who visit are primary and must be respected. To argue otherwise would be to insist that it is acceptable for federal agents to break the laws that govern the management of designated wilderness. It would be a while before I understood that these laws are broken all the time, not necessarily by the handpicked group I hiked with that day but by superintendents, district rangers, directors of agencies, and other high-ranking employees of the National Park System, the Forest Service, Fish and Wildlife, and the Bureau of Land Management.

The next day, buses carried the conference participants down the mountain to catch the ferry to Field's Point. In just four days I'd had an invaluable hands-on education about wilderness. Several line officers had invited me to visit them and offered to take me out in the areas they manage. Omar, who works in the summers as a seasonal ranger, invited me to come to the Mount Hood Wilderness, where he is responsible for monitoring the activities of legitimate hunters, backpackers, day hikers, mushroom gatherers, packers, and climbers as well as poachers, fugitives, and vandals. He explained that in a large wilderness near a major city such as Portland, a lot goes on that is never witnessed.

There were no more conferences while I was at Holden, and for the next ten days I lived my dream life. I woke early and made it to the communal dining room by 7:00. During meals and on the trails, I met scientists, writers, and other folks who had come to Holden for a variety of reasons—to monitor the snow melt; to take samples from the water and mining tailings; to photograph, track, or hunt the animals; to find solace after a traumatic loss; to practice the violin or set up an easel in the out-of-doors; to eat simply, rest often, and otherwise retreat from overly complex lives. Most days I spent the morning working on a writing project I'd promised to send my publisher by the middle of October. Then I'd grab my day pack, pick up my lunch, and walk out of the village into the Glacier Peak Wilderness. There was no changing of clothes for different occasions, no wasted time deciding what to wear. I dressed the same way every day—in one of two pairs of olive-green hiking pants, a shirt with pockets, and a vest for carrying film, sunscreen, and a notepad.

One afternoon I hiked to a spot high above Copper Creek. Up to the right I could see water dancing in bright sunlight over rocks and boulders as it fell rapidly down its steep streambed. To the left the creek—really more of a rushing river—disappeared into the dark conifer forest below. The air was warm enough for me to take off my sweater to use as a pillow as I stretched out on the ground. I gazed up at the deep blue sky, the deep greens of spruce and fir, the bright gold of the mountain ash, cottonwood, and quaking aspen. The air temperature was perfect. For three hours I lingered there, and although I had a book and notebook along, I soon abandoned any intention of reading or writing.

I'd been told that this seemingly pristine water was still polluted by chemicals used in processing the ore taken from the mines. A popular hiking trail up to a place called Honeymoon Heights crisscrosses the extensive tailings left exposed by the mining operation. Rainwater and melting snow still carry toxins from the tailings down to the creek below. There were few if any fish in the part of Copper Creek that is contaminated by the tailings. Perhaps because of the pollution, I'd not seen many birds at Holden, but that afternoon I encountered dozens of mountain chickadees as they settled in a nearby bush, filling the air with their hoarse, whispered calls.

I was dozing when I heard a loud crash and then a rustling of leaves nearby. When I looked up I was staring into the eyes of a doe. With her were two gangly teenage fawns. They gave me a wide berth then bounded into the trees, returning to the trail some fifty yards away. Then, hearing another crash, I looked around and saw a young buck with asymmetrical antlers looking directly at me. We stared at each other for some time before he dropped his head and walked slowly down the trail.

I look back at that afternoon as a milestone in my journey. I lay there grounded on the earth, energized by the penetrating rays of the sun, soothed by the gentlest of breezes, and cleansed by the rushing water below. I let my mind wander to the people I'd left behind. It was 4:00 P.M. in California, and Laura was probably absorbed in a paper she was writing for graduate school. It would be 1:00 P.M. in Atlanta, where Jerome would be leaving his office to walk over to the hospital for lunch with his colleagues. My parents would have finished lunch by now, and my father would be getting ready to go to the golf course; Mother would be settling down for an afternoon with her watercolors. Monica would be hard at work, and Richard could be teaching a class or painting in his studio. I couldn't imagine that my presence in almost any of these settings would have been particularly welcome.

My mother was the exception. She always enjoyed my company in the long afternoons as she waited for my father to return. Unlike the others, she just might be thinking of me as I was of her. She would have enjoyed being here and would have loved the birds, the deer, the golden light and rushing water. It made me sad to think about her at home alone, but I knew that the sadness came more from my love for her than her need for me. My mother loved her life, and she loved me. Whenever I called to say that I wanted to see her but it would be a while, she would say, "Don't worry, honey, you have a good time. I don't have to hold you in my lap to love you." I look back on that afternoon as a time of pure contentment that had nothing whatsoever to do with learning, striving, or interacting and everything to do with being one creature among others quietly and temporarily sharing the same spot on earth.

At dinner a few days later I met Jim Addington, who had come to lead a workshop on "Spirituality and Creativity." Jim was looking for a hiking partner to walk with him up to one of the lakes in the wilderness the next day. I agreed to go. We put in an order for two sack lunches so we could spend the whole day hiking. At dawn I looked out the window at fog, mist, light rain, and snow on the high peaks.

"Looks like our hike is off," Jim said when I saw him a few minutes later at breakfast.

"Well, let's wait and see what it's like in an hour."

Sure enough, an hour later the sun was shining through a clearing in the clouds. We grabbed a day pack for the lunches and headed out. Wearing brightly colored T-shirts pulled over darker fleece jackets, I assumed we were protected from hunters and the cold. As we entered the wilderness, a pair of does came down the trail, moved off into the trees to wait for us to pass, then returned to the trail. Animals blazed many of the trails in this part of the Cascades long before humans began to use them. Off in the woods a large six-point buck was visible standing motionless while we passed. I'd seen hunters heading up the trail the day before, and several days later I encountered them walking into the village. All but one was empty-handed.

At first we walked through a heavily forested area. Within a mile the forest gave way, and we were high on the side of a mountain looking out. From previous hikes I recognized two peaks, Copper Mountain and Bonanza Mountain, both named during the mining boom. Two miles of switchbacks brought us increasingly awesome views and led into a forest of spruce and fir.

Stunned by beauty, I didn't notice that the snow was getting deeper and clouds were rolling in until we came to a spot where the trail disappeared completely. About that time we came on large fresh tracks, too large to be deer or elk. Excited by the prospect of seeing a moose, we pushed on. A single set of tracks meant there was no calf. Probably we were following a bull moose; probably he would not attack as a cow with a calf would. Assuming that the moose was on a trail, we followed the tracks in silence for another mile or so, even though the wind picked up and heavy snow began to fall. The dazzling beauty of the day, the excitement of stalking a large animal, and the effort of climbing uphill were enough to make me ignore the increasing cold. It didn't even occur to me that we should turn back until my companion stopped in his tracks and looked at me in bewilderment.

"Aren't you cold?" he whispered through chattering teeth, then paused before adding slowly, "I'm real . . . real cold."

Only then did I pay any attention to how Jim was dressed. First I noted wet running shoes and white, presumably cotton, socks. Then a cotton turtleneck under a fleece jacket. Gloves that seemed to be made of some kind of plastic. Instead of a wool cap, he had on a cotton baseball cap. I suddenly remembered Ken's instructions, embellished with horror stories, about hypothermia: "Always take an extra jacket, wool socks . . . if you don't need them, someone else may . . . had a buddy, almost died . . . only forty degrees . . . windy . . . wet and chilled to the bone."

I looked in my day pack and found food, a first-aid kit, and a flashlight. None of this would be much help to Jim, who was much too cold to function. He cooperated when I led him to a log, where he sat quietly while I took off his wet shoes and socks and wrapped his feet first in my woolen mittens and then in my jacket. Not knowing what else to do, I insisted that he eat a peanut-butter sandwich while I kept my arms wrapped around his bundled feet. Jim had little fat over his muscles, and for once I was glad for the extra five pounds I'm always battling. Even more, I appreciated the wool socks and waterproofed hiking boots that I wore whenever I hiked. I looked around for anything resembling dry wood and realized I probably couldn't get a fire going in all this snow. Besides, the temperature seemed to be dropping and more snow appeared likely. Getting off this mountain as quickly as possible seemed essential, and we had to do so with care. A sprained ankle could have devastating consequences.

Jim's shivering subsided enough for him to put back on the wet socks and cram his still-cold feet into wet shoes. Going downhill did not generate the heat that climbing had, so we walked as fast as we could without inviting a fall. Finally the sun came out, and a few minutes later we reached a relatively dry trail. Soon we felt almost warm. As we emerged from the wilderness, Jim looked at me and shrugged.

"Next time, I think I'll bring boots," he said in a playful tone of voice.

Next time, I thought, I'll make sure I have emergency supplies. Next time I'll remember how quickly mild hypothermia can change to a severe condition with mental confusion and rigid muscles. Next time I'll think twice before going out in the snow under a threatening sky with someone wearing running shoes and cotton socks.

When we returned to the village, I went to my room, quickly changed into a bathing suit, and headed for the large outdoor hot tub, which—along with the sauna—is Holden's only gesture to luxury. I found Jim already up to his neck in the very hot water. Only then did I talk about what I'd learned from Ken about the process of freezing to death. People exposed to cold lose heat mainly from the extremities and the head; body temperature can drop from 98.6 to 95, the zone of mild hypothermia; if it drops down to the mid-80s, victims often hallucinate. Just before losing consciousness, they often feel a sensation of extreme heat and tear off their clothing; people rescued in this state can easily die from being rewarmed too rapidly.

I don't think Jim ever did believe that he was in serious trouble. He assumed that even if he had been unable to walk out, I probably could have gotten help before he succumbed to coma or frostbite. As we emerged limp as noodles from the hot water, Jim, who is from Minnesota, couldn't resist teasing me about my know-it-all lecture on the dangers of freezing to death.

"Tell you what—let's pack all our emergency gear, take extra everything, and go back tomorrow and find that moose."

"Wrong," I said, and made a counterproposal. "Let's take another trail below the snow line and find whatever we find."

After a morning's work the next day, Jim and I hiked up to Honeymoon Heights, named for the cabins that newlywed miners once occupied there. From the top we could see the whole of the village rimmed with astounding peaks of the North Cascades.

September 20 was the last day that the Jacuzzi would be open. I was reading myself to sleep when I heard a large crowd gather not far from my window for one last soak in the soothing waters. At closing time, 10:30 P.M., they all sang "Auld Lang Syne." Thirty minutes later the village was quiet. I'd been in Holden a week, but I was not ready to leave. The next day I made arrangements to stay another seven days.

Except for the possible toxic legacy from the mining days and the lack of medical services, I couldn't really think of anything wrong with Holden. It was as nearly utopian as any place I'd ever been. The wholesome food—pastas and casseroles, vegetable salads, fresh baked breads and muffins, and seasonal fruit—was certainly better than my usual fare at home, and I loved having no more clothes than I could carry in my backpack. I suppose that once winter set in, I might want to go out for a movie, a play, a concert, or a glass of wine. I might miss having the *New York Times* at breakfast, but I could probably adjust to reading back issues in the library. The quality of my life was no poorer for having to wait several days to hear the latest news from the Middle East or the New York Stock Exchange.

The absence of telephones, television, or any other instantaneous form of communication means that the people of Holden are a little behind on what is happening in the outside world, and they look forward to letters from friends and family. There were a few times at Holden when I felt like a homesick kid at camp, dutifully writing postcards home. And once in a while I missed being able to call Jerome to tell him how I loved the pared-down simplicity of daily life in this place where the most exciting event was an encounter with a wild animal or an unexpected snowfall. Most of the time, though, I was glad for the isolation.

While I was at Holden, I thought a lot about how wilderness affects attitudes toward money and consumption. Certainly the folks who live year-round in the village had little need for the material goods that clutter the lives of so many urbanites. When there are no stores nearby and everything people have must come in on the ferry and then be brought up in a bus, excessive consumption is absurd. Living near and spending time in the wilderness, eating in a communal dining room, and sleeping in small quarters, the guests and residents of Holden have no choice but to live simply.

Before I left home, I'd heard people talk about feeling "complete" and "balanced" and I'd thought I knew what they meant. Looking back now, I don't think I did. In Holden's peaceful setting, I felt my emotional, physical, and rational faculties merge into one. No one part of me seemed to be at war with another. I experienced no inner turmoil. This is not to say that I didn't feel sadness, fear, or anger. I did, but when I had those feelings, I didn't feel anxiety about them.

It was in Holden and the Glacier Peak Wilderness that I felt myself recover from years of energy-depleting living. In that community of strangers, no one made any requests or demands of me. Although a few people asked me to join them for hikes, I usually went alone into the wilderness. Sitting on the edge of Hart Lake, in a grove of ancient trees or on a ridge overlooking a whole range of snowcapped mountains, I felt energy return that I didn't even know I'd lost. Before I left Holden, I resolved to do whatever it takes to use that energy for what seems most valuable to me.

Bear Poachers and
Mushroom Wars

〰〰〰 TAKE MY WORD for it. Bear poachers are scary people, and so are folks who kill each other for mushrooms. There are hazards in any wild place, but in the Glacier Peak Wilderness the only time I was afraid was when Jim Addington developed hypothermia. Only a small number of hunters had come into that side of the wilderness, and they seemed like sensible, cautious men. There are so few grizzlies in the North Cascades that I didn't even consider the possibility of a bear attack, but the day after I left Holden, I found myself in a very different kind of wilderness.

Thanks to the slow ferry ride, reentry into the world of automobiles was gradual. I left Holden in the late morning, and it was late afternoon when I retrieved my van and headed south toward Oregon, where I expected to meet with Omar, the ranger who had offered to take me along on his rounds in the Mount Hood Wilderness. Heading south from Chelan, I passed through miles of apple and pear orchards. It was harvest time, and the roads were lined with empty crates that would soon be filled with fruit to be shipped all over the world. There was little traffic on the road, but the quiet of the evening was occasionally broken by the buzz of low-flying aircraft spraying the fields with what fruit growers call "plant protection products." About dark I turned into a campground outside Yakima.

The next morning I turned south and drove on Highway 97 through the Yakima Indian reservation to Interstate 84, then west through the Columbia River Gorge and south on Highway 35 on the edge of the Mount Hood Wilderness. Kim, a young ranger with a confident air, was skeptical about my camping alone in the wilderness.

"Set up camp in one of the national-forest campgrounds," she advised. "Then take day hikes. There's a lot of activity in the wilderness right now. It's hunting season, and the bear poachers are out. We'd appreciate your letting us know if you see any poachers. We can't possibly patrol the whole area."

"How would I know a poacher if I saw one?"

"Well, you won't see just one. They go in pairs in four-wheelers. The back of the vehicle will be caged off for the dogs. Bear dogs. You might find the vehicle at the end of an old logging trail. They like to get out in a hurry once they get a bear. You may also run into a carcass. That can be a pretty gruesome sight."

"Why would they leave a carcass? I don't understand."

"They don't want the bear. They just want the gallbladder and the feet. Gallbladders bring a thousand dollars in Asia, where they're sold for their medicinal powers. In fancy restaurants in some Asian countries, a cup of bear-paw soup sells for as much as eight hundred dollars. That's to improve sexual performance. The claws are sold as souvenirs."

Kim sold me a map of the wilderness and recommended a trail up Mount Hood. Then she gave me some final advice. "Look, I go in there all the time by myself, but I've learned to sense danger. Trust your instincts. Pay attention to what you're feeling. People still have extrasensory powers that they don't use. The other day I was hiking along and suddenly I felt chill bumps all over my body. For no reason, I was stopped in my tracks by fear. I walked slowly a few more feet, and just around the bend I saw a large black bear with a cub. She looked at me, and I slowly backed down the trail. I wasn't so afraid of her as I was of the hunters who might be stalking her."

At that point a tall, middle-aged ranger wandered into the office and joined in the conversation. "You telling her about poachers? No point in calling those guys hunters," he said. "They're killers. They don't pay attention to anybody's rules."

"I guess I'm safe," I said. "I'm dressed in brown and green and I stand pretty tall. Nobody's going to mistake me for a bear."

"Be careful, lady. There's deer poachers out there too. There's folks who'll do anything. Shoot anything. Take anything. Kill each other for mushrooms. Besides, everything in the forest is brown or green. Why would you dress like that?"

I looked down at my olive-green hiking pants and tan shirt and vest and thought that averaged together, my clothes were about the same color as a ranger's uniform. But I did wish I had an orange hunting vest, or at least the bright yellow T-shirt I'd borrowed to wear in Glacier Peak Wilderness.

Noticing my growing concern, the second ranger tried to re-assure me. "You'll probably be okay. Just be careful. Make a lot of noise so nobody will mistake you for a deer. And be sure to let us know if you see any of those poachers," he said over his shoul-der as he went out the door.

"I didn't want to say anything until he left," Kim said, "but look out for men, and don't worry about women you see out there. It's a macho thing. I've never known a woman to kill a bear, or even want to."

"What's this about mushrooms?"

"Harvesting mushrooms on federal lands can be very lucra-tive, and folks who go after them sometimes go after each other. People have died for mushrooms not so far from here."

I thanked Kim for her advice and asked her to check on me if I didn't come by in the morning, but she explained that rangers couldn't do that. Too many people go into the wilderness, come out safely, and forget to check by the station. Noticing my wedding band, Kim suggested that I call my husband, explain where I was going, then call him back when I came out. The For-est Service would respond if he called the next day and explained that I didn't return when I said I would.

A few minutes later I was driving up the road to Cloud Cap. When I parked the car at the Tilly Jane Campground, there were no other cars in sight. Then I headed up Mount Hood on Trail 600 A, a steady uphill pull to Cooper Spur Ridge. There in the late afternoon light, with the face of Mount Hood looming directly behind me, I looked through clear air at a string of volcanoes—Mount Adams, Mount Rainier, and Mount St. Helens. The bear poachers, I convinced myself, had probably done their dirty work early in the day. And there I was, the last on the trail, looking down at that amazing landscape in utter solitude. I had packed survival gear in case I sprained an ankle and couldn't get down—water, food, a sweater, matches, a Gore-Tex jacket, and a space blanket. If I had to stay up there until other hikers arrived the next day, I could survive. Before long a full moon would rise in the east. As much as I wanted to wait for the moon, I knew I should get down off the mountain before darkness fell.

It was fully dark by the time I pulled into the first of several national-forest campgrounds looking for a place where I would be comfortable enough to spend the night. All the campgrounds were officially "closed" for the season, which means that rangers no longer patrol them and there's no toilet paper in the pit toilets. The first time I pulled off the road and drove down the pitted dirt road into an area set aside for camping, I was surprised to find it totally abandoned. No tents, no fires, no cars—nothing. After what the rangers had told me about this part of Oregon, I wanted to find a site near a family with children. Instead, in the next campground there was only one party. Four men. Two four-wheelers. I didn't take the time to look for cages in the backs of the vehicles, but I did see a couple of dogs by the fire.

My last chance to find a place that seemed safe in the national forest was the Still Creek Campground. My heart sank when I pulled in to total darkness, but as I came to the end of the loop, there was a campfire and one vehicle—a Chevrolet sedan with Georgia plates. I stopped and jumped out to greet the people sitting around the campfire. Then I heard a growl and saw a large Doberman. As my eyes adjusted to the firelight, I saw two men and a woman. Women don't kill bears, I thought.

"Look, I just want to introduce myself. My name's Melissa, and I'll be camping nearby."

Silence. Finally the larger of the two men stood up, put a hand on the dog, and told him to quiet down. The dog dropped to the ground but didn't take his eyes off me. It occurred to me that these people were as uneasy about who I was—and who might be in the back of the van—as I was about them.

"I noticed you have Georgia plates. I'm from Atlanta, and I'm here by myself," I said in an appeasing tone I'd grown to hate in myself but that seemed appropriate at the time. "Okay with you if I camp nearby?"

"Sure, lady, whatever you want to do. The dog won't hurt you unless I tell him to. He does what I say. We're from Savannah. Came out here to go to cooking school, and we're living in the woods till we can make enough money to rent a place in Portland."

How, I wondered, were they making money? I felt only slightly safer than I had in the other campground. The woman and the smaller man never said a word to me. There was something weird about these folks and their dog, I thought, as I prepared dinner. From time to time the dog would growl, whether at me or at some other potential intruder, I never knew. I do know, however, that of all my nights in the woods, that was the time that I was most afraid. I never even set up my tent but instead covered the windows in the van with makeshift shades, and I crawled into my sleeping bag as soon as I'd cleaned up. Just as I was drifting off to sleep, I was startled by a knock on the front window.

"You in there?" a male voice said.

"Yeah, sure," I answered.

"My dog and me are just making rounds. Wanted to make sure you're okay. Sam here'll protect you. He don't like it when strangers come around."

Obviously I wasn't the only person who felt I needed protection in that wild part of Oregon. I slept fitfully, and the next morning when I climbed out of the van around 6:00 A.M., I was greeted by a low growl. If Sam had really been instructed to protect me, he hadn't quite gotten the message. He stood glaring and growling at me in the early morning light as if to warn me not to come near his territory. I gave him a wide berth when I headed for the pit toilet, but when I returned to the van, he growled again. Sam, I concluded, was confused, but somehow I managed to pack up my cooking gear, pull on my clothes, and drive quietly away without waking his people. As I pulled out onto the highway, I turned on the radio. The top item on the local news gave me a chill. A German tourist had been pulled from his white van parked in a rest area on nearby Interstate 5 and murdered just north of Grants Pass. Well, I could say for sure that the strange people I camped near were not the killers, since I knew they had been at the Still Creek Campground all night. Even so, I had a feeling they weren't up to any good.

I drove north a few miles until I found a country store serving coffee and fresh baked breads. I called Jerome from a pay phone to let him know I was okay, then turned back to the wilderness, where I took another trail up the mountain. I had a whole day to explore what could only be a small fraction of the Mount Hood Wilderness. In spite of deer and bear poachers as well as licensed hunters, I felt safe as I headed up a frequently used trail. I expected to be overtaken by more ambitious hikers, but it was late morning before I saw another human being—a lone backpacker coming down from a three-day trip. Shortly after we passed on the trail, I suddenly felt a rush of adrenaline. I was not conscious of hearing, seeing, or smelling anything; but I was consumed with fear. I took a few deep breaths and told myself I was being silly. I walked another twenty-five yards before I looked down and saw fresh tracks. Bear tracks. I stopped to listen. Silence. Nothing. I reasoned with myself. If there were anything to fear, I would certainly hear something. As I stood there in the silence, I remembered the ranger's warning: "Pay attention to what you're feeling." I looked down at the fresh bear tracks going from left to right across the trail in front of me. Then I noticed other tracks. Dog tracks. I turned around and walked steadily down the mountain. After about ten minutes of walking, I heard a single shot from the direction I'd come, followed seconds later by two more. I stopped again to listen. The forest was totally quiet. No squirrels scurrying, no birds singing. Nothing.

That afternoon I returned to the ranger station and reported that I'd seen bear tracks and heard shots nearby. I learned that poachers who make a kill in the morning are long gone by afternoon and that participants in the mushroom wars also get out of the wilderness in a hurry. The Forest Service issues mushroom permits in the area to people who collect mushrooms for the international market. Those who know what they are doing harvest hundreds of pounds of this extremely valuable commodity. Matsutakes, the most valuable of Oregon's wild mushrooms, ripen in the fall. Ordinary-looking white mushrooms with a pinkish base, they sell for as much as $60 to $100 a pound retail. Pickers may be paid as much as $25 a pound for top-of-the-line matsutakes. The more common morels bring pickers between $3.50 and $4.75 a pound. While the average picker makes about $100 a day, some earn as much as $1,000 or even $2,000 a day for a big find during a bumper crop. Real money is made by the folks who set up buying stations on the fringes of national forests. In one season buyers pay millions in cash for freshly picked mushrooms, which they then sell at considerable profit to brokers who send them on to Canada, France, and Japan. In 1993 the total annual crop of wild mushrooms in national forests in Oregon was worth more than thirty-five million dollars, but the market fluctuates, and pickers can track its ups and downs on the Internet.

"We're talking big money," the ranger said, "and people are shooting at each other out there. My guess is that most people who go into the wilderness pack heat." As I was about to leave, the ranger reached into her files and dredged up copies of newspaper articles that recounted several violent incidents in which armed robbers had held up collectors and taken their mushrooms in the forests. In less than a year, two Cambodian pickers had been shot dead in the field.

Then I learned one more piece of chilling information.

"I guess you've heard about the skinheads out here."

"Don't tell me."

"Okay, I won't. But they're here and they're armed. They come out at night just to shoot automatic weapons into trees."

"Thanks for not telling me."

There were good reasons why I felt frightened in the highly charged atmosphere of wild Oregon. Anyone breezing along near the Hood River exit of Interstate 90 could have been at my campsite in thirty minutes and out of there and back to Portland in little more than an hour, whereas there was no easy access to the Glacier Peak Wilderness. Entering that wilderness from Holden, I could check in at the hike hut early in the morning to report where I planned to hike that day; if I had not returned by dinner hour, someone would come looking for me. Here rangers and law-enforcement officials were too busy dealing with poachers and the constant threat of violence to do anything else.

The closer a wilderness is to a city, interstate, or well-traveled highway, the more degraded, overused, and dangerous it is likely to be. Wilderness in the Everglades is close to Miami and other highly populated areas of south Florida; Joshua Tree is near Los Angeles, San Diego, and Palm Springs; the Desolation, Ansel Adams, and John Muir aren't far from San Francisco, San Jose, Sacramento, and even Las Vegas. The Olympic, Mount Ranier, and a cluster of other wildernesses in the North Cascades are an easy drive from Seattle and Bellingham; the Never Summer, Flat Tops, and Indian Peaks from Denver. Bandelier and the Pecos can be reached before sunrise by early risers from Santa Fe and Albuquerque. Some de facto wildernesses that have yet to receive official designation are locked inside national parks that have thousands of visitors in a day. The Grand Canyon, Glacier, and Yellowstone are among them.

Ready for a good night's sleep, I decided to spend the night on the rim of a different volcano. I drove south, passing just to the east of the Mount Jefferson, Belknap Crater, Three Sisters, and Mount Thielsen Wildernesses. I didn't stop until I came to Crater Lake National Park. I arrived there in the late afternoon, the time when the angle of the sun creates perfect reflections on the lake. I sat for some time on the edge of the crater, confident that no one was likely to shoot at me or mistake me for an animal with a thousand-dollar gallbladder. Nearby was a young woman sitting in a meditative pose. In front of her on the ground was a copy of Thoreau's *Walden*. A fellow traveler, I thought.

Later I pitched my tent in the park campground, washed clothes in the laundromat, and cooked a pot of lentils and rice. Then I slept soundly, grateful for the illusion of safety I felt in a national park campground, where families with children slept peacefully nearby.

Since leaving home, I'd mostly been immersed in the wonders of the natural world. The marvels of geology, weather, and living things had invigorated my body and spirit in mysterious ways; but the closer I looked at what was in front of me, the more I saw the degrading effects of human activity.

It was in California that I became aware of what was lost with the construction of the Hetch Hetchy Reservoir and the ugly commercial establishments in Yosemite Valley; in Wyoming that I saw the damage done by grazing stock on public lands; in Montana that I smelled the toxic fumes emanating from pulp mills along the Clark Fork River; in Washington State that I saw the horrendous devastation of clear-cuts and the ugly wounds and poisonous tailings left by mining operations; and in Oregon that I felt threatened by violence.

Road building and clear-cuts near and around wilderness destroy corridors that maintain genetic diversity by connecting the wildlife of one wilderness with that of others. Road construction and timbering also choke waterways, annihilating habitat for fish and other aquatic creatures. They open pathways for illegal snowmobiles, off-road vehicles, and other motorized encroachments on the wild. Grazing, mining, and overuse degrade vegetation, pollute the water, and destroy riparian areas. I was beginning to think that for federal lands to be, in fact, public lands, the public would have to lay claim to what is legally theirs. To do so will require knowing the laws that govern these lands and, in the appropriate public forums, demanding that the laws be respected as well as enforced. I had learned in Holden that the Wilderness Act requires that the agency responsible for administering a wilderness must operate from a wilderness management plan that has passed through public review and comment. Protection of the 106 million plus acres of designated wilderness is a job for many people; no one person could have both the big picture and intimate knowledge of more than a few of the 600 plus wildernesses in the Lower 48, Alaska, and Hawaii. It is the responsibility of those who use and care about wilderness to see that it stays wild—a task that will last as long as there are public lands to be protected.

Canyons and Slickrock

～～～ QUESTIONS OF safety had been in my face since I'd left home. Is it "safe" to trust a stranger to be my guide, to cross a wobbly log spanning a cold rushing creek, to drive over a mountain pass at night in the snow, to hike in grizzly or mountain-lion country, to set up camp next to some weird folks with an aggressive Doberman guarding their camp, to go into the woods with bear poachers and mushroom rustlers? The truth is, I'd concluded that there is no such thing as safety for mortals. We're always at risk for an accident, a mugging, disease, or for that matter a bolt of lightning, but I was learning to hedge my bets—to assess the lay of the land and pay attention to what was around me.

I could play it safe, but I couldn't know for certain that I was safe. When I jogged through wooded areas in public parks, I looked for threatening-looking people the same way I looked for snakes in the Georgia woods. Wilderness had not taught me to be fearless but rather to pay heed to feelings of apprehension and to remember that normal fear is an essential part of the wildness of the human species. We share it with all feral creatures that go scurrying through the bushes when we approach. To deny it is to ignore a powerful tool for survival.

It was about 6:30 A.M. when I finished breakfast in a truck stop near Ashland, Oregon, and asked the cashier for the best route to Salt Lake.

"Oh, that's easy. My sister has a motel in Utah, so I've been there. Get on Highway 140 and stay on it a long time."

"How long?"

"Oh, you know, three hundred miles or so. Be careful, some places it dead-ends and jogs around. There's a good hundred-and-fifty-mile stretch at the end with no gas. You're not likely to see many cars either—just desert."

Entering a part of the country I'd never seen, I had that "on the road again" feeling as I passed through five totally different landscapes. I watched the sun rise in an early morning fog in the Rogue River Valley. As the fog lifted, I climbed into a series of national forests—the Rogue, the Winema, and the Fremont. The Forest Service has the habit of leaving a few large trees standing along the side of the road, giving travelers the illusion that they are passing through vast forests. I'd learned enough in Oregon to know that just beyond the fringes of the highway would be clearcuts. The only vehicles I saw on the road that early in the morning were logging trucks sagging with the weight of huge trees.

From the forests I emerged into orchard country and then grazing lands. By the time I reached the high desert, I'd climbed to six thousand feet. High on a ridge, I pulled into a turnout and gazed through clear air at the distant horizon. No sign of human activity except a lone truck coming over the ridge from the opposite direction. Just after entering Nevada, I stopped at a gas station/casino to fill up and fortify myself with a Coke and candy bar. The route was easy, and I was making good time until a young blond woman standing in the middle of the road holding a stop sign interrupted my journey. For forty-five minutes on Highway 95, I waited for a highway crew to do whatever it was they were doing ahead. Ahead of me was a pickup truck. When three shirtless men got out and walked over to the side of the road to urinate, I looked away until they went back to the truck for another beer. I was not comfortable—something about the beer, something about the tattoos—but they had given me no reason to be afraid. Besides, there was a highway crew ahead, and one of the crew was a woman.

When it dawned on me that we might be there for a while, I turned off the engine and got out to stretch my legs. The fellows in the truck took that as an invitation, and in a matter of seconds they began some serious harassment. Noting my Georgia plates, one started a "Georgia Peach" routine that I hadn't heard in years. Another saw my car phone and asked if he could make a call. When I told him it wouldn't work in this deserted place, he offered to fix it.

About that time a man driving a large newish sedan pulled up behind me. Just as one of the shirtless fellows reached for my car phone, the man emerged from his Oldsmobile and walked toward me.

"My name's Paul," he said, extending his hand. Without saying another word, the guys settled down and drifted back to their truck.

Paul and I chatted for some thirty minutes. When I asked him how he happened to be in this isolated place, he responded as if he had been waiting for days for someone to talk to. He told me that he had taken ten days off from his high-pressure job as a college administrator and that in just four days he'd traveled all the way from eastern Tennessee to the coast of northwest Oregon. In five more days he would return home.

"I wish I'd done this years ago," he said. "I had no idea how beautiful this country is. I'm a changed man." I smiled to myself at the idea of such a rapid transformation, thinking how I'd been away for two months and my own journey seemed to be going in slow motion. When I asked Paul how he thought he'd changed, he hesitated.

"I have to do things differently," he said slowly. "Not just some things. I mean everything. Otherwise, I'm going to die."

"Look at this," he said with a sweep of his hand. "How can you look at all this beauty and emptiness and not be changed? Our lives are so small, so short. Back in the sixties I thought I was going to do something important with my life. Make a difference. Make a better world. Somehow I lost my way somewhere between earning a living and raising a family. Damn it, I haven't even seen the Grand Canyon."

Paul's eyes misted over, and I became uncomfortable. Before I could think of anything to say, he began to talk again—about his wife finishing law school and urging him to quit his job, and how this trip was just a beginning. I thought of telling him about how the whirlwind trip I'd taken a few months earlier to the Chiric- ahuas had been a new beginning for me, but in the end I resis- ted talking about myself.

Just as the woman in the neon-orange suit released us, I heard myself say, "Sounds to me like you're ready to make some changes. Maybe it doesn't matter what you do as long as what you choose needs to be done and you can do it . . . "

"Do it with heart?" Paul filled in.

"Yes, with heart, with love, with . . . "

"Spirit? That's it. I've lost my spirit."

As he walked back to his car, the guys in the pickup pulled away and Paul called out to me. "Don't worry about a thing from here on. I'll follow you all the way to Salt Lake. Just keep it under seventy-five miles per hour. I've already been stopped once."

I stayed in front of Paul until I was about thirty miles outside the city. Then, with salt flats on either side as far as I could see and absolutely no place for a cop to hide, I decided to play it safe with Paul. I blew the horn, waved, accelerated to eighty-five, and gradually left him behind.

That night I camped in an urban campground under a lone Chinese elm tree. I had driven the 760 miles from Ashland, Oregon, to Salt Lake in twelve hours. Except for the delay on Highway 95, I had only stopped twice, both times for gas, a Coke, and a Snicker's candy bar. That night I slept soundly, lulled by what I thought was a gentle, intermittent rain. When I woke in the morning, I dis- covered that the soothing sound I'd enjoyed during the night was actually made by leaves falling from the overhanging elm.

When I picked up Jerome at the Salt Lake airport later that day, it had been a long four weeks since we'd seen each other. I was so glad to see him that I didn't complain when he filled the back of the van with an excessive amount of gear. Our plan was to camp first in Arches National Park and then in Canyonlands. From Salt Lake we drove straight to Moab and asked around for a good rest- aurant. The Central Café, we were told, was the best restaurant in town. I was eager to celebrate Jerome's birthday with a good meal. He stuck to his low-fat vegetarian regime and ordered field green salad, pasta, and wild berries for dessert, but I threw caution to the wind and feasted on a wild-mushroom appetizer, a rich dessert, and for an entree—don't ask me why—elk in a burgundy sauce. Jerome was puzzled.

"Look," I told him, "anybody who spends as much time as I do in the wild should know how wild game tastes." I'd grown up eating wild dove, quail, and duck, but I'd only rarely eaten venison and never elk. "Besides, this is a celebratory dinner, and I'm ready to indulge myself with something special." We ordered a nice bottle of merlot and began a prolonged celebration that ended a week later with our twenty-ninth wedding anniversary.

The first night we camped in Arches, Jerome built a campfire in the fire pit provided by the Park Service. Even after a light drizzle had begun to fall, we cuddled next to the fire under an umbrella and talked about what was hard about being apart.

"I hate it when you call late at night and then I can't get to sleep," he said.

"I hate it when you go to bed before I find a place to call you," I countered.

"I hate it that you're three time zones away."

"I hate it when you don't seem happy that I've called."

"Why should I be happy? You're three thousand miles away. I'm stuck at home, dealing with all kinds of difficult stuff at the office and then coming home to an empty house and no dinner. Then on top of that, I have to take care of the dog and keep up with the house renovations. Sometimes it's almost too much."

"Yeah, I know. I remember what it was like to be the one stuck at home. It's not that I'm trying to pay you back for all those years when I was handling everything. It's just that it's my time."

"I'm okay with that. It is your time, and I know how important it is for you to be doing this. But it's not always easy for me to know you're sleeping in the woods and I don't even know where you are."

"Jerome, do you understand that this is about changing the way I live?"

"I think so. But I'm not sure how it's going to turn out."

"Neither am I," I said. Then I asked him to tell me what he liked about my being gone.

"I've had a lot of time to think. Maybe I'd like to make some changes too, take more time off, spend more time in places like this."

"Do you feel like you need to be alone out here?" I asked.

"No. I like being with you—here in these canyons, so different from anything I've ever seen. Sometimes I like being at home alone, being able to do things my way, when I want to, and not having to think about what you want. But I've had enough of that."

Knowing how often "change" for a man means looking for a new woman, I became uneasy. "Do you want me to come home?" I asked.

"I can't ask you to do that. In the long run it's good for me to know that you're doing what you want to do. And I'm proud to have a wife who can go for what she wants."

"Are you sure about that?"

"Yeah, I'm sure. I like telling people about your adventures. I'm just ready for some adventure of my own."

Jerome never said that he missed me terribly, was really lonely, or wished I'd come home. I think he understood that what I was doing was important to me, and he knew better than to say anything that would get in my way. After we crawled into our tent, the drizzle turned to a driving rain—a rare occurrence in canyon country in the fall.

The next morning the sky was clear, and we got out early and hiked to Sand Dune Arch and Broken Arch. As we wound back to camp on the bottom of the canyon floor, we came to a large pool of water from the night's rain. The surrounding sand was decorated with animal tracks—deer, rabbit, fox, porcupine, and coyote. One set of tracks was much larger than the others, and Jerome guessed they belonged to an extra large coyote. I knew that coyote tracks, like dog tracks, include claw marks; cats retract their claws when they walk. I examined the larger tracks carefully. There were no claw marks.

Thinking that a mountain lion would have found easy prey among so many thirsty animals, I looked around for evidence of a struggle—hair, bones, a scuffle preserved in the sand. Nothing. Maybe the lion came for water and saved the prey for another day.

I urged Jerome to help me follow the tracks. Without paying much attention to where we were going, we followed them up one of the many openings between the strange vertical rock formations known as fins. As we turned a blind corner, I half expected to find a sleeping animal, but instead the sand turned suddenly to the red sandstone called slickrock. We walked a bit further, turning this way and that. Finally we dead-ended into a rock wall, where we found a large pile of relatively fresh scat shaped something like a frozen Dairy Queen dessert with a curl at the end. I got down close and pulled it apart with the edge of a rock; it was full of hair, tiny bones, even teeth. Backtracking to get out of the corner, we found another sandy area where I hoped to find more tracks.

"What are you gonna do if we find that cat?" Jerome asked with a smile that suggested he thought I was on a wild-goose chase. I was too absorbed with tracking to think about the reality of a large predator, and I guess I never really expected to find the elusive nocturnal animal that is so rare in these parts. We were still laughing at my reckless pursuit of a mountain lion when Jerome suggested we go back to camp for breakfast.

Feeling a little disoriented, I asked, "Which way?" I could almost always count on Jerome to know, but he looked around and seemed confused too. We'd left no tracks on the slickrock, and there were three possible ways leading out from where we stood. Neither of us had paid attention to the position of the sun when we started out. There we were surrounded by red and yellow pinnacles, spires, and odd-looking rocks balanced on more peculiar structures. We had eaten the granola bars and drunk all the water we'd brought. We had broken all the rules, and we were surely lost.

"Don't panic," Jerome advised. "We can figure this out." We scouted the immediate area; since there were only three ways out, all we'd have to do is try one after another until we came to the place where we'd seen the last tracks. Then we could follow the tracks to the watering hole and from there find the trail. We calculated that we had walked about ten minutes since we last saw tracks, so if we took one path at a time and walked for fifteen minutes we would surely find them. When we turned back the second time, we were getting discouraged and uncomfortably thirsty. Jerome was reassuring. "It's got to be the next one." In about ten minutes I spotted the first set of tracks, and in less than an hour we were enjoying breakfast at our campsite. Later that morning we went to the visitor's center to report what we'd seen.

"There are a few lions in the canyons," the ranger told us, "but we rarely even see tracks. You probably saw coyote tracks. There's lots of them. Most of the mountain lions in this area were cleared out years ago by ranchers." He brought over pictures of tracks, and I showed him what I'd seen. "Larger than coyote," I insisted, "and no claw marks." Still not totally convinced, he said he would go back in there to see for himself. "Be careful," I said. "You may get lost if you follow lion tracks up to the slickrock." I felt foolish as soon as the words were out of my mouth, but his response surprised me.

"You're right," he said. "Anybody can get lost in there. I wish more people thought the way you do."

Late that afternoon Jerome left me alone across from Balanced Rock while he walked up the Devil's Garden Trail to take pictures. I sat on what I'd concluded, from reading and talking to folks, was the spot where the writer Edward Abbey had parked his trailer during the three stretches he spent there in the late fifties and early sixties as a seasonal park ranger. The sun was low in the sky behind me. It was the time that photographers call the "magic hour," and Balanced Rock was taking on the glow of that amazing light. How many feet did that pedestal and rock soar into the sky —a hundred, two hundred feet? More? I scanned the landscape and imagined Abbey shivering alone on the steps of his trailer, mesmerized by the snakes that visited him there, looking at this weird, amazing wilderness of rocks.

Back at the campground, we made a fire for warmth and cooked supper over the camp stove—boiled potatoes, beans, and rice. After eating, we were sitting by the fire sipping a cup of hot chocolate when a young woman in uniform came over to urge us to come to the ranger show at the nearby amphitheater. "Slim Mabry's talking," she added. "You won't be sorry."

Mabry, then in his eighties, had been Abbey's boss at Arches and then later his friend. After his presentation about the early days when much of this area was unexplored, he began to talk about Abbey, whom he criticized as "too radical for his own good" but whom he was obviously proud to have known. The ambivalence he felt came out in other ways: he couldn't resist telling us that Abbey's *Desert Solitaire* was not exactly authentic since the writer had his wife and baby with him a good deal of the time.

Later that night Jerome and I took turns holding the flashlight and reading *Desert Solitaire.* The trails in Arches, Abbey claimed, were easy to follow, and a person would have to really work at it to get lost. Hmmm. Maybe, I thought, getting lost was different from not knowing where you are? Maybe Abbey was concerned about being permanently, irreparably, fatally lost. Even that didn't seem too difficult to me. In fact, two days later we came pretty close.

We'd set up camp on the rim of Squaw Canyon near the Needles section of Canyonlands National Park, a spot where people camp before going into the backcountry. There are no telephones and no running water. Every trail into this area drops down into a wilderness so rugged and beautiful that I couldn't imagine coming that close and still seeing it from afar.

It was only 10:00 A.M. when we finished setting up camp, so we assumed we had plenty of time to hike. Without looking at a topo map, we took the advice of another camper and descended into the canyon, expecting to enjoy a "moderate" hike. We carried only about a quart of water, apples, and a couple of energy bars.

Without a thought of danger, we set out to explore one dazzling scene after another—the brilliant yellow of the autumn cottonwood leaves; the reds, oranges, and ochers of the sandstone sculpted into bizarre swirls and shapes; and the deep green of the piñon pines—all set off by the intensely blue, cloudless sky. Forgetting how little water we had between us and ignoring the skull and crossbones carved into the wooden sign marking the trailhead, we decided to add a loop and go into Lost Canyon. What started as an easy saunter down a well-marked trail soon turned into a hands-and-knees scramble up slickrock that left me trembling from exertion and fear. But those early scrambles up well-grooved and slightly tilted rock seemed like child's play by the time the day was over.

When we came to the first steep climb, we met a couple about our age from Salt Lake. They were the only other people we saw all day. Elsa and Doug were about to turn back, but we talked them into going all the way into Lost Canyon. To provide access to the bottom of the canyon, the Park Service had bolted a steel ladder to a sheer rock face, but we found no such help getting back out. About six miles into the hike we realized we would have a considerable climb to get out of Lost Canyon, as we were surrounded by three-hundred-foot vertical rock walls. We could backtrack and climb out on the ladder, but to do so we would have to go back six miles rather than the three or four miles we had remaining. With no water and only three hours of daylight left, we decided to press on. Eventually, we found a way into a narrow side canyon, picking our way over rocks up a dry wash, sometimes stooping down low to get under overhangs and squeezing through narrow openings, always watching carefully for rattlesnakes. To reach the rim of the canyon, we had to make our way up a narrow, slanting ledge of rock a little more than a foot wide in places, at two points jumping over crevices in the rock that appeared bottomless.

The trail was marked by cairns placed across and up the slickrock by park rangers. Following what we assumed was the official trail, we found ourselves perched in a sitting position high on a narrow ledge that angled steeply toward the canyon. I inched my way sideways toward the next cairn. Jerome and Doug had gone mountain-goating ahead, but once they got across the ledge they realized that Elsa and I were having a hard time making the crossing. There was no way for them to help us: the ledge was barely wide enough for one person. Elsa was frozen in a curve of the cliff about ten feet ahead of me. Knowing that a slip could lead to a tumble into the three-hundred-foot abyss below, I fought panic and watched Elsa take deep breaths. Before this she had been un-affected by the heights; now she looked at me and said in a sooth-ing voice, "You don't have to move yet. This is real scary. I won't leave you."

I relaxed slightly and leaned back against the cliff face, occa-sionally peeking below. With Elsa just ahead of me, I found the strength to continue my sideways movement to the point where I could hoist myself up one ledge at a time to the top of the canyon. From there I stood up and followed the cairns—first across slickrock leading into Squaw Canyon and then back out a much easier trail to camp. As we reached the rim, the four of us, parched, headed for the tank of water provided in this waterless place by the Park Service. For a few minutes we stood there drink-ing, laughing, and talking about our adventure together, enjoying the euphoria that comes after being really afraid. Jerome and I said good-bye to Doug and Elsa and climbed up a rocky ridge to watch the magic light spread out to the horizon.

When I asked a ranger the next day why the Park Service would route hikers across that hazardous trail, he didn't seem to understand my concern and insisted that the hike should be clas-sified as moderate. He reminded me that a moderate trail in the backcountry is very different from hikes labeled "moderate" in easily accessible parts of national parks. He got out a topo map and pointed out the route out of Lost Canyon. When I described the ridge where we had to sit down and inch our way across a nar-row ledge slanting down into a three-hundred-foot drop-off, he finally got the picture.

"You followed the cairns all the way?"

"Oh, yes," I responded. "I wonder what would have happened to us if someone went out there and moved them."

"I think somebody did. We need to get down there and check it out," he said.

It had not occurred to me to worry about vandalism in Canyonlands until I realized how totally dependent we were on the good will of others who descended into that magical but po-tentially deadly maze. Later I learned that it's not uncommon for vandals to go into the canyons and move the cairns around to confuse hikers. Who? I wondered. Kids on a lark who barely even thought about the consequences of their pranks? Sadists?

When I left Jerome at the airport at Salt Lake City three days later, we promised each other that we'd come back to Utah for our thirtieth anniversary. We would go to Zion, maybe stay at the lodge, and take easy day hikes up well-marked trails where it's impossible to get lost.

When I headed south on Interstate 15 from Salt Lake, I had just enough daylight left to make it to Bryce Canyon before dark. I was glad to be alone again, though I knew that when I put up the tent that night I would wish Jerome were with me. But not now, and not the next morning, or the morning after. I could hardly wait to escape the interstate, and when I turned off on Highway 20 just south of Beaver, Utah, I felt that I'd returned to the wild. There was no sign of human habitation on either side of the road, only miles and miles of desert sage dotted with piñon and juniper. A light rain began to fall. Some five miles in, three does crossed the road ahead of me; a mile or so later I saw a young deer lying dead by the side of the road. I'd seen far more roadkills on busy highways, where a deer that bounds in front of a car is doomed. At least on winding back roads traffic was slowed enough to give the animals a chance. On a particularly steep grade, I passed a familiar road sign:

ROUGH NARROW ROAD LOOSE GRAVEL
STEEP GRADES
BLIND CURVES
DO NOT EXCEED 15 M.P.H.

I was climbing to seven thousand feet when the now-steady rain began to change to snow that quickly turned to slush. Add slush to a "rough, narrow road, steep grades, loose gravel, and blind curves" and there you have it: DANGER. I'd grown quite accustomed to one kind of danger or another. Why, I wondered, were some dangers more acceptable than others? Why, for example, was I more comfortable negotiating a slippery road than I was clinging to a ledge of slickrock in Lost Canyon? I imagined that I was more likely to skid off the road than to fall from the ledge, where—except for my panic—there was nothing to trigger a fall. Yet inside my van, comforted by Merle Haggard's "I Had a Beautiful Time," I felt much calmer driving the hazardous road than I had creeping along a dry ledge on a sunny afternoon.

When I entered Red Canyon, I couldn't resist slowing down to notice the sight of that red rock intensified by the whiter-than-white snowflakes. The walls of Red Canyon were to rocks what the feathers of the vermilion flycatcher are to birds. The reddest of reds, red like blood. I made it to Bryce Canyon National Park in time to set up my tent in the campground near the rim before darkness fell. The snow let up long enough for me to boil water for instant soup and fill a Nalgene bottle with hot water to put in the bottom of my sleeping bag. I'd learned a lot about staying warm since that stormy night six months before in Madera Canyon when I shivered in a summer sleeping bag as snow and sleet swirled around me. These days I brought both Thermarest pads and two pillows along with me, and, warmly dressed in layers of Polartec and wool, I climbed into my winter sleeping bag.

Propped up on two pillows, with a light hanging from the top of the tent, I opened *Desert Solitaire* and read good-night stories to myself as the snow fell outside. The next morning I awoke with the book beside my head. I had fallen asleep somewhere in the middle of "The Dead Man at Grandview Point."

Death in the Navajo Nation

〜〜〜 SOLITUDE IS exceptionally sweet at a campsite in the early morning. That first morning in Bryce Canyon National Park, I made myself a thermos of tea, walked to the edge of the canyon, and sat cross-legged waiting for the sun to bring warmth and the light that would transform the shadowy realm below. I had yet to see the sun rise over the Grand Canyon, and sensations I had that morning were as pleasurable as any I'd experienced in the natural world. Looking at photographs of Bryce, I'd been struck by a range of colors not quite like anything I'd ever seen. That morning I saw those spires and nameless formations brushed with snow metamorphose moment by moment as the changing light of the rising sun revealed colors of the flesh of fruits and vegetables—peach, cantaloupe, apricot, pumpkin, grapefruit, sweet potato. As the sun rose higher, the colors of Bryce Canyon reminded me of the hybrid daylilies in my own garden, though less bright, more changeable, and quieter. Later in the day, as the snow melted, I hiked to the floor of the canyon. Neither words nor paint could begin to evoke the experience of wandering in that place. Every turn in the trail brought a new perspective on the dazzling natural sculptures, their colors made all the more intense by the deep shades of the evergreens—ponderosa pine and Douglas fir— and the bluer-than-blue cerulean skies.

The roadless backcountry of Bryce Canyon National Park, like most of Utah's canyon country, is not protected by federal legislation designating it as wilderness. The designated wildernesses in Utah are much smaller than the extensive de facto wildernesses there, which still lack full legal protection. Although there are a half-dozen small wildernesses in the lower part of the state, the only extensive one is the High Uintas, just east of Salt Lake City. When I visited this area in June of 2000, I learned that it suffers from overuse. If the Uintas and other wildernesses near large population centers are to retain their wild character, the managing agencies will have to limit access. The wildlands within the national parks in Utah and the recently designated Grand Staircase–Escalante National Monument in southern Utah are protected from mining and mineral development, but they still lack the protection of a wilderness designation.

Snow covered the ground as I drove down Highway 67 through the forests and alpine meadows of the Kaibab Plateau toward the Grand Canyon. The golden aspens were at their peak, quivering in a light breeze under an overcast sky. When I arrived at the north rim of the Grand Canyon, I literally had the place to myself for a while. All the facilities were closed—the lodge, the campground, and the ranger station—and when I walked out to Bright Angel Point, I sat shivering in utter solitude at a comfortable distance from the edge of the rock jutting out into the canyon. I'd learned that respecting three rules would guarantee solitude or near solitude even in the most popular wild places: get up and out before others have breakfast; go out while others are thinking of dinner; and visit very popular places in the snow or out of season.

Back in the van I studied the map. It was already mid-afternoon. I would be heading east to New Mexico, and there was nothing between here and there except the vast Navajo Nation. Planning to stop early at the first campground I came to, I traveled first north on 67 and then east on 89. To entertain myself I listened to an audiotape of a Tony Hillerman novel, *The Blessing Way,* that I'd bought in Moab, Utah. I entered the Navajo Nation just as 89 turned south again through the Painted Desert and just as Detective Joe Leaphorn of the Navajo Tribal Police began following a horrifying trail of murder. It started off with a body high on a desolate mesa, much like the territory I was passing through. No tracks, no clues. I finally headed west again on Highway 160 just as Leaphorn discovers a second body. Darkness had fallen, and I'd seen only two or three gas stations and nothing vaguely resembling a campground. Ahead was Tuba City, Arizona. I would stop there and ask about a place to camp, though I feared there were no campgrounds in the Navajo Nation.

Just outside Tuba City I pulled into a gas station/convenience store. I bought a loaf of bread, cheese, and a couple of overripe bananas, enough to see me through until morning. Then I looked down at the news rack in front of the checkout counter and saw the headlines of the *Navajo Times:* NAVAJO ACTIVIST MEETS UNTIMELY DEATH. I reached for the paper and paid for it along with the groceries. The cashier told me that she didn't know of any campground along the highway, but that there was one in town.

I pulled into the campground, a large asphalt area with elevated chemical toilets and hot showers, and parked next to the only other campers, a retired couple with two dogs in a humongous RV. There was no point in pitching a tent in this place. After I'd eaten, taken a shower, and settled in my sleeping bag in the back of the van, I opened the *Navajo Times.*

Leroy Jackson, a Navajo environmentalist, had been at odds with many of his own people who were cutting the forests he wanted to save. He was found dead in his white Dodge van with shades drawn over the windows. It was parked at Brazos Bluff Lookout near Tierra Amarilla, New Mexico, less than forty miles from the tiny town of Vallecitos, where I planned to go in a couple of days. Officials who found the body, like those in *The Blessing Way,* were unable to determine the cause of death. Lt. Leaphorn, I was sure, would solve the mystery; he always did. I, on the other hand, had every reason to let this alone. I was not a detective. I'd never even been in the Navajo Nation, and I knew no one there. It was none of my business. If Jackson was murdered, then anyone going around asking questions could be in danger. Besides, here I was about to fall asleep inside a white Dodge van with the windows covered. Before I closed my eyes, I promised myself I'd leave the case of Leroy Jackson alone.

When I woke the next morning at dawn, I was really hungry. No tea and oatmeal this morning, I thought, and I didn't have to go far to find a real breakfast. Across the street was a restaurant with half a dozen pickup trucks parked in front. I ordered an omelette, potatoes, toast, and coffee. Then I got out the maps of Arizona and New Mexico and found the town of Shiprock, New Mexico, where Leroy Jackson's wife had waited for him to join her and their children at the Northern Navajo Fair. Then I found the road in northern New Mexico where he was found dead in the back of his van.

The waitress, a small Indian woman, asked where I was going. "Shiprock."

"You got business over there?"

"Yeah, I want to learn something about Leroy Jackson." So much for minding my own business. I asked if she knew anything about him.

"A little." she said. "I read the papers, and I know some people think he was murdered. Some people think he should've been."

"What do you think?"

"I don't think anything," she said dismissively. "You want more coffee?"

As I headed east through the Navajo Nation, a love of adventure swept over me. I knew that in a sense I was pretending to be an investigative reporter spurred by memories of the imaginary Indians of my childhood play, but this was more than play. Leroy Jackson was an environmentalist whose values clashed with those who wanted to profit from the same wild lands he wanted to save. That night I found a campsite in the Navajo reservation at Canyon de Chelly, and I spent the next day traveling around the Four Corners area, asking questions, and trying to find out something that would help me understand how and why Leroy Jackson had died. I even drove down one of the loneliest roads in New Mexico and passed by the Brazos Bluff rest area where he was found, but I didn't have the courage to pull into that deserted spot in a white Dodge van. The murder—if it was a murder—was too fresh. The autopsy report was not even completed, and most people I talked to knew little more than I did. A few, however, responded to my questions with a question: "Why do you want to know?" Or "Who do you work for?" I didn't know at the time that bringing up the name of the recently dead was taboo in Navajo culture.

The death of Leroy Jackson continued to haunt me, but it was months before I learned more about him. A leader and one of the founders of Diné Citizens Against Ruining Our Environment (Diné means "The People" in Navajo), he had worked to reduce timber harvesting in the Chuska Mountains to protect the sacred groves where the Blessing Way ceremony was held and to save the places where traditional herbs grew. His success in reducing the timber harvest and in delaying future sales helped put people out of jobs and created enemies for Jackson. Navajo protesters hung him in effigy; there were threats of violence. Angry loggers threatened with losing their jobs demonstrated outside the mill, holding signs that read, "LEROY JACKSON, KEEP YOUR HANDS OFF JOBS . . . OR ELSE." Jackson disappeared a few days before he was to have flown to Washington to meet with officials at the Department of the Interior and Bureau of Indian Affairs to protest logging practices in the Chuska Mountains.

Four weeks after the body was found, the medical investigator concluded that methadone found in his system was the cause of his death. The death, announced the coroner, was accidental. Friends and family members contested the finding, insisting that Jackson never used drugs.

Some eight months after Jackson's death, another tribal environmentalist disappeared. Fred Walking Badger—of Pima and Zuni heritage, from Arizona's Gila River Indian Reservation—had been campaigning against harmful and careless pesticide use, which he believed was contaminating the water and wildlife on the reservation. Badger left his home on May 21, 1994, to run an errand near Sacaton, Arizona, and never came back. His car was found burned in the desert, but his body to date has not been found. Badger's wife, like Jackson's, believes that her husband's activism led to his death.

By the time I left the Navajo Nation that first time, my feelings were similar to those I'd had when I first saw the Grand Canyon. I knew that I was looking at the surface of a world so deep, so old, so alien to my experience that I could never really understand it.

Canyon de Chelly is a canyon of human scale. It has been home to Native Americans for centuries, and to this day is occupied by Navajos who keep sheep and sell jewelry and pottery to tourists who hike to the bottom. My friend Carol Light was on vacation in the area, and when I called her from the road, we made plans to meet and hike there. After my escapades the day before chasing the story of Leroy Jackson, relaxing with Carol in that exquisite place was the ultimate comfort. Solitude has its pleasures, but the joy of companionship with a close friend in such a place is hard to beat. Like the afternoon I spent alone outside Holden on the banks of Copper Creek, that day stands out from others—golden autumn foliage, intense blue skies, picnic perched on a log by the side of a stream, and endless, nourishing talk. By the end of the day, we'd filled in the gaps in our knowledge of each other's stories. Carol and I both think of that time as a breakthrough in our friendship.

This Is Texas

~~~~~ THE LARGEST state in the Lower 48, Texas falls far short in designated wilderness. There are five small wildernesses in east Texas, including Big Slough, Indian Mounds, Little Lake Creek, and Turkey Hill. The largest of the five, Upland Island Wilderness, is only twelve thousand acres. All are second-growth recovering forest; Indian Mounds preserves a few acres of old-growth trees. The Guadalupe Wilderness, within the Guadalupe National Park in southwest Texas, is adjacent to the Carlsbad Caverns Wilderness in southern New Mexico. After I left Carol, I visited this harsh terrain and, along with hundreds of other visitors, entered the chilly caverns, descending to ever more bizarre formations of stalagmites and stalactites.

Far more interesting to me, however, was the desert wilderness that climbs up to Guadalupe Peak at 8,747 feet above sea level. Few visitors to the caverns venture into the forbidding desert. Exploring the fringes of this alien world, I identified the common plants—mesquite, ocotillo, Parry's century plant, rabbitbrush, and the ever-present sagebrush. I was surprised to see the strange creatures that have adapted to such harsh conditions of heat and dryness: Gambel's quail, greater roadrunner, and the broad-necked darkling beetle. I heard but did not see what I assumed was a western diamond-back rattlesnake.

I left the daunting high Chihuahuan desert of western Texas to drive to El Paso, where I would meet my friend Marjorie, who had lived for more than a year in the Kalahari Desert. What was alien to me about deserts was familiar and even comforting to her. Before I'd left home, Marjorie and I had agreed that she would join me toward the end of my trip if she had a lull in her cancer treatment. I called her from Arches, and she jumped at the chance to join me for a few days at Big Bend National Park. She had just finished a round of chemotherapy and was beginning to feel good again. It was late in the afternoon of October 30th when I picked her up at the airport in El Paso. She wore jeans, hiking boots, and a bandana to hide her baldness. In spite of all she'd gone through, she managed to look nothing less than beautiful. She seemed strong, in good spirits, and ready for adventure. As soon as we were in the car she began to talk. I insisted that she tell me about her most recent ordeal, but it soon became apparent that hashing over the details of cancer treatment was the last thing she wanted to do.

"Just give me the bottom line," I said.

"I'm anxious much of the time; I've been sick as hell, weak, and scared. The worst has been looking at my children and thinking I may not get to see them grow up."

I reached over and squeezed her hand and waited for her to say more.

"That's all I want to say. Right now I'm in a good place. I feel good, and I want to make the most of it."

Marjorie and I became friends in the summer of 1984. She was thirty-nine and I was forty-two, and she was a big part of my life at the time I began my journey nine years later. I first met her at a party. She and her husband, Mel, walked into a crowded room. They seemed a charmed couple, radiating warmth and light. Shortly after we met, she called to set up a tennis game. We met on the courts the next day, and afterwards we sat in the sun and talked about our lives. In the beginning we had common concerns and passions—the outdoors, physical fitness, writing—and we often talked about what we were going to do with the rest of our lives. Marjorie judged herself by what she was going to do, not what she had already done. I was impressed, though, by the life she'd led and what she'd accomplished. When she was in her early twenties, she and Mel had gone to Botswana as anthropologists. Living with Bushmen in the Kalahari Desert, she did the research that led to *Nisa: The Life and Words of a !Kung Woman,* a highly acclaimed book that provoked envy from me and other women who longed for more exciting lives.

In the early days Marjorie told me of her desire to go back to Africa and to reconnect with Nisa, but she couldn't imagine how she could leave her three children to make the trip. I told her that I wanted a task in life that seemed important enough to engage all my energies. She understood what I meant when I talked about merging commitment and passion, and I understood something of the pain she felt in being pulled by opposing desires—to be a good wife and mother and to resume her work in Africa.

In the early years of our friendship, Marjorie and I grew from jogging buddies to confidantes. In the time that came between "let's play tennis" and "there's something I haven't told you," we talked about our youthful adventures, our work, and our hopes, our parents, our childhoods, childbirth, and children. We gave each other advice about hair color and clothes. We talked about books, sex, and the wonders and limitations of men. For a long time the serious and the not-so-serious were about evenly balanced.

As time went by and our children became older, our lives didn't change very much. My children went to college, hers to a neighborhood school. We were both writing books, and we talked a lot about how to find the time and solitude for our work. "Somehow, someday, we've got to figure this out," one of us would say. In the early days, we talked about the future with a lightheartedness that Marjorie's discovery of a lump in her breast wiped out forever. Not surprisingly, one of the gifts of that dreaded diagnosis was that Marjorie was no longer willing to compromise. She did go to Africa, found Nisa, and began a book about the experience—one that her husband would finish after her death.

As we traveled south on Texas Highway 90, a huge pumpkinlike full moon rose from behind the mountains and illuminated the bleak Texas landscape. Marjorie asked me where I'd been when I saw the last full moon. I told her that in late September I'd seen the full moon rise behind Mount Hood as I searched for a place to camp in a national forest in Oregon. I didn't tell her how afraid I'd been that night.

"And before that?" she asked.

"The moon before that was a blue moon, the second moon in the month of August. I was driving south through a deserted part of Montana. There was wilderness all around." I didn't mention the scary people in the truck who'd nearly blocked my way.

"And before that?"

"The early August moon I saw in the Great Smokies when Jerome and I went on a camping trip right before I left. I guess the next one I'll see will be in Atlanta."

"How do you feel about being at home again?" Marjorie asked.

"I'm not sure. I don't know how I'll adjust to being back in a world of walls, telephones, and electricity, but I know I want to live more simply, spend less money, have fewer things." I didn't tell her that I feared losing everything I'd gained in the wilderness.

It was too late for us to go all the way to Big Bend National Park, so we checked into a motel in Marfa, Texas. We were too restless to sleep. For dinner we ate a huge bag of Guiltless Gourmet corn chips with salsa and a bag of fat-free cookies; then we drove out of town and parked the van in a place where the night clerk had told us we might see "the famous Marfa lights." I'd never heard of the Marfa lights before, but scientists and tourists come from all over the world to investigate these mysterious lights that rise up and fade over the range south of Marfa. There was no question that Marjorie and I saw greenish and orange lights glow and disappear across the landscape, and I would never doubt the existence of the Marfa lights. Whether they are produced by gases seeping from the earth, an energy field, or something else, I couldn't say. But I can say that we saw them and that, following the elusive lights that night, we laughed so hard we cried. And when the day came that we could no longer laugh together, I thought back to that night and was glad that we'd once had so much fun.

The next morning we chose a campsite in a remote area of Big Bend on the banks of the Rio Grande overlooking Mexico. Only one other campsite was occupied, and signs warned of robberies in the camp and hinted at illegal crossings and drug deals. Undeterred, we pitched a tent as close to the river as possible. But then we did go to the ranger station to ask about our safety in this isolated spot. The ranger, an attractive young woman accompanied by a German shepherd named Judge Roy Bean, told us that there was nothing to worry about.

"Of course there are some illegal crossings, poor people from the village of Santa Elena. They snoop around the campground during the day looking for anything of value. You won't see them, though. They wait until the campground is empty."

"Will we be safe in our tent at night?" Marjorie asked.

"I've been here five years, and we've never had any violence — only harmless daytime robberies."

"Then why the dog?"

"Oh, the Judge is a narc, trained to sniff out marijuana and cocaine. He's doing a pretty good job."

As we walked out I was prepared to move camp if Marjorie was uneasy, but when I asked her what we should do, she didn't hesitate. "Let's take our chances."

That night Marjorie slept out under the stars in spite of what I'd told her about tarantulas and snakes. I crawled into the tent feeling strangely safe. The odds were on our side. I zipped up my sleeping bag, hung a small light from the top of the tent, and settled down to read. Then the night sounds began. First a pack of coyotes howled and yipped as they do at dusk and dawn. Then two great horned owls began their nightly call. I gradually drifted into a deep sleep.

Then I heard roosters crowing across the river in Mexico. Not wanting to disturb Marjorie, I got up quietly and walked a short distance up the river. The bushes along the banks were alive with birds. In a matter of minutes I saw a hummingbird, three male vermilion flycatchers, a pair of doves, and a flock of goldfinches, some already dressed in winter plumage. Swallows skimmed insects from the surface of the water, and an American dipper, rarely seen so far east, sat on a rock, rhythmically dipping up and down and singing its bubbly trill.

When I returned to our campsite, Marjorie was still sleeping. Time for a jog. Remembering how much fun we had once had jogging together, I felt sad going off without her. When I first left home, I was barely able to run a mile. Now I could keep up a steady pace for three miles, and that morning I managed to run for thirty minutes and still make it back before Marjorie woke up.

Later that morning, we went to the small general store near the Castillon ranger station to find out about the best hikes in the area and the possibility of crossing the Rio Grande into Mexico. David Martin, who worked in the store, told us that he frequently goes across to the little town of Santa Elena for an authentic Mexican meal in one of the town's two restaurants. Before I knew what had happened, Marjorie had asked David to take us with him that night. Santa Elena, David warned, was totally unprepared for tourists: there'd be no one selling trinkets, no cantinas, and no mariachis. We had just enough time to hike the Lost Mine Trail before meeting David back at the store that evening.

By the time we piled into his reconditioned 1949 Plymouth, night had fallen. In a matter of minutes, we arrived at what locals call "the gate." Two steel poles with a crossbar prevented the passage of motorized vehicles to the banks of the river, so that smugglers as well as those who had come over for legitimate transactions were required to carry whatever they were transporting along the quarter-mile sandy road to and from the water. At the gate four men were loading what appeared to be groceries into a wheelbarrow.

When we arrived at the river, it was completely dark and a couple of hours before the moon would rise. There were no lights and no dock, and to reach the water's edge we had to climb down a steep bank with loose, rocky soil. Our only light was my gradually dimming flashlight, which David used to signal to a boatman across the river. We waited for several minutes there in the dark until we heard the sound of oars striking the water. At last an ancient rowboat appeared, navigated by an even older man. After a few minutes of strenuous rowing, he deposited us on the opposite shore in total darkness.

With the help of my fading flashlight, we made our way down

FROM HOME TO WILDERNESS

a rocky dirt road to the village and the "restaurant" that David regularly patronized. We stopped in front of a modest house. There were no lights, and David decided that Maria had closed up early. Just as we were about to move on down the street to the only other eating establishment, lights came on and a voice called out:

"David, tu quieres comer? Espere un momento."

Within minutes we were seated around what seemed to be the family table drinking Carta Blanca and eating beans, eggs, tortillas, cheese, and salsa. Halfway through the meal we were joined by David's friend Kathy, a volunteer ranger whose job was to capture the wayward horses and cows that crossed the river and wandered into the national park. She explained that Mexicans paid dearly for failing to keep their horses and cows confined: not only did they have to go through the bureaucratic hassle of traveling to a nearby town and filling out forms, but they had to pay substantial fines—about one hundred dollars per animal, barely under replacement cost. Of course the animals had to range freely in order to find enough to eat, and there was no way to teach them about borders or prevent them from noticing that the grass was decidedly greener across the river in Big Bend.

Kathy was an attractive woman with long, thick blond hair. She told us about a recent encounter with a mountain lion and how she liked hiking in the nude. When she told us about riding her horse alone, Lady Godiva style, through a remote canyon on Halloween night, I had no trouble imagining the scene.

As we were leaving Maria's, we stumbled over what appeared to be a very sick little dog, heaving and convulsing with such intensity that I feared it would drop dead any minute. After much animated conversation with Maria, I finally understood that the dog, Vanessa, is especially fond of enchiladas cooked with jalepeño peppers and is willing to endure the heaving and convulsions in order to enjoy her favorite food. Maria insisted that the dog, like everyone else in the family, has to have hot peppers to be happy.

After we left Maria's we walked down the main street of Santa Elena, population three hundred. Intermittent streetlights illuminated small areas, but the general impression was one of darkness and silence. Shadowy figures lingered in some doorways, and I could just imagine how I would have experienced this walk if it were not for David. Yet I felt at ease. We ducked into a tiny general store and bought a large bottle of Mexican vanilla, which David insisted was much better and cheaper than anything available in the States.

The ancient boatman was waiting at the river to row us back across the strong current in the dark. A few minutes later, I scrambled up the loose and sandy soil of the steep bank, stood safely on the American side, looked back at Mexico, and thought about borders and how an openness to serendipity had made such an experience possible. Again, Marjorie slept under the stars and I crawled into my tent pitched close to the edge of the Rio Grande.

The only other person in the campground that night was a man in a locked camper complete with an alarm system parked some hundred yards away from the river. The next morning as we were making breakfast, he came to our campsite to warn us that smugglers crossed through there at night and that sleeping in the open was dangerous.

Marjorie and I looked at each other, smiled, and shrugged.

"You at least ought to have a gun," he said. "This is Texas. Everybody's armed."

I wondered how many times I would have to explain to a well-meaning person that I was not interested in carrying firearms. Rather than argue, we invited him to join us for a cup of tea, and in a matter of minutes he was talking about other wild places in Texas and urging us to go to go to Aransas Wildlife Preserve to see the whooping cranes.

After he left, Marjorie and I sat at the river's edge facing south, looking out at the three-tiered view of water, mountains, and sky beyond. We sipped tea and talked about the people we'd met in Santa Elena and the tiny black-and-white shaggy dog with a fondness for jalepeño peppers.

Leaving Big Bend wasn't easy. We joked about staying longer, but Marjorie had to get back to her children and I was beginning to feel the pull of home. On our last day we hiked the Window Trail in the Chisos Mountains, and at sundown we left Big Bend and headed north on Texas Highway 385 before turning east on highway 90. We saw more wildlife that night than I had seen since I roamed the high range in Wyoming. As we turned onto the northbound highway, a pair of robust canines sprang into view, paused briefly in the middle of the road to stare into my headlights, and then trotted off into darkness. At first we thought we'd seen wolves, but unlike the occasional dippers, wolves have long ago been eliminated from Texas. I had a hard time convincing Marjorie that the animals we'd seen were unusually healthy coyotes. Looking back, I'm sorry I tried.

Deer season was in full swing, and there were so many deer along the sides of the road that I wondered whether they were running from hunters. I slowed down considerably to avoid killing one of the many animals that crossed our path. Even so, shortly before we stopped for the night I attempted to straddle a skunk, only to hear a thumping sound as I hit it with a back tire.

Marjorie was determined that we would find a place to sleep outdoors on our last night together. Looking for the perfect spot, we followed the signs down a deserted road to a primitive campsite on the shores of the Amistad Reservoir, formed by a dam on the Rio Grande. We pitched the tent on the edge of the lake in the dark, not sure of where we were. The next morning I realized that Mexico was again little more than a stone's throw away. There were hundreds of ducks on the lake, as well as a healthy population of geese, herons, and other waterbirds. In a nearby tree perched yet another bright red vermilion flycatcher. Like the one that so astonished me in the Chiricahuas, this one seemed to hold his perch for my pleasure.

While Marjorie and I were preparing breakfast, a man emerged from a camper a hundred yards or so away. The only other person around, he came over to chat and offered us water, since there was none available. Cheerful and generous, he was typical of people I had met in remote campgrounds. Later his wife emerged, and together they headed for a small fishing boat. "Have a good day," Marjorie called out to them.

The man paused, looked back at us, and said, "At my age, I don't have time for anything but good days."

"Nobody does," Marjorie said quietly to me.

Our days in Texas were the last really happy ones Marjorie and I would share. Shortly after I returned home, she resumed another round of debilitating treatments, and after that, round after round. When things were especially tough, I sometimes tried to distract Marjorie from her pain by recalling Big Bend and other days of play and laughter. But in the end, the laughter and even the memories faded, and I was left with a deep ache in my heart for my friend.

After leaving Marjorie at the airport in San Antonio, I turned onto Highway 87 and traveled toward Victoria, Texas. I was pessimistic about finding a place to camp in this flat, barren country dominated by chemical companies, oil refineries, and other industrial installations spewing God-knows-what from huge smokestacks. Further west I could at least count on finding a place to camp in a national forest, but in eastern Texas I rarely saw trees, let alone a forest. By the time I got to town it was dark, and there was no sign of a campground. I passed a Honda dealership, wheeled in, and asked the salesman for help.

"Sure, we have a campground here, just down the way near the golf course in the public park."

"Great. I'll give it a try."

As I was pulling away, he came running after me. "Seems to me I remember somebody saying that they never built facilities there. The city put in the hookups for RVs, but they ran out of money before they built a bathroom. But check it out anyway. I may be wrong."

Sure enough, the campground was empty and there wasn't even a pit toilet. It was time to spring for a motel. After checking into the local Best Western, I went outside to explore the town. The balmy Texas night air, after the dry, thin air of the high altitudes further west, felt like home. My skin was damp with perspiration and my hair was curling again. I finally found refuge from the warm night in a nitty-gritty Mexican restaurant where I sipped a margarita, worked my way through piles of chips and hot salsa, and then ate about half of a huge plate of traditional Mexican dishes, the "$4.95 Special."

Then I stopped in at the bar attached to the motel to get directions to the Aransas Wildlife Refuge, where I would go the next morning. The bartender, a pretty young woman in her early twenties, came over and whispered in my ear, "Am I glad to see you! I haven't had another woman in here in weeks. These jerks act a lot better when there's a lady in the house. Stick around, will you?"

I had not intended to stay, but I ordered a light beer, the seventy-five-cent Thursday-night special, and nursed it for a couple of hours. Things did get interesting.

For directions to Aransas, Maria referred me to Gerry, a one-time oysterman, now a car salesman. Gerry, sitting on the stool next to me, took care to give me detailed directions through the deserted back roads that lead to the refuge. He also advised me to get up early and be there before dawn.

"You know the area well?" I asked.

"Well, I guess I do. My family has been in the oyster business down that way for three generations. I've spent a lot of my life on oyster boats. But no more."

"What happened?"

"Goddamned environmentalists ruined it for us. They don't know what they're talking about. Just crazy extremists, all of them. First they talk about pollution, then contaminated water, then the red tide. They don't know shit. 'Scuze me, ma'am. I forget you're a lady."

When I told him not to worry about his language, Gerry continued, "No one has ever been able to prove that oysters make people sick. All those people that claim they got hepatitis from eating oysters? Not so. They got it somewhere else and they blamed it on oysters. Yep, the environmentalists have ruined things for a lot of people. Take the lumber industry out in Washington and Oregon. If that goddamned spotted owl is so valuable, why don't they protect it? Put it in a cage, put all of them in cages."

Sitting next to Gerry was Tom, a young man who earned his living reclaiming vehicles from people who had failed to make their payments. "A dangerous business," he said, and explained that later that night, about 2:00 A.M., he would drive his tow truck to the delinquent person's house, back up to the vehicle, make a quick hookup, and drive away as quickly as possible. The whole process would take about two minutes. Then down the road he would stop and make sure the load was secured, call the police, report that he had reclaimed the car, and tow it back to the motel, where he would sleep before taking it to the dealer's parking lot the next morning. For the night's work, he would earn six hundred dollars plus expenses. I wondered if expenses included the steady stream of beer he was consuming.

Tom and Gerry eventually asked me what I was doing in their part of the country. When I explained that I was traveling in my van seeing the wild places in America, they became concerned. Both men were trained mechanics and wanted to know if I was taking good care of my vehicle. I told them that I was driving a new Dodge minivan with only twelve thousand miles on it and that I had in fact had the oil changed at the correct intervals. Almost in unison, they both asked, "But do you check your oil?"

"Well, no, I didn't think that was necessary if I'm having it changed every three thousand miles."

The two men shook their heads in sympathy for my ignorance. Then Tom asked if I was properly armed.

"You mean, do I have a gun?"

"Yeah, lady, we're talkin' guns here."

"Actually, I'm not carrying a gun, and in fact I feel safer without one."

"Lady, listen to me," Tom said in an authoritative voice. "You need a gun. This is Texas."

"Yeah," Gerry chimed in, "This is Texas, lady, you better get yourself a gun."

At this point Tom broke in excitedly, "You know, you're the only woman I know, maybe the only woman I've ever known, who doesn't check her oil and who doesn't carry a gun."

As I got up to go, Gerry handed me his card and said, "It's been a real pleasure to meet you, ma'am. Now, you be real careful and write me a letter sometime."

The next day started when I awoke at 4:30 A.M. to reach the Aransas Wildlife Refuge before dawn. By five I was zipping along on Texas Highway 87 looking for the cutoff that would take me south and east to the Gulf. Somehow I managed to negotiate the back roads, following directions that included "Take a cutoff across the fields, go to a dead end, look for three silos, and turn right in front of them." Just before 6:00 A.M. I pulled into the parking lot of the visitor's center. It was still dark and there was no one around. No cars, no light, the only sound that of hundreds of swarming mosquitoes. In my months in the West, I had not encountered a single mosquito, though I'd been warned that in Yellowstone they were "the size of wild turkeys." Swatting the mosquitoes that quickly covered my bare hands and face, I located a box with maps of the refuge and decided to park and walk the Heron Flats Trail through the tidal marshes.

I had come here to see a whooping crane, one of the rarest creatures in North America. Once reduced to only twenty-one specimens, this five-foot-tall white bird has recovered to a population of 150 that migrate between Canada and Aransas every year. In late October they begin to arrive in Aransas, and in the spring they migrate north again. There are a few whooping cranes in captivity and two other smaller wild groups.

I set out at dawn with just enough light to see the many animals I would flush in just a few minutes on the trail. First a snake that made a sudden and strange escape, not by slithering along the ground but by turning itself sideways and upright, ever so briefly forming a giant, rounded *M*. I had never seen a snake that looked or behaved like this one, but I was certain it was not a rattler, a moccasin, or a copperhead. It seemed a rather playful though skittish animal. Surely not poisonous. Then came a herd of feral hogs, followed by a pair of collared peccaries (javelinas) exuding a strong skunklike scent. Before I left the refuge I had heard the rustling of an armadillo and seen deer, alligators, and innumerable waterbirds—great blue herons, egrets, pelicans, ducks, and geese. I had suffered dozens of mosquito bites. But though I hiked several trails and waited patiently alone on the observation tower, I never saw a whooper. As I was leaving, I spotted a ranger walking to his truck in front of the otherwise deserted visitor's center.

"Where are the whoopers?" I asked.

"They could be anywhere. I saw three this morning in the marsh down by the observation tower. It's really hard to miss a five-foot-tall white bird. We counted forty-four yesterday."

But miss them I did, and I drove away thinking that I'd have the whoopers some other time. That is, if they survived until I could get back this way. Since many tankers ply the waters adjacent to Aransas, the greatest risk to the birds here is an oil spill.

At 9:30 A.M. I was back on the road with the radio tuned to local news from Corpus Christi. A whooping crane had been found shot and wounded. It had been flown to San Antonio for treatment, but local vets predicted it would lose its wing. The person responsible had not been found. This is Texas, I thought.

Settling In

~~~~~ FROM ARANSAS I headed north on Highway 35 and stopped for gas at the first full-service station I could find.

"Fill it up," I said, "and check everything you can check."

I went inside to get a Diet Coke and came out to the station attendant's solemn face and stern words:

"You're mor'n a quart low, lady. You shouldn't let it get so low. Bad for your engine. These little four-cylinder jobs only take four quarts in all."

By lunchtime I was through Houston, and by dinnertime I was stuck in the afternoon traffic in Baton Rouge. Although I was getting hungry and had nothing but an apple to snack on, I didn't stop. By bedtime I had left Mobile behind me and was traveling north on Highway 65 toward Montgomery. Forty miles into this deserted highway, I began to get really sleepy, and when I saw a Best Western sign in the middle of nowhere, I stopped, determined to sleep until I couldn't sleep anymore. I had traveled some eight hundred miles that day. The desk clerk promised me that a spacious room in the back of the motel would be quiet. I bought a candy bar from a vending machine, took a hot bath, and fell gratefully asleep around 11:00 P.M.

Some hours later I woke suddenly to a rustling sound. Unsure of where I was, I felt around me, identified sheets, and realized that I was in a bed in a room, not in a sleeping bag in a tent. Then I remembered stopping miles from nowhere in southern Alabama. When I turned on the light the rustling sound stopped. "Maybe I dreamed it," I thought, and turned off the light. Immediately the sound returned. I decided it must be coming from the wastebasket where I'd thrown the candy wrapper. Then I knew there was a rat or mouse in my room.

Having dealt with bears outside my tent and a mountain lion screaming in the night, I could surely handle this. Again I turned on the light and the noise stopped. I would take the wastebasket out in the hall and then call the front desk and report what I had done. But when I picked it up, either a large mouse or a small rat jumped into the air and ran under the bed. I was wrong. I couldn't handle it. I called the front desk, explained what had happened, and asked for another room.

"I'm sorry, we don't have any more rooms. Maybe the security guard can kill it."

I tried to imagine this scene and hesitated only briefly before saying, "I think I'll just check out and head for home."

The desk clerk was very solicitous. "I'm so sorry this happened, but to tell you the truth, it happens every year when they plow the cotton fields next door. No matter what we do, some of them get into the rooms. I'm real sorry. I hate it when they do that."

By 3:00 A.M. I was on the road again. Still in the middle of nowhere, I stopped only once for gas and bought a Diet Coke, a moon pie, and a sack of boiled peanuts. I was heading for the barn.

The road in front of my house dead-ends into a dirt lane. I pulled into my usual parking place just as Jerome and Hugo were coming out of the house for their morning jog. It was 8:00 A.M. Saturday, the sixth of November 1993. I looked out at a perfect fall day, and although many leaves had fallen, the woods were still aglow with gold and red. They rushed down the stairs to meet me, and we engaged in a three-way embrace with much hugging, tail wagging, kissing, barking, sniffing, and laughing.

Jerome could hardly wait to show me the improvements he'd made in the house. There were new windows and carpet upstairs; decking and some siding had been replaced; the holes in the fence had been repaired. There were new bookcases and desktops in my study. Finally I had enough workspace. Surely I would want to stay at home.

That first morning at home I was so restless I couldn't sit still. And I couldn't stay inside. I made coffee, and we went out into the garden. I'd missed the sweet-smelling autumn clematis that blooms in September. The late-blooming phlox, rudbeckia, and sedum were long gone, but there were blooming asters, lantana, and butterfly bushes. Still no frost. A flicker and a cardinal came to the bird feeder. Then the phone rang.

"Let it go," I said, stopping Jerome before he went back inside.

"I'll just listen to the message," he insisted.

"Please don't tell anyone I'm home yet. Not until Monday. I need some time."

Except for calling my parents and Jerome's mother to let them know I was home safely, I didn't talk to anyone that weekend. With Jerome's help I unpacked the van and began the slow process of reentry. I walked around the house opening doors and drawers. The refrigerator was empty except for a bottle of champagne; on my desk was a laundry basket full of mail.

"I can't do anything about this today," I told Jerome.

"Then let's just play. Take a walk, go out to lunch, go to bed early."

"Okay with me. Just promise me you won't answer the telephone."

"That's a promise."

On Monday morning I dived into my closet and started making piles of things I didn't need. This was the first time in my life I'd taken a serious look at my closet. There were the remnants of former lives, skirts and jackets of my dressed-for-success days as a college professor, dinner suits I wore for fund-raisers and medical-society functions, a black sequined gala jacket with velvet pants, preppy outfits I'd jokingly referred to as my PTA clothes, the navy-blue suit I was saving for jury duty. For fun I put the clothes in different piles according to the function they served, and I realized how many lives I had been trying to lead. How, I wondered, had I held together such contradictory roles. After living happily for three months with no more clothes than could be stored in a small bin under the platform in the back of a van, I couldn't possibly tolerate so much stuff.

I sorted the piles again. There was a pile for Goodwill and another pile of blazers, skirts, and suits for Laura to wear in her new job as a counselor. I set aside the largest pile for a friend who was about my size and needed clothes.

I kept various shirts and sweaters, one skirt, a selection of slacks, one suit, and my best shoes. I kept a silk dress for weddings, a black knit for everything else, and my "Don't fuck with me" dress, an olive-green wool gabardine with big shoulder pads and brass buttons to wear when I felt I needed the upper hand. I saved a few of my favorite summer garments, sweats, a bathing suit, and hiking clothes. Suddenly my once overcrowded closet seemed roomy, and there was nothing left hanging that I didn't like. I had gotten rid of everything that I'd hung on to just because "I might need it someday."

It took several days to go through the mail, straighten my study, and file the various maps, cards, pamphlets, and books I'd brought home with me. There was a letter from the motel manager in Alabama apologizing for the "unpleasantness" and reassuring me that the mouse in question had been captured. A letter from Mr. Rambo—yes, really—of ECOLAB in Houston, Texas, explained that the Pest Elimination Division of his company is constantly working to create pest-free environments for those establishments it serves. There is nothing they can do, however, until a pest actually enters a building.

I tried to imagine Mr. Rambo supervising the "elimination" of the unnamed animal he called "the pest." I imagined a bloody scene or the spreading of lethal chemicals. Surely a high-tech company from Houston did not include a mousetrap in its arsenal of "all necessary steps." I began to feel guilty for failing to catch the mouse and return it to the cotton fields it so foolishly left.

During that week I checked in with friends, visited my par-

ents, and had dinner with Richard and Monica. Already I was trying to do too much; city time was rapidly replacing wilderness
time, and I didn't like it.

Late one afternoon about two weeks after I returned, I'd met my
friend Cecylia at the gym for a workout around 4:00 P.M. We like
to have at least two hours to do aerobics, weights, stretches, and
the hot tub. That day, Jerome had made a point of saying he'd be
home by 6:00 and that he'd like to spend the evening with me,
maybe go out to dinner. I countered by volunteering to fix a nice
dinner at home. At 5:30 I left the gym in order to get home in time
to finish dinner preparations. Jerome wasn't there when I arrived,
and at 7:00 P.M. he still wasn't home and hadn't called. At 7:15 the
phone rang.

"Hi, honey," Jerome said in a somber voice. "I have a very sick
lady in the hospital, and I've got to take care of her before I can
come home."

I'd learned through the years that when Jerome started talking about having "a very sick patient," he was always covering for
something else. All of his hospital patients were sick. Otherwise
they wouldn't be in the hospital. When I questioned him, Jerome
confessed that he'd been at a meeting that he'd forgotten about
when he made a dinner date with me that morning. And he had
not yet made his late afternoon rounds at the hospital. I was furious. Not so much because he had forgotten our date or failed to
leave me a message, but because I had cut my workout short and
wasted an hour or so expecting him to come in the door any
minute. But more than that, I was angry because I'd done something like this many times in the past, and for many years I'd gone
into neutral in the late afternoon and squandered time dallying
in the kitchen, listening to "All Things Considered," waiting, waiting, waiting.

Six months before, I probably would not have registered a
complaint. After all, what's thirty minutes or an hour? My attitude
toward time had shifted. The three months I'd spent free from time
pressures and other people's schedules had made me appreciate

the value of pursuing my own interests on my own time. Jerome never comes home when he says he will. He wants to please, and so he tells me what he thinks I want to hear. By the time he finally came home around 9 P.M. that night, I had made up my mind never to put myself in this position again.

"Look," I said as soon as he walked in the door, "you never know for sure when you are going to be able to get away. It makes no sense at all for me to structure my days to be available just in case you get home when you say you will. From now on, unless we have specific plans to be together at a particular time and you know for sure you can make it, don't even bother to tell me when you think you'll be home. I'll do what I want to do, and you take all the time you need. I'll see you when I see you."

By the time I got all this out, my anger had subsided. Jerome admitted that he hated feeling pressured to be home at a particular time, and that he really didn't like making promises he wasn't sure he could keep. Eventually we agreed that it would be much better for both of us not to have any expectations about seeing each other in the late afternoon or early evening except on weekends and one weekday when neither of us was especially busy. That day Jerome would come home early, and I could count on him to be there. We would have dinner together. The other four days we had no obligations, and if we both happened to be home at the dinner hour, we could make a salad or run out to a nearby restaurant for burritos or pasta.

It took going into the wilderness and having all my time for myself to discover how I'd spent much of my life being available to my family and friends; how often I'd answered the phone just because it rang; how many times I'd rushed home just in case Jerome needed me. What he gained from our new arrangement was freedom from time pressure and from promises he couldn't keep. I gained late afternoons and early evenings for what I wanted to do. Eventually he found ways to cut back on his work and take more time off. But there will never be any guarantee about what time he gets home, and I am never standing over the sink wondering where the hell Jerome is.

Shopping

〜〜〜 FOR THE FIRST ninety days that I was away I had only occasionally gone into stores. Every week or two I found a grocery store, where I bought fruit, oatmeal, yogurt, bread, carrots, and green peppers. Combined with the dried beans, rice, and protein powder I kept as staples, these items provided me with a balanced diet. Occasionally I bought books, batteries, stamps, and postcards. I was at home before it dawned on me that I hadn't purchased anything else in three months—not even lipstick, a new hat, or a pair of socks.

I had grown accustomed to the simplicity of the out-of-doors —a campsite near a river, no other campers in sight, the sound of birds in the morning, dinner cooked over a backpacking stove, and only a few possessions. My traveling wardrobe included two pairs of outdoor pants, one pair of sweatpants, assorted shirts, one sweater, running shoes, socks, and hiking boots. In the bottom of the clothing bin in the van were a black knit dress and a pair of black flats. The bin where I stored my clothing would have fit into a corner of my closet, but still I had more than I needed. By the time I returned home, I had decided to find out what it would be like not to go shopping until August 9, 1994, a full year after I'd left home.

There was a time when shopping was a form of recreation. At least once a month I would stop by the mall on my way home from work and check out the sales. Every spring and every fall for as long as I could remember I had added a few items to my already overflowing closet. I also passed a few things on to Good-will. But after I cleaned out my closet this time, I had no desire to add another item to it, and I didn't for another full year.

Shortly after I returned, Jerome made plans with our friend Ernie Fokes, visiting Atlanta from Idaho, to meet for lunch at a restaurant in Lenox Square, a popular shopping center. Since I wanted to see Ernie, who was in town only for the day, I went along. Walking through the mall to the restaurant, I tried not to focus on the carefully exhibited wares—the latest food processor at Williams-Sonoma and the unidentifiable objects at Sharper Image. Wafting from the door of a bath shop were familiar fragrances. "Bear bait," I thought. Black bears and grizzlies are attracted to perfumes. When we finished lunch and wandered through Macy's on the way back to the parking lot, I began to feel very uncomfortable. Passing through the cosmetics and perfumes, I recalled my morning grooming ritual at the campsite: brush teeth and hair, wash face, apply sunscreen and lip gloss. But when I looked in the mirror, I wondered if I had made a terrible mistake by not using the expensive anti-aging cream that a company representative was hawking. Then I passed through rows and rows of purses before coming to the high-priced leather goods locked inside glass cases. For thirteen weeks I'd kept credit cards, traveler's checks, and an extra car key in a small cloth zipped pouch that I wore like a necklace tucked out of sight under my shirt. Toiletries and a comb I stuffed into pockets. I'd had no need for a purse.

That day I decided to make it a year before buying anything except groceries, books, and necessary household and office supplies. I had long been the household shopper, so Jerome readily went along with me and agreed not to shop on his own before the year was up. Friends and family members helped out when I found myself really needing some small item. When my cosmetics ran low, my daughter-in-law rummaged through her unused free samples and found a lipstick and blush that would do. One friend gave me a drugstore Timex watch after mine broke.

There were times when I wanted to cheat, and I would tell myself that no one would ever know if I slipped into a store to buy a Chanel blush or a Lancome mascara. Once I rationalized that merchandise in the grocery store didn't count, and so I bought six pairs of white socks and a mop at the supermarket. But except that day with Ernie and Jerome, I did not go to a mall, and except for the socks and a new mop, I didn't bring any new objects into the house.

I didn't expect to become totally indifferent to this activity I had once enjoyed, nor could I imagine idly resuming recreational shopping. What I hoped to do was to become a much more conscious consumer, to buy quality merchandise that serves real needs (or desires so strong I couldn't possibly resist). I did notice as time went by that when I was anxious about something, the urge to go shopping would be activated. But resisting it was relatively easy. All I had to do was think of the piles of clothing I'd just discarded and the unpleasant sensations I'd experienced the last time I was in a mall.

If I really wanted to go shopping, I could do so—on or after August 9, 1994. But where would I be on that day? Maybe deep in the woods somewhere far from a shopping center. At that time I would be free to travel to the nearest town and buy whatever I wanted, but I would also be free not to. As it turned out, I woke up that day camped on the banks of Sheridan Lake in the Black Hills of South Dakota. Shopping was the last thing I wanted to do on that golden morning. There was nothing I could have bought that would have added to the quality of my life.

FEBRUARY 1994

WILD FLORIDA

A Long Road

≈≈≈ ONE THING wilderness had taught me was the value of an unencumbered life, and while I'd done a lot to eliminate excesses and complications from my own, much remained to be done. By February I was ready to go back on the road with no more belongings than I could comfortably fit in the compartments under the platform of the van. I wanted to sleep in a tent and crawl into my sleeping bag every night with nothing but a book, a flashlight, a notebook, and a pen. I was impatient to get to a place where no one could call me on the telephone.

Early in February 1994 I took off for Florida, unsure of what kind of wilderness I might find. Florida was close to home; I'd been there dozens of times. Jerome and I had taken our children to the Florida Keys for family vacations, most recently when they were both college students. From 1969 to 1971 we lived in the Florida panhandle, where Jerome was stationed in the navy.

When we moved back to Atlanta, going to Florida usually meant taking off on a cold winter day and driving as far south as necessary to find warm ocean breezes. When Laura was still a toddler, she called to Jerome from the backseat of the car as we drove toward the Keys. "Dad," she said, "I don't like this. Florida is nothing but a long road." This time I was on that long road in order to find something more than sunshine and a relief from winter, though I certainly wanted that as well.

The day was overcast when I left home, but just about the time I crossed the Florida line, the clouds opened up and within an hour there were blue skies. By the time I came to the outskirts of Orlando, the smell of orange blossoms permeated the air, but I still had not fully recovered that "on the road again" feeling I'd had on my journey west. Laura was only partly right. This Florida was actually a complex maze of superhighways connecting urban centers surrounded by endless developments of houses, golf courses, condominiums, and mobile homes.

I spent that first night with my friend Roselyn and her husband Wilbur in Winter Park. She and I had been friends since high school, we'd roomed together in college, and we'd shared an apartment with two other "girls" the year after graduation. In 1963, when we graduated from college, we didn't think of ourselves as women. We were still girls, and what binds us together after all these years is not so much shared interests or even shared values, but that we were girls together. And when we get together and talk about our lives, we are girls again.

I knew Roselyn's husband before she did. I dated a friend of his and had a short fling with Wilbur. I remember one particular night during spring break at Daytona Beach when Wilbur and I and a few other people went fishing for mullet. Probably going fishing was an excuse for taking a boat out at night, but I do remember hundreds of mullet in the water, some of them even jumping in the boat. I have a vague memory of a fish fry, but that may have been another time.

To this day Wilbur's great passions in life are hunting and fishing. One room in their home is known as "Wilbur's room." It took me a while to adjust to what I was seeing when Wilbur showed me around. There were huge elk antlers, the head of a Dall sheep, snakeskins, a coyote rug, a wildcat attacking a wild turkey, a marlin and swordfish crossing bills, a lamp base made from the head of a large alligator, and numerous other heads and antlers—all skillfully preserved by a taxidermist. Wilbur's special room is also a showcase for his guns, the beautifully crafted knives he has made, a collection of wild-turkey callers, and other hunting and fishing paraphernalia. Though we come to it from very different directions, Wilbur and I share a love of wilderness. Over dinner we swapped stories of our adventures, though his account of tracking Dall sheep in Alaska only to be tracked in turn by a grizzly topped all of mine.

The next day another friend from college days drove down from Valdosta, Georgia, to join Roselyn and me for lunch. The three of us had met only occasionally in the three decades since we'd lived together with one other friend in a two-bedroom apartment, made even more crowded by the comings and goings of the various men in our lives. As always we fell into easy intimacy, as if only a few hours had passed since we had last talked.

Sue knew about my interest in wilderness, but Roselyn was puzzled. "It just doesn't seem like you to be sleeping alone in a tent outdoors, let alone in some of the wild places you've been." She said she thought I'd be afraid, and like many people, she was concerned that I was not carrying a gun. I confessed that sometimes I was indeed afraid, but that my feelings of fear were not so intense that they stopped me from doing what I wanted to do.

"Fear comes and goes," I said.

"You ought to be more afraid," she declared. "Terrible things happen out there."

"She'll be all right," Sue said, having long given up trying to persuade me to carry a gun.

"I'm sure you know this, but I can't help but remind you that this is Florida," Rosie concluded.

First Texas, now Florida—a state legendary for murders, it seemed. German tourists gunned down for no apparent reason, five college students brutally murdered by a serial killer in Gainesville, their murderer on trial as we spoke. A few days later he would plead guilty. Eight days later, on February 19, a college student would be murdered and his sister raped in the Ocala National Forest—a place I intended to visit—by two men who befriended them in the campground and invited them to go on a hike. In Atlanta I paid little attention to the evening news "body count," but on the road I seemed to be keenly aware of murders. Supervigilance may be one way I kept the debilitating aspect of fear at bay.

I had to confess that I was more uneasy in Florida's wild places than in national forests and wilderness areas in Wyoming and Montana, not so much because of the highly publicized murders but because there was so little buffer between Florida's wilderness areas and its many overpopulated towns and cities. In my weeks in Florida I was rarely more than an hour from a major highway, and I was usually relatively close to an urban area. I had good reason to feel less comfortable in Florida than in sparsely populated areas of the West, but I tried to reassure Roselyn—and myself—that I would be as safe as she is in the parking lot of a Winter Park shopping center.

A few nights later I was asleep in my tent in a campground on Sanibel Island. I'd come to see the Ding Darling Wildlife Refuge, but there was no such thing as a remote campsite on the crowded island. Sometime after midnight I was awakened by what sounded like a man's voice: "Hello, hello there," the voice repeated several times. I froze and realized that I had nothing to protect myself with—no personal alarm, no pepper spray, not even a stick or a large flashlight. I was certain that the insistent "hello" was directed at me, since there were no other tents nearby. But it was not long before the only sounds I heard were trucks passing on the nearby highway.

The next morning when I crawled from my tent just before dawn, I noticed that I'd left a light on inside the van. Perhaps someone had tried to warn me that I might wake up to a dead battery. I walked over to a nearby aviary, where the owners of the campground raise tropical birds. I noticed a large green parrot that looked at me, cocked its head, and in a very human-sounding voice said, "Hello there. Hello there." Fortunately the battery was not dead, and I arrived at the refuge just after sunrise. In addition to the vast 1,296,500-acre Marjory Stoneman Douglas Wilderness in the Everglades, Florida has sixteen other wildernesses totaling 125,825 acres. Of these, 2,619 acres are in the northern end of the J. N. Ding Darling Wildlife Refuge. Visitors drive, bike, or walk outside the southern edge of the wilderness, and crowds are hard to avoid in the winter unless you leave the road and walk down one of the trails—Indigo Trail, Shell Mound Trail, or South Dike Trail. That morning I saw flocks of roseate spoonbills, wood storks, great and little blue herons, an assortment of ducks and moorhens, and—most impressive of all—the elegant and rare red-dish egrets.

After leaving Sanibel and heading south on I-75, I turned east on Route 846 to the 11,000-acre Corkscrew Swamp Sanctuary. It was the middle of the afternoon when I arrived and nearly dark when I emerged from this strange wetland where some of the oldest trees in eastern North America live. Thanks to the Audubon Society, which maintains the sanctuary, I was able to walk along a boardwalk through the sawgrass and sedges of the wet prairies. Some of the dense broad-leaved trees of the ham-mocks were adorned with delicate tree orchids. Large swamp ferns grew on high ground. Water lettuce almost completely cov-ered small lakes. Most arresting of all were the stands of great bald cypress, some of them 8 feet in diameter, 130 feet high, and about seven hundred years old. Perhaps because it was so late in the day, there were no other people around, and I was alone with the trees.

I remembered a time almost two decades before when I was called by a full moon from my room in a youth hostel in Balus-trand, Norway. I'd come there with Laura at the end of May with the idea of getting as far north as possible. Balustrand turned out to be our stopping point, since the road beyond was blocked with snow and ice. Leaving my sleeping six-year-old daughter behind, I hiked out alone into the forested countryside, not knowing where I was going. About a mile down the narrow dirt road I came to a grove of giant fir trees, and I left the road to wander among them. The floor of the forest was covered with needles, and there was no underbrush. I was suddenly struck with a powerful feel-ing I couldn't describe. At first I felt there might be someone lurk-ing in the shadows cast by the moon. I made myself breathe deeply and peer through the spaces between the great trees. There were no other people, but I was in the presence of some-thing, and whatever it was held me there. I didn't want to leave. Eventually I felt myself relax, and after a while I walked back to the road and returned to my sleeping child.

The memory of that incident has returned to me from time to time through the years, but never with quite the same intensity as it did when I stood in that cypress grove. The two ecosystems could hardly have been more different: one tropical, the other alpine. Through much of the year, the great trees in northern Norway stand in snow, which melts in the spring and drains into the fjords of the North Sea. The giant cypress stand in the dark, still water of the swamp. Nevertheless, in both places I felt a mysterious sensation, a prickling of the skin, a shortness of breath, and a vague sense of being watched by something or someone.

The next day I drove east across the state on the old Tamiami Trail to its intersection with State Highway 997. Then I turned south and drove through fields of strawberries, corn, and tomatoes to reach the eastern edge of the Everglades National Park. The thirty-eight miles from the park entrance to the dead end at Florida Bay is dotted with self-contained and very different worlds. Several miles down the road is the Pa-hay-okee Overlook, where I saw for the first time the vast saw-grass prairie, once thought to be impenetrable, stretching from horizon to horizon. Further along is Mahogany Hammock, a subtropical tree island made accessible by a boardwalk that meanders through oaks, mahogany, and strangler figs, some laden with resurrection ferns. There were no other visitors to the hammock while I was there, and I lingered for an hour or so. When I emerged out of the deep shadows of that junglelike world into the light of day, I noticed a lone white ibis standing with a large brightly colored reddish-orange snake in its beak, probably a Florida king snake or Florida scarlet snake.

I stopped to watch, wondering how the bird would manage to eat the writhing creature. Holding the snake in the middle of its two-foot-long body, the bird tossed it up into the air over and over again without letting go. Eventually the two parts of the snake twisted together. Only then was the ibis able to gulp down this more manageable prey.

At the end of the Florida peninsula I set up a tent on the edge of Florida Bay. It was late afternoon. I pulled on a long-sleeved shirt and applied insect repellent to my hands, neck, and face. Then I made a cup of tea and settled down at the edge of the water. While in Florida, I was asked to write an article about Marjory

Stoneman Douglas for *American Nature Writers,* a two-volume work published by Scribner's. I was thrilled at the prospect, since to me Douglas's life and work are exemplary, not in the sense of being flawless but in serving as a model for others. In two weeks I would travel up to Miami to interview this woman whose passion for a place was strong enough to focus her efforts for nearly eight decades. Until then, I would explore the watery world she had given so much of her life to save.

Once again I was disconnected from home. To use the telephone, I had to go to the ranger station. The only obligation I felt was to be attentive to this place. For reading I brought Douglas's classic *The Everglades: River of Grass,* a volume of her short stories, and *Freedom River,* a novel she would later tell me was her best work. During those two weeks I hiked through the coastal prairies, paddled a canoe through canals and ponds, and slogged in tennis shoes through the shallow water. On the edges of the saw-grass and salt marshes are the mangroves—the black mangrove, with curious sticklike protuberances that allow the plant to breathe, and the red mangrove, supported by entwined roots arching up through the water into the air. Both species stabilize and hold marine sediments and eventually form new land. Many marine and estuarine organisms begin their life cycle in nutrient-rich mangrove waters, and they provide habitat for most wading birds—herons, egrets, ibis, and storks—as well as clapper rails.

Late one afternoon I joined three other people for a boat trip through the small islands in Florida Bay to see the rookeries and nesting grounds of thousands and thousands of birds. Offshore we saw crowds of white pelicans on sandbars feeding; eagle and osprey nests (and midair battles between these two dominant raptors); and in the distance, a dozen or so flamingos standing in a long line.

Most of the 1,296,500 acres of designated wilderness inside Everglades National Park is covered with water. Those who have taken a canoe through the ninety-nine-mile wilderness waterway that extends from Flamingo to the Ten Thousand Islands on the west coast may complain about mosquitoes, but they remember the wonder of sharing this watery world with alligators, porpoises, manatees, and a myriad of birds—herons, storks, ibises, egrets, skimmers, snail kites, and many more.

One day I hitched a ride on an airboat with a Florida Fish and Wildlife official—I'll call him Max—on his rounds to check on a remote part of the glades outside the National Park. An airboat is a god-awful contraption that makes a noise loud enough to disturb any living thing capable of hearing, and we wore mufflers to protect our ears. Except for the odd alligator and occasional birds rising to fly in front of us, we saw little life until we stopped on an island once inhabited by the Mikasuki Indians, probably dating from the late eighteenth century. There we explored the remains of an Indian settlement, where we found shell middens, pottery shards, even a tool made from shells. As we hiked around the island, we saw limpkins and a least bittern, two wading birds I'd not seen before. Limpkins are in a family of their own, having no close relatives. Once hunted almost to extinction, they have recently made a fair comeback. The two we watched were foraging for snails, their primary food. The least bittern crept through a cluster of reeds at water's edge.

In addition to monitoring the backwaters of the glades, Florida Fish and Wildlife has a wide range of responsibilities, including capturing exotic animals that escape from their cages. Max entertained me with the story of a boa constrictor he captured in a school yard and brought to his own house, only to have it escape and disappear. To her horror, his wife found it days later under the mattress of the bed they slept in. There were tales of monkeys raising families in the trees of subdivisions and a pet-shop employee who released dozens of animals in a public park. Max prefers dealing with wild creatures, though that, too, can be a challenging job.

In the late afternoons I would visit Eco Pond and then come back to my campsite and watch flocks of white ibises sail overhead, heading for their rookeries in the mangrove islands in the bay. Most nights I crawled into my sleeping bag around 9:00 P.M. and settled down to read and write until I fell asleep an hour or so later. I would usually wake up around 5:45 A.M., with plenty of time before sunrise to walk the quarter mile to the van, gather cooking gear, and light my stove. By the time I was settled down with a cup of tea, I would notice a faint light in the east. A few minutes later the birds that fished from the mud flats just in front of my tent began to arrive. Around 6:20 a great white heron came flying in from the mangrove islands out in the bay where it nests. This giant bird—the white morph of the great blue heron—is found year-round only in these waters and in the Florida Keys further south. Though it spends most of its life wading in the shallows, it would sometimes choose to start its day stepping gingerly around my campsite and cocking its head to check out what I was up to. About the time the sun rose, it would wander down to the edge of the sea and begin the day-long task of catching fish.

Next would come a little blue heron and several snowy egrets, followed by flocks of little gray sea birds. Overhead ibises soared inland to their feeding grounds in the saw-grass and mangrove swamps. As the sun broke the horizon, a lone brown pelican sailed in and landed on the piling twenty feet or so out in the bay, where it sat patiently facing inland waiting for breakfast to swim by.

The last to come were the two black vultures that took up residence around my campsite. Carrion is the natural food preference of a vulture, and while a rotting hamburger might qualify as carrion, there was no garbage near these walk-in campsites. I couldn't understand why the vultures were there, but biology tells me there must have been something in it for them. They eyed me as if they were trying to assess my state of health, and since I gave little evidence of life so early in the morning, they may have had hope.

If I died unnoticed in this place called by some "The End of the World," I would provide a feast for these patient birds. I wondered how many I could feed, whether they would pick my bones clean. Given the history of murder in the Everglades, they may have had human flesh before.

Eco Pond

〰〰〰 DURING THE TIME I spent camping out in the Everglades, Eco Pond became my Walden. A few minutes after sunrise
other campers would emerge from their tents, and one or two
might wander down to the mudflats to watch the birds. About
this time—7:00 A.M. or so—I would gather my cooking gear, store
it in the van, and walk down the road to explore what was really
a man-made evaporation pond. Birds by the hundreds came there
to feed, nest, or just rest on their way to and from their rookery
in Florida Bay to feeding waters further inland.

Eco Pond is small, about a half mile around, yet my first stroll
along its shore lasted for hours. Just as I arrived a flock of white
ibises arranged themselves in the buttonwood trees on an island
in the middle of the pond. With them was one lone roseate spoon-
bill. Hiding in the grass near the edge of the lake was an American bittern, a secretive bird larger than the least bittern that even
serious birders are thrilled to see at close range. On the first quarter of the path around the pond I passed a green-backed heron,
various egrets, a tricolored heron, and a smooth-billed ani, a peculiar black bird with a floppy tail and parrotlike bill.

As I was watching the bittern creep about in the grasses at the
edge of the water, I heard a roar that left me chilled to the bone.
Scanning the water, I spotted a ten- or twelve-foot gator just in
time to hear the fearsome sound again as the huge creature called
for a mate. Thrusting its head and tail out of the water, it arched
its back and somehow managed to bellow without opening its

mouth. I watched in frozen fascination as the immense animal moved slowly through the water, stopping from time to time to arch its head and tail and roar again until it disappeared in a thicket of cattails some fifty feet away.

I knew that I was not at risk even though there was no barrier between this creature and me. Alligators will occasionally attack children and dogs, but hardly ever go for adults walking along a dry path ten feet away. What I felt was not so much fear as the thrill of witnessing the beginning of the process that would result in mating, nesting, eggs, a cache of about thirty eggs, and finally, months later, a dozen or more baby alligators. Eco Pond could never support such numbers, and even the one or two young that were likely to survive might have to migrate or be relocated to new waters.

I lowered my binoculars and continued to walk around the pond, but suddenly stopped again. There, only a few feet away, was another large alligator completely out of the water. In its mouth was a soft-shell turtle as big as a dinner platter. There was no evidence that the turtle was damaged, but it didn't take much to imagine what was happening to its soft underside. For some time I watched the predator slowly consume its prey. Throughout it all, the turtle moved its front feet as if it would eventually escape. With head extended and eyes bulging, it crawled in place as the alligator slowly crushed its shell.

Every twenty minutes or so, the gator would open its jaws and in a fraction of a second move the turtle around two or three inches to a more vulnerable position. With each of these rapid movements, I would hear the sound of shell cracking and watch the turtle's head progress slightly closer to the gator's teeth. I stayed riveted to the scene until the head of the turtle was an inch from the crushing teeth. I'd seen enough. Taking deep breaths I gradually dispelled the tension I'd been accumulating while watching this common event, made uncommon only by my presence. I left the pond around 10:30 and returned in the early afternoon. The only sign of the bloody scene I'd witnessed was a ten-foot swath of flattened grass at the edge of the water. A ranger had told me that the turtle would be all the food the alligator would need for at least a week. If this gator were female, I thought, then perhaps she would now be available for the bellowing bull I'd heard earlier in the day, and the turtle would provide the energy necessary for the strange underwater copulation that would result in eggs a couple of months later. I couldn't help but wonder what Thoreau would have written had he spent a year—or two— at such a pond.

Mosquitoes

〰〰〰 KNOWING HOW to limit the damage done by biting insects is an important survival skill in any wetland area of the Southeast, but it's essential in the Everglades, where a few minutes of exposure can result in dozens, even hundreds of bites by mosquitoes and the invisible but devastating no-see-ums. Both male and female mosquitoes drink nectar, but only the females pierce skin and drink blood. A blood meal is necessary to bring the eggs to maturity. I'd begun to suspect that biting mosquitoes prefer the flesh of females, since I have always suffered more bites than Jerome on our trips together. But when I asked the Everglades mosquito expert about this, he just shook his head. "No way. I've seen plenty guys almost eaten alive out here."

At night, when I climbed into my tent, mosquitoes always came in with me and waited for skin to appear. Even in February it's warm enough most nights in south Florida to sleep with little or no covering. I usually slept on top of my sleeping bag and under a loose knitted cotton blanket, which mosquitoes easily penetrated. Several times during my first night I woke to the dreaded buzz, turned on the flashlight, and swatted what I thought must be the last mosquito. By morning I had almost fifty bites, but the next day I talked to a ranger and figured out how to avoid another miserable night. By the time I left the Everglades, I had learned the rules for surviving mosquitoes:

1. When outside, always wear a hat, a long-sleeved shirt, and pants tucked into boots, and apply insect repellent to all exposed skin.
2. Leave openings to tent zipped shut at all times except when getting in and out.
3. Learn to get in and out of the tent in a matter of seconds.
4. Never remove hat, boots, or clothing until you have killed all the mosquitoes you can find.
5. Use a flashlight to find mosquitoes. They usually hide at the top of the tent.
6. Use either hands or a flyswatter to kill mosquitoes.
7. Accept the inevitable: one mosquito will always survive the slaughter.
8. Apply cortisone cream to new bites.

It is the mosquito that escapes that is the most irritating. Sometime between midnight and 2:00 A.M., expect to be wakened suddenly by a painful sting you know is the work of a mosquito. You will try to cover yourself only to find that you've left a vulnerable spot or that the critter has gotten under the cover or into your sleeping bag with you. You may think you have no choice but to turn on the light and begin the search-and-kill maneuver all over again, but there is another option that will eliminate the problem, at least for the night. A mosquito whose feeding is interrupted prematurely will inevitably bite again, and every unsuccessful swat may mean a new bite. When you feel the mosquito bite, grit your teeth and let her feed. It takes a mosquito about two minutes to take all the blood it can hold. After that, she will not bite again for some hours and you should be able to sleep.

The White Heron

≋≋≋ THE MOON WAS full and bright and the night was full of sound—woks, croaks, clacking, squawks, and once a piercing wail. I was having trouble sleeping, so around midnight I crawled from my tent and walked down to Eco Pond to see what was going on. *See* is not quite the right word. Even with so much moonlight, I was not able to make out the shapes of birds on the water or in the trees. No matter. Their voices told me they were there, along with frogs, insects, and other creatures singing and calling in the night. During one moment of near silence the dark shape of a medium-large bird appeared in front of me and uttered a deep-pitched squawk as it passed. The pitch of its call indicated a black-crowned night heron.

An hour later I crawled back into my tent, did battle with the few mosquitoes that had followed me in, and tried again to fall asleep. No dice. I was wide awake and hyperalert. I looked out the mesh window of my tent at Florida Bay, where the water was still and only the slightest breeze stirred. I took up Marjorie Stoneman Douglas's *River of Grass* and turned to the opening passage: "There are no other Everglades in the world. They are, they have always been, one of the unique regions of the earth, remote, never wholly known. Nothing anywhere else is like them: their vast glittering openness, wider than the enormous visible round of the horizon, the racing free saltness and sweetness of their massive winds, under the dazzling blue heights of space. They are unique also in the simplicity, the diversity, the related harmony of the forms of life they enclose."

I read about resurrection ferns, small green tree snakes, and the now endangered swallow-tailed kite that feeds exclusively on one species of tree snail. In the midst of a passage about strangler figs, I drifted off to sleep to wake again at 6:30 A.M. When I peeked out at the water, I spotted the great white heron with its seven-foot wingspan wheel slowly in and land on the piling usually occupied by a brown pelican. When this more homely bird arrived a few minutes later, the heron held its place while its rival circled and circled before landing in the water nearby.

The full moon was low in a pastel western sky; the eastern sky was a garish pink and orange. The tide was high and fuller than usual, but the birds arrived in their usual order, beginning with the white heron and ending with vultures. They gathered among the mangroves to wait for the water to recede and expose the mudflats where they fished.

Then came the children: two boys eight or nine years old loaded with fishing gear took over a spot near the birds and me. In a matter of minutes the smaller of the two boys had hooked what turned out to be a medium-sized eel. By the time they reeled it in, it had wrapped the line around its body several times and seemed hopelessly tangled. Sure that they had caught a snake, the frightened boys cut it loose and left it still alive and writhing in the shallow water.

I explained that what they had caught was an eel, not a snake, and that they should at least remove it from the water and bury it. Otherwise a bird, perhaps the heron or the brown pelican, would surely eat it, swallow the hook and line, and eventually die. But my chiding had no effect. The boys stuck to their story: they had caught a snake, and they weren't going anywhere near it.

I jogged to the nearby ranger station to report what had happened, but the young man I talked to was not very interested.

"We don't have the personnel to handle this kind of problem. Besides, the eel could do some damage to anyone who tried to free it."

"Well, couldn't someone at least go talk to the boys about responsible fishing? You know, explain to them that if they hook something they should remove the hook and if they can't do that, take the animal out of the water?"

"I'm sorry, but we really don't have the man power to do that sort of thing. If I talked to every fisherman who needed talking to, I wouldn't have time for anything else." With that the ranger began fingering Hemingway's *The Green Hills of Africa,* which he had been reading when I interrupted him.

I headed for my morning walk around Eco Pond and for a while forgot about the eel. About three quarters of the way around I noticed a great white heron with a fishhook hanging from its beak. In a few minutes I was back at the ranger station reporting yet another animal in distress. The story was the same.

"There's really nothing we can do. The bird would never allow itself to be caught," the ranger explained.

"Couldn't you watch it, wait for it to get weak, and then catch it? Throw a net over it, maybe?" I asked.

"No, we really don't have anyone who can do that. Besides, it takes time. The bird would never cooperate."

"Since you said it 'takes time,' that must mean that it's possible to catch the bird and remove the hook before it dies," I persisted.

"Well, I guess it is possible. Folks down on Sanibel Island—a group called CROW—rescue a lot of birds, but we really can't do that here. You have to understand, this happens all the time."

Remembering the time that the evening news was dominated for days by the drama of two whales trapped under an ice floe, I realized that people would rally by the millions to save animals— when they are large, charismatic megafauna and when the media dramatizes their plight. But if death is common, if it "happens all the time" as it does after oil spills or as a consequence of irresponsible fishing practices, we throw up our hands and say that the job is too big. If we saved one heron, we might be expected to save them all. To solve this problem, fishermen would have to change their habits, taking care to retrieve fishing lines when bait is taken by what they consider undesirable life-forms; rangers would have to enforce the rules and regulations that are so widely ignored in the Everglades. I met no one in the glades who would even talk about taking on this project.

Park rangers and administrators seemed to be stuck in resignation. "There's nothing we can do about the fishermen" had been generalized to "there's nothing we can do about anything" —about an eel, a heron, or any other wildlife damaged or killed by careless people. Later I talked to Carol Lowenstein, the staff rehabilitator at CROW, the Clinic for Rehabilitation of Wildlife on Sanibel Island. She told me that, indeed, wounded birds can be helped and that with the help of two staff veterinarians as well as student interns, they treat 3,700 birds and animals a year, about half of which are successfully restored to the wild. The difficult part of the work is capturing animals, which often can't be accomplished until they are too weak to escape—and sometimes too sick to recover.

I returned to the bay to check on the eel. It was gone, and so was the great white heron that regularly patrolled the water where the eel had been. Had the heron eaten the eel? Was the heron I saw at Eco Pond the one that sailed in to my campsite every morning? If so, then wasn't I partly responsible, since I could have found a way to remove the eel from the water and dispose of it out of reach of the birds? But like the boy who caught it, I was squeamish and thought a professional should do the job. At the information center I talked to Steve Robinson, the ranger who seemed most knowledgeable about wildlife in the Everglades. When I described the eel, he concluded that it was probably a spoon-nose eel, a common breed in Florida Bay. Steve also warned that since the eel was in distress, it might have bitten anyone who tried to rescue it.

Late that afternoon I wandered down to the marina, where two young women were trying to catch a pelican that had something large lodged in its throat. Nearby was a shed where fishermen cleaned their fish. Disregarding the small sign warning them not to feed the birds, some fishermen tossed fish remains to the pelicans that line up on pilings nearby. These birds have no trouble swallowing a good-sized live fish, which slides cleanly down their large throats. But a bony carcass often gets caught,

　　　　　　　WILD FLORIDA

and unless it is removed, the bird will die. It's no small job to catch a pelican and remove a fish carcass from its throat, but these young people who worked in the canoe concession regularly patrolled the area to identify and help any birds in distress. The rangers, the young woman told me, rarely take the time to help, and no one enforces the rule, "Don't feed the birds."

Back at Eco Pond in the late afternoon, I waited along with a group of birders for the flocks of ibises to arrive. As I wandered along the shore, I found myself wondering which bird would be the next victim of a fishhook. Then I spotted a rarely seen sora rail creeping along the edge of the cattails. Just as the rail disappeared in the reeds, a flock of white ibises appeared overhead, and right in the middle was a flash of red as bright as the vermilion flycatchers I'd seen in the West. Just in time I raised my binoculars, and there it was. "That, madam," I heard a nearby birder say with a British accent, "is the rare and wondrous scarlet ibis." He told me that eggs from this glowing red South American bird were brought to Florida from the Caribbean in the 1960s and placed in the nests of white ibises. The experiment failed to produce a new generation of scarlets, as the transplanted hatchings matured mostly to breed with the white ibises, producing a small population of rosy hybrids. But at least this one survived.

I woke about 5:30 the next morning. Waiting for dawn, I sipped tea and scanned the horizon. The stars were still out and the moon was low in the west, but both soon faded as the eastern horizon began to lighten. Then I saw white wings swimming through the heavy air, and in moments the great white heron landed in front of me as if it were standing for inspection. I sighed with relief when I realized that there was no fish line dangling from its beak. "Reprieve," I thought. My bird had not eaten the eel, and at least for now it was free to feed and preen in this small part of Florida it had staked out as its own.

Looking at the bird I thought of as my own, I laughed at myself as I recalled how the day had begun with my fruitless if not foolish attempts to save the tangled eel and the white heron with a fishhook in its throat. The impulse I'd felt to save these two doomed creatures was intense, but misdirected. Far more important,

I realized, was saving the Everglades themselves so that all creatures there would have a chance to survive.

By the end of the two weeks I spent camped on the shore of
Florida Bay, I had begun to think of the thousand or so square feet
around my tent as my personal territory. I had readily resumed
the simple life I had fallen in love with during my first three
months on the road. I could look out at water, mangrove islands,
sky, and birds without seeing any other humans. I was virtually
alone, a condition I'd learned to cherish. To restore my spirit, such
solitude seemed necessary. My days were all my own.

The Next Fifty-two Years

~~~~ ON THE LAST day in February I traveled west across the Tamiami Trail to Everglades City, which is just beyond the northwest border of Everglades National Park. In about twenty-four hours I would drive back to Miami to interview Marjory Stoneman Douglas for the article I would write. There is no campground in the western section of the National Park, so I checked into a motel for one night. Until recently this seemingly sleepy little town was a port of entry for huge quantities of illegal drugs, but in the 1980s law-enforcement agents successfully carried out Operation Everglades, which slowed the drug traffic and sent around a hundred of the town's five hundred residents to jail.

I arrived late in the afternoon in time to take a boat ride among the mangroves. The local guide pointed out birds that were now all familiar to me. The immature white ibis, known in these parts as a "swamp chicken," he said, makes delicious eating. Though it's against the law to kill these birds, he didn't hesitate to tell me that local people routinely kill and eat them.

Back in town I treated myself to a fish dinner and went to bed early. The next morning I woke as usual before sunrise. When I switched on the light, I felt slightly nauseous at the sight of white walls, brown-and-yellow printed bedspreads, and the smell of cleaning chemicals and insecticides. I hurried outside and jogged through the unguarded gate of the National Park, then sat at the edge of the water looking out at the Ten Thousand Islands surrounded by shallows that merge with the Gulf of Mexico. I saw several gulls but few other birds. Sitting at the edge of the water near the boat docks, I closed my eyes and imagined the great white heron wheeling in from the east over in Flamingo to begin a day of fishing.

I was not ready to leave the glades. I longed to take my ritual walk around Eco Pond one more time, but even more I wanted to talk with Marjory Stoneman Douglas, who had been fighting to protect the Everglades for some seven decades. In the final chapter to *The Everglades: River of Grass,* first published in 1947, Douglas wrote of the balance that still existed in the glades between "the forces of life and of death." She believed that there is also a balance in human nature that sets courage and will and the ability to work with others against "greed . . . inertia . . . and foolishness."

I was scheduled to interview Douglas at three o'clock that afternoon at the house in Coconut Grove that she had built in 1926. On April 7, 1994, a few weeks after I met her, Douglas would be 104 years old, exactly twice my age. She was five years older than I when she published *River of Grass.* I had been warned that she couldn't see at all and could barely hear but that she loved to talk about her work and about the Everglades. I arrived right on time to be greeted at the door by Medina, the woman who cared for her. I waited in the living room, the one large room in the small cottage. I looked around at the bookcases, photographs, carvings of birds, and the many objects that covered the tabletops of the house she had occupied for nearly seventy years. I was uneasy and unsure how I might relate to this blind and nearly deaf woman whose work and life I admired. I had never met anyone nearly 104 years old.

In a few minutes Medina led Douglas into the room, guiding her through the maze of tables and chairs to her favorite chair. In order to be heard, I had to sit on the arm of the sofa, lean over toward her, and shout into her hearing aid. I began by thanking her for taking the time to talk with me.

"Yes indeed," she said. "I have all the time in the world."

When I heard those words, I relaxed. I couldn't remember when I'd met anyone who had "all the time in the world." Even when I met a friend for lunch, we usually began by setting time limits. "I have about an hour" was a common beginning point. This woman, however, had time for me, and I expect she'd always made time for conversations to develop or play themselves out.

I had read about Douglas's feisty spirit and endurance in a fight. There's a story going around about the time in the early eighties when she spoke to a meeting of the Dade County Planning Board held in a hot, stuffy school auditorium. Attending the meeting were some thousand or so landowners who were demanding that the board approve further draining of the east Everglades to make room for more development. When Douglas, then 91, came to the podium, some of the audience heckled her. In her usual crisp but determined manner, she informed her opponents that they might as well sit down. "I've got all night," she said, "and I can take the heat."

What would it be like only to do things that are too important to be rushed, to sit with a friend until the purpose of our being together is fully served, and to leave enough space between activities so that there is no need for hurry? I thought how shocked my friends or family would be if I began a visit with the announcement that "I have all the time in the world." Marjory Stoneman Douglas had somehow learned to live on wilderness time in the midst of a booming city.

In the hour and a half I spent with her, Douglas's responses ranged from gracious and kind to irritated and angry. She never tried to answer a question until she was sure she had heard and understood it, and this often required my repeating it several times. If she didn't like my question, she said so emphatically. When I asked if she had a favorite bird, she let me know exactly what she thought. "What nonsense," she said. "Don't be silly. Why would I have a favorite bird?"

After I told her that I'd felt attached to the great white heron, she told me about the nuptial flight of the white ibis as "a great wheel of white birds floating over the country—an amazing thing." I suspect that in human affairs as in nature it is the big picture that interests her, not the small, private worlds of individuals. I worried sentimentally about the fate of one bird; she thought in terms of ecosystems and the large community of living things.

Douglas showed no evidence of being affected by those who opposed her work. When I asked her to talk about the people who made her work difficult, she responded without hesitation: "They didn't make it hard for me especially. They just made it hard for the Everglades."

When I asked her if she was getting tired, she answered irritably, "I don't get tired." Somehow I believed her and persisted a bit longer to ask her questions about the past and the present.

I asked her opinion regarding what we should do about the pollution of the glades by sugar growers, and she explained that she was still fighting them but that I might do better to talk to other members of Friends of the Everglades, the organization she had started in 1970. Then she paused and said without any sadness in her voice, "I've pretty much retired from active work. I'm old and I'm blind. I can't see to read. So I am not so useful as I used to be." Before I left she would repeat these words again. What struck me about this comment was what was unsaid. Marjory Stoneman Douglas didn't say that she had completely retired, only that she had "pretty much retired." She did not say that she was "useless," only that she was "not as useful" as she used to be.

I had begun the day complaining about waking up in the sterile white walls of a motel room and longing to be outdoors where I could see the sunrise and the birds sailing in. Marjory Stoneman Douglas could not even see the walls of the house she'd built so long ago. She had gone to Washington a few months before to receive the Medal of Honor from President Bill Clinton, but she couldn't see the color of the walls of the room she stayed in at the White House or what her host and hostess looked like. Yet she told me she liked Bill, spoke of Hillary as a very nice girl who had gone to the same college she had, and observed that Al Gore had not made much of an impression on her. These things she mentioned in passing, without ever suggesting how limited the experience must have been to someone who can't see and can barely hear. In fact, in the hour and a half I spent with her she didn't complain once—maybe in part because she can still call forth the sight of the nuptial flight of hundreds of white ibises wheeling across the sky.

Marjory Stoneman Douglas left a powerful and lasting impression on me. With a strength of character that transcended her frail body, she emanated power. Straightforward and plainspoken, she had no time for nonsense. Hers was a vigorous spirit. When I reluctantly left her that day, I felt I'd learned something about what it means to focus and stay the course. I hoped that, like her, I could learn to take the heat.

When I was born in 1941, Marjory Stoneman Douglas was a few months shy of 52, and her major work was ahead of her. *River of Grass* would not be published until 1947, the year I entered the first grade. Being with her made me think about how I would live if I knew I had as much ahead as I have had behind—if I had another fifty-two years. What long-term projects would I take on with so much time ahead?

Douglas had all the time in the world for me not because she thought she would live another fifty-two or even five years—in fact she died four years later at 108—but because she believed that talking to me was worth her time. I was a writer doing an article for a book about American nature writers. Talking to me was important to her, and she did so with the attention and leisure she thought the project deserved.

I wondered what it would be like to live with a determination to make each day count while at the same time taking the long view—to wake up every morning knowing deep in the bones that on the one hand we have no time to waste and on the other we have all the time in the world. Those of us who are energetic and healthy have the luxury of both short- and long-term perspectives. The hypothetical "if I only had a year" position forces me to choose carefully among the many possible ways to spend a day; the equally hypothetical "how to spend the next fifty-two years" stance allows me to commit to projects that might not be completed before the middle of the twenty-first century. Taking on long-term projects like saving the Everglades or any other wild place requires working with others who will continue the project after we're gone.

Fifty years ago, when *River of Grass* was published, Marjory Stoneman Douglas knew that the battle she was waging would be a long one. When I met her, she let me know that the struggle to preserve what remains and recover at least some of what has been lost will never end. Two days after my visit with Douglas, the *Miami Herald* ran her picture on the front page and quoted her most recent criticism of what she saw as the Florida state legislature's capitulation to the sugarcane growers. She made it clear that there will always be some people who are determined to use the glades for short-term profit and that if her "River of Grass" is to be restored and preserved, there must always be others willing to fight them and able to take the long view. Maybe the feeling of having all the time in the world came with the belief that others would continue her work after her frail body finally succumbed to mortality.

Voices

〰〰〰 By the time I came home, winter was retreating and spring making its first display. Our house is set on the side of a hill surrounded on three sides by woods—red oak, white oak, yellow poplar, and loblolly pines with an understory of dogwood, redbud, and bottlebrush buckeye. There is no lawn. What I call the garden sweeps up from the street, flattens out behind the house, and then climbs the remainder of the hill to the top. There are really four sections to our garden—the lower shade garden, under a large red oak; the sunny front hillside; the four partly sunny raised beds in the flat back area; and the mostly evergreen shade garden on the upper slope.

On the first morning at home, I went out to find daffodils, forsythia, drifts of snowdrops, and bloodroot already in bloom. Wild azaleas were in full bud, and my neighbor's Japanese magnolia was covered with blooms. By early April ferns, blue woodland phlox, bleeding hearts, and Solomon's seal would fill in the shady spots, while a cluster of deciduous azaleas—cream, pink, and yellow—would saturate the air with fragrance. Mid-April would be the showiest time, with dogwood, redbud, evergreen azaleas, and flowering cherry providing the backdrop for dianthus, candytuft, and veronica. Rhododendrons bloom in early May, followed by hydrangeas, Siberian irises, astilbes, and a flush of sweetheart roses so vigorous that that they cover a six-foot wooden fence, spilling over both sides and climbing up the house. Only three vines produce more than a thousand fragrant and delicate blooms in the month of May.

I spent the spring and early summer of 1994 mostly at home, writing the article on Marjory Stoneman Douglas and enjoying a simple, predictable routine. I would get up at the usual hour and go out in the garden with the *New York Times* and a pot of coffee before beginning work upstairs in my study. For convenience I drank tea at campsites, but Jerome and I both enjoy coffee at home in the mornings. Before I'd left home the previous summer, I had rushed through the news, reading headlines and skimming articles. No more. I give myself ample time with the paper and at least a half hour to tend the garden—watering, weeding, and deadheading. Gardening I do on wilderness time, by setting myself a manageable task and letting it take as long as it takes to complete.

In June and July the spring flowers have been surpassed by more flamboyant summer bloom—daylilies, purple coneflowers, blindingly bright rudbeckia "Indian Summer," and scatterings of shade perennials. By midsummer much of this bloom is gone, and I'm left with the grasses, hosta, ferns, lantana, and butterfly bush.

In late July Jerome and I went to Highlands, North Carolina, to be with my parents, who had spent a month there in the summer for decades. That year was particularly poignant to me, as I faced up to my parents' aging and realized that it might be the last time they would be able to come to this place they loved so much. Mother was eighty, and Daddy four months short of eighty-five. On what turned out to be our last visit together to this beautiful place, Mother and I spent the mornings on the deck overlooking the tops of trees. We had no agenda other than being together, breathing the cool mountain air, watering the flower boxes, and watching the birds come in to feed. I mostly remember hummingbirds—the ruby-throated and one my mother insisted was the rarely seen Rufous hummingbird.

When I told my parents I was getting ready to go back out west, they again offered encouragement and a little advice. Mother, who approved of my plans to write a book about wilderness, gave me her usual support and urged me not to worry about her and Daddy and to "get going while the getting was good." Daddy gave me a hug and advised me to learn to change a tire before I left this time.

The first morning back in Atlanta, I took my coffee into the garden, sat down on the deck, closed my eyes, and listened to the sounds of nature. The Carolina wrens were feeding a noisy clutch of young, and squirrels were disrupting the birds on the feeder. In the distance I heard the raucous call of the pileated woodpecker. These sounds began to fade as I turned my attention to the voices in my head. There I found the same questions I'd encountered a year before and that still emerge when I'm about to take off on a journey: Why not focus on your life at home, start a new writing project right here, work on local environmental problems, nurture your friends and family—especially your aging parents? Take better advantage of urban pleasures—restaurants, concerts in the park, movies? Pick up tennis again or take dancing lessons with Jerome? Why give up all that you enjoy here even for a short time? Why go off alone to meet with strangers when the people you love are here?

For a moment I thought the noise in my head was subsiding, but it came back with a different refrain: Leave well enough alone. You were lucky last summer. You were not attacked by a wild animal or struck by a lightning bolt, and you escaped without harm when you encountered scary people. Yet when I conjured up memories of bears outside my tent, thunderstorms, the night cry of a mountain lion, the sound of gunfire, and icy roads on a mountain pass, I felt more exhilaration than fear.

The voice urging me to stay at home was growing faint. I took a deep breath to make sure it had subsided. Then I heard another voice: Your garden is a private place. You come here in the early mornings to be alone, and in the evening you sit here with Jerome to talk over the day. It's a place for daily renewal. Digging in the dirt, sowing seeds, pulling up weeds, enjoying the beauty of it all gives you energy and prepares you for what's next. Your life here is the foundation for more life. Home is the place you come from and go back to. You will once again sit with your mother in her quiet house holding her hand and comforting her, but remember she wants much more for you. You'll find a different kind of renewal in wild places and voices that are not available to you in this tame garden. There are many places you want to be, and there's a lot more for you to learn about wilderness. Your work requires that you go. In the end, this voice prevailed.

Later that day I was at a service station lying on the concrete under the van, my hands covered with grease. Kenny, who had taken care of my cars for years, was teaching me how to change a tire. It took an hour to locate the jack under the hood, discover the spare hidden up under the back of the van, find the gadget necessary to lower the spare to the ground, jack the car, remove one tire, replace it with the spare, and then reverse the procedure. When I finally stood up, the deed done, I was almost euphoric. Last year I'd gone out on the road with no idea where the jack was kept; now I could change a tire. At least I could change one in broad daylight on flat concrete in a gas station with Kenny and his assistant coaching me all the way.

I washed my hands in the sink at the back of the garage. Then I walked out into the sunshine and looked across the street to the corner where I'd had the fateful encounter with the yuppie more than a year before. I smiled as I remembered the sense of victory and disbelief I'd felt as the BMW drove away. I waved good-bye to Kenny, Sam, and the other fellows at the station.

"Call us from the road if you need help," Kenny said with a characteristic twinkle in his eye. "I'd like to make a road call in Montana."

"Thanks, guys," I answered confidently, "but I'm not going to need any help. I'm going to be just fine."

Leaving home for the second extended period was much simpler than the first time. I packed the van with probably half the supplies I had taken the year before. Everything fit with room to spare in the bins under the flat platform that sometimes served as my bed. Stashed carefully under the passenger seat was my notebook computer. In pockets built into the sides of the van, I stored maps, field guides, and a few other books. I could think of nothing else I would need or miss having.

The morning of the day I left, I repeated the rituals of the year before. I had breakfast in the early August garden and then walked from the top of the hill to the street, surveying the plants and trees. I would miss the asters, chrysanthemums, and autumn clematis, but I expected to come home in early November just in time for fall pruning and putting the garden to bed. I took my elderly golden retriever for a last walk. I called Jerome at his office and left messages on the answering machines of a few friends. Then I called my parents.

I half jokingly told my mother to stay well while I was gone. "No crisis until I get back," I said. Then came those reassuring words that I'd heard so many times.

"Don't worry. . . . We're fine. . . . Your daddy's on the golf course. . . . Remember, you can have a good time or a bad time, but I know you always choose the good."

"By the way, tell Daddy not to worry. I learned to change a tire."

I knew that my parents wanted me to follow my passion, but this didn't make it any easier to leave them.

AUGUST 1994

BACK TO THE WILD

Free Rein

~~~~~ THERE ARE NO designated wildernesses in Kansas. Neither are there any in Connecticut, Maryland, Rhode Island, Delaware, or Iowa. States with less than 20,000 acres of wilderness include Indiana, Kentucky, Louisiana, Maine, New Jersey, and Rhode Island; those with less than 10,000 are Massachusetts, Mississippi, and Pennsylvania. The only federally designated wilderness in New York is 1,363 acres on Fire Island. Ohio's only wilderness is a 77-acre island off the shore of Lake Erie. On the way back to the wild, I had come to what must surely be the most tamed and trammeled of American landscapes.

Thirty hours after I left home, I was setting up my tent in a campground at the edge of a recently cut wheat field outside Salina, Kansas. At first I was a little uneasy. The only other campers were a party of four men riding Harleys, but they seemed to be interested only in their bikes and their plans to make it to South Dakota in two more days. After organizing my belongings, I headed off down a sandy dirt road that cut through the fields and connected the widely spaced farmhouses.

I took long strides, breathed deeply, and watched the late afternoon sun settle gradually on the horizon. A lone red-tailed hawk soared above the drying fields of cut-over wheat. Stretching to the horizon, the road was marked with the tracks of a very large dog going my way, tracks that had been made since the last vehicle passed. Soon two more hawks appeared to scan the fields for mice.

A century and a half ago prairie grasses covered a million square miles of North America, and this particular part of Kansas was home to the diverse mixed-grass prairie. Where I stood looking out at cultivated fields was once a wilderness of sturdy grasses interspersed with flowers—Blackfoot daisy, butterfly milkweed, Dakota verbena, prairie spiderwort, and in the spring, blue false indigo. Prairie dogs and black-footed ferrets went about their business, and hordes of migrating buffalo swam through the belly-high grass. The Wichita Indians, just one component of the vast ecosystem, roamed these parts. Then came the first settlers, who brought in plows to cut the living net of roots that held it all together.

I had been walking down this dusty road for an hour or more, and not a single vehicle had come along in the lingering twilight. About halfway back I stopped and dropped down cross-legged in the middle of the road to wait for the evening star. I planned to return to camp when it appeared, but Venus was not enough, and I began to wait for one star and then another. Slowly they came— ten, twenty, then too many to count. Suddenly I was swept back to childhood. The only memory I have of my maternal grandfather—I called him Sim—must have taken place shortly before he died, when I was not yet four years old. Astronomy was his hobby, and after he died, I loved studying his celestial globe. My mother, my grandfather, and I were lying on a quilt in the front yard on a moonless night waiting for darkness and for the first star to appear. Bats swooped across the yard, snatching insects as they flew. In those days the air was clear and there were no streetlights. As each star appeared, I was the first to see it, or so I thought. Sim was teaching me to count—one, two, three, twenty, a hundred, then thousands of stars. I'm sure I didn't make it past three, but I remember the counting and his instruction—Venus, the North Star, the Big Dipper, the Milky Way. Had he not died so young, I might have become a tolerable amateur astronomer; but that magical night in Kansas I could not go much beyond what my grandfather had taught me.

I considered how much of my inner landscape had altered in just a little more than a year, and I wondered what it would take for humans—and for me in particular—to chart a path through life that would be as sure as that of the stars. What most distinguishes me from a grizzly or a planet in orbit is choice. I can choose my path. To relinquish that choice and allow others to dictate the particulars of my journey would be to renounce the very essence of my being, my own peculiar, irreplaceable spirit.

As I headed back to the campground, I began to feel a little uneasy. My eyes were sufficiently adapted to the dark to distinguish the road from the fields, but I would not have seen a rattlesnake coiled in front of me. When I finally climbed into my tent, I fell into a deep sleep. Around dawn I was jolted awake by a violent thunderstorm. I peered out at black clouds on the horizon where just a few hours before there had been a clear, starlit sky. One especially dark spot looked like a tornado, but then it dispersed and mingled with the others. I counted the number of seconds between the bolts of lightning and the thunder. One one thousand, two one thousand, three one thousand: this thing was close, and I was lying on the ground in an open place fast turning into a bog. Clutching my sleeping bag and pillow, I dashed barefoot through the rain and jumped into the van, feeling much safer perched on top of four rubber tires.

An hour later I stepped out into a newly washed landscape, made tea, dried out my tent, and took a jog on the road through the fields I'd walked along the night before. As I reached the first farmhouse, a large dog appeared and fell in step behind me. When I turned around, he stayed right at my heels. I had many hours of driving through Nebraska and into South Dakota before I'd see a landscape included in the National Wilderness Preservation System, but wildness is everywhere, even in Kansas. It resides in the thunderhead, in the stoop of a hawk aiming for prey, in the genetic coding of seeds waiting for rain in a remnant prairie, and in this domestic canine striking out through the fields as if on a hunt.

In the distance I saw a truck approaching. I hailed it and asked the driver to return the dog to the next farmhouse. He looked at me with puzzlement, then opened the door and the dog scrambled in.

"That dog's mor'n a nuisance," he said. "I thank you for looking after him, but he roams all over this county. No way I could fence him in. You're not from these parts, are you?"

"No, I'm not. I'm from Atlanta, and I'm heading west."

"Looks to me like you don't want to be fenced in either."

"You're right about that."

We chatted for a few minutes about the crops he raises—wheat and milo, a form of sorghum—and about the storm that had come up so suddenly early in the morning. Farming, he said—even in the breadbasket of North America—was becoming increasingly expensive and risky.

"Sometimes I wonder why I farm," he said as he pulled away. Then about twenty feet down the road, he stopped suddenly and called back to me, "Hey, you look like you need company. What's the chance you'd like to take this old cur with you?"

"Not a chance in the world," I said as I waved good-bye, not sure whether he referred to the dog or himself. Picking up my pace, I felt a surge of energy. I was ready for whatever came next.

Hogs in the Wilderness

〜〜〜 IT WAS LATE afternoon when I wound my way into a primitive backcountry area in Badlands National Park in South Dakota. The campground there was immediately adjacent to the Sage Creek Wilderness, more than sixty-four-thousand acres of virgin grasslands. Twenty or so tents were arranged in a circle like covered wagons. I found a space and merged with the circle, and like the other campers faced my tent outward so that I could see the grassy plains without seeing tents or people. Looking out from the front of my tent, I had the illusion of solitude.

Some five hundred buffalo make this wilderness their home, and I'm told often wander into the campground to graze. When I asked a ranger if the bison ever attacked campers, he told me that they only charge people who approach them.

"Leave them alone and they'll leave you alone. You may not see many buffalo now. The rut's starting and all the stray individuals are joining the herd. Buffalo never stay in one place very long."

The same must be true for Harleys. I arrived in the Badlands the week of the famous Sturgis motorcycle rally and races. For the first full week in August, Sturgis becomes the largest community in South Dakota, its population swelling from eight thousand to more than two hundred thousand. What started as a race has grown to a major "happening," with events including concerts that feature famous rock bands, weddings, contests, and continuous parties. The word *Sturgis* refers not just to the town but also to the accumulation of all that has happened and will happen there. Sturgis has been going on without interruption for more than sixty years. Bands of men and women roar down the highway dressed in full black leather regalia, many sporting elaborate tattoos. For most of them, Sturgis is the end point of an annual pilgrimage; getting there is the main thing. They come from every state in the United States and from some thirty other countries. For the week before and the week after the rally, the celebrants of the motor-driven festival dominate highways and back roads in that part of the West.

A steady stream of bikers traveled along the loop road of Badlands National Park, and a fair number made it up the bumpy dirt road to the Sage Creek Wilderness, where I had come to reenter the wild. Most, however, did not stop, and only one party of bikers spent the night.

The next morning, I looked out from my tent at the largest intact mixed-grass prairie remaining on the continent. About fifty yards away, a bull buffalo was grazing, and beyond him, a female with a calf. Four bison trails radiated from the flat circular basin used by campers. The buffalo, apparently genetically programmed not to spoil any more of their grazing land than necessary, use the same trails year after year, generation after generation. There were no manmade trails in this particular designated wilderness. Following one of the buffalo trails, I hiked to the top of the highest accessible peak and looked out at the remnant of a vast prairie that had covered most of the central part of the continent. I searched the horizon for the herd, which remained—I guess—just beyond the farthest ridge that I could see.

Back at the camping area, a few other campers were starting breakfast. As I was making tea, one of the bikers walked over to my campsite and asked if I'd seen the buffalo grazing on the hill. He said his name was Tony, that he was a high-school math teacher, and that he was traveling to Sturgis with three buddies.

"You ought to go up there," he said. "It's quite a sight. They close the center of town to all traffic except bikes. There'll be thousands and thousands of bikes lining Main Street, and every Harley is different."

Interested, I asked him what kind of people I'd find in Sturgis.

"All kinds. Doctors, lawyers, accountants, teachers like me. And then you'll find the real bikers. Mechanics, welders, electricians, construction workers—men who live, eat, and breathe bikes and spend most of their money on their bikes. If you decide to go, be careful."

"What do you mean?"

"Well, just remember that not everybody's what they seem. There's always a bad element. Most people will tell you one percent, but I say five percent. Be careful who you talk to. Ninety-five percent of the people you meet are fine folks, just out having fun. Then there's the others."

Well, five percent of two hundred thousand is ten thousand —a substantial number of the "bad element." But I was too close to Sturgis to miss this mass happening. Later, as I was cleaning up from breakfast, Tony and his buddies revved up their bikes and waved to me as they were leaving. I broke camp, left the Badlands, and headed in the same direction.

I found a place to camp on the shore of Sheridan Lake in the Black Hills National Forest. Only a few of the thirty-odd campsites were occupied. There were two families, two groups of biker couples, the camp hosts, and me. The nearest campsite was some distance away from mine, and I looked out at the water and the heavily wooded Black Hills beyond. Not quite ready for Sturgis, I drove to nearby Mount Rushmore that afternoon, sharing the road all the way with hundreds of bikers.

Later, as I sat on the terrace overlooking the mountain, I watched group after group approach the monument and study it with a kind of reverence. After paying their respects to the famous sculpture, many bought ice cream and other refreshments at a nearby concession and lingered on the terrace below the mountain. Most of the crowd were bikers, and all seemed to be having fun. Noticing that I was alone, a woman invited me to join her and the three men she was traveling with. One of the guys—Larry— jumped up to get me an ice-cream cone, and I sat down, feeling relieved to be part of a group. By the time Larry returned, the others were telling me their stories—how they became bikers and what their bikes mean to them. Jobie, the most forthcoming of the group, explained that his bike is worth fifty thousand dollars and that the average Harley owner has about thirty thousand dollars invested in his bike. Larry talked about what his bike means to him.

"A bike is an extension of personality. Every Harley is different. You could say a Harley is a work of art. An artist expresses his feelings with painting or sculpture. We express our feelings with our bikes."

We laughed and talked for almost an hour. As my four companions got up from the table, Larry looked me directly in the eye and said, "You want to understand bikers, think of us this way. We're really cowboys. We've just swapped our horses for Harleys."

Leaving Rushmore, I drove to Custer State Park and stopped off at the Sylvan Lodge for a beer and a nice meal. There I met what Larry had somewhat scornfully called "Yuppie bikers"—two doctors, a dentist, an accountant, and a group of men and women whose business was programming and/or servicing computers for satellites. Unlike the live-eat-breathe bikers who talked mainly about bikes, races, and other rallies they'd attended, these folks talked about their work, their children, the stock market, and about the meteor shower they'd seen the night before. But in the end the talk always returned to bikes. One woman mentioned a friend who constantly warns her that someday she's going to die on a bike.

"Every time she does this to me, I point to her cigarettes and remind her that we're all going to die. She's the one killing herself. I'm just having a good time."

Death was decidedly in the air around the Black Hills. By the fourth day of the rally, there were six fatalities. The hospital emergency rooms in Sturgis and surrounding towns saw a steady stream of serious and not-so-serious injuries. Some patients were shipped home to hospitals better equipped to deal with major injuries. Others in critical condition could not be moved and—if they lived—would probably spend some time in Custer, Deadwood, or Rapid City.

It was dusk when I returned to my campsite on the far side of Sheridan Lake, a mile or so away from the highway. I could still

BACK TO THE WILD

hear the muffled roar of the bikes heading back to Sturgis. Some would be going to the opening-night concert of the rally, reputedly the wildest musical event in the West. I had heard on the radio that public nudity absolutely would not be tolerated this year. A group of bikers told me that the police make this announcement every year to no avail. When I asked if it would be appropriate for me to go to the concert, one of the bikers said, "Honey, don't you even think about going over there unless you go with all five of us." As I slipped into my sleeping bag around 9 P.M., just as the concert was beginning, I noticed that the roar of bikes had ceased. At last the night was quiet.

I woke early the next morning and jogged twice around the mile-long loop of the spacious campground. The few occupied campsites were quiet, and I enjoyed about an hour of silence and solitude before the rumbling resumed in the distance. The hogs were waking up.

About 9 A.M. I drove up the road to another national-forest campground that had a laundry and hot showers. There, with the help of tepid water, a blow-dryer, makeup, and clean clothes, I spruced up for the world-famous Sturgis Rally and Races. Then on a sudden impulse, I hung two cameras around my neck. If doctors could pass for welders and factory workers could pass for lawyers, I could surely pass for a photojournalist, which is exactly what I did. "New York Times," I would shout when I wanted to stop traffic to get the perfect shot. Most people enjoyed the game, but one woman dressed in a see-through black-lace bodysuit looked at me with an exaggerated sense of boredom and complained, "I'm so tired of having my picture taken."

There were more wild things in Sturgis than I had seen in all my time in the wilderness: heavily bearded men with complete buffalo hides or other animal skins covering their bikes; extremely attractive, perfectly built young women with long blond hair wearing black jumpsuits with numerous cutouts strategically placed; not-so-attractive women who managed to be both legally clothed and virtually naked at the same time. There were bikes with jump seats or sidecars for animals: dogs wearing goggles, a Vietnamese potbellied pig, a bobcat, and a rabbit with its own customized helmet. There were bikers wearing helmets adorned with antlers of various kinds, and bikes with every imaginable accessory. One bike had a sidecar shaped like a bathtub, complete with a real live bikini-clad woman taking a bubble bath.

After a couple of hours of wandering through the sea of bikes, I decided to check out rally headquarters, located above the police department in the Sturgis Community Center. There at the hospitality desk I met Joyce, a schoolteacher from nearby Rapid City. When I asked Joyce how she got involved in motorcycles, she explained that she was once married to a biker, and though they divorced, she "got hooked."

"I don't have a bike now. I'm a single mom, and I can't afford it on a teacher's salary. I hate to ask guys for a ride, because they always want something in return. They expect you to put out, or at least give them money. But all men are that way, not just bikers. They think with their dicks."

"I hate it when they do that," I agreed, feeling glad I hadn't accepted the offers I'd had to go for a ride.

"I still take rides," Joyce added, "but one day I'm going to ride into this town on my own Harley."

At the Oasis Lounge on a corner of Main Street, I met Doreen and Patty, who worked at a pizza parlor in a small town in Iowa. They had come to Sturgis on the backs of their boyfriends' Harleys.

"We have so many friends here," Doreen told me. "Every year we meet more people, and we plan to meet again the next year. We always stay in the same campground. Last year me and Tommy planned to get married here. But then we didn't. I don't know if we will now. I'd like to get married in the campground with all our friends around."

Later I met a couple from West Virginia. Mike, a fireman, had earned enough money to come to the rally by working sixteen-hour days battling a major fire in a steel mill. This was his second trip to Sturgis. Debbie, who had never been west before, was mightily impressed by the beauty of the mountains, canyons, and open range. You can see the country, she told me, so much better on a bike than in a car.

The two were curious about why I had come alone to Sturgis, and when I explained how I happened to be there, Debbie gave me their address and invited me to come see them so they could show me the wild places in West Virginia.

I strolled back along Main Street, weaving in and out of the bikes. Not quite believing that there are no two Harleys alike, I searched in vain for a pair of twins. No such luck. Each did seem to be unique. Then I came on a light-blue Harley with a Garfield figure for a logo. The owner, a clean-cut young man with sandy-colored short hair, saw me eyeing his bike. His name was Steve, and he was from nearby Rapid City.

"You're wondering about Garfield. That's for my boy. He died seven years ago of leukemia. He was three years old. Garfield made him laugh."

"We never get over those losses," I responded, not knowing what else to say.

"No, never. But riding my bike I feel alive. Most of all I love to feel the wind in my hair and smell the alfalfa during mowing time."

Everywhere there were provocative messages on T-shirts, ranging from the unspeakably obscene to the most predictable. The most common, however, was one I'd seen on bumper stickers as well. In white writing on a black background with the Harley logo was this message: "IF YOU HAVE TO ASK WHY, YOU WOULDN'T UNDERSTAND." I've often been tempted to give this response to people who ask why I want to go into wilderness areas. Why would I sit on the shore of a pristine lake deep in the Popo Agie Wilderness in the Wind River Range of Wyoming and watch the sun set and the stars come out? Why would I hike into the Mount Hood Wilderness and climb up to the base of that snow-covered volcano? Why follow the tracks of a moose in newly fallen snow in the Glacier Peak Wilderness in the Cascades? Why take off early in the morning on a buffalo trail in a virgin prairie in the Sage Creek Wilderness? Why would I want to see the mating rituals of alligators or hear a mountain lion cry out in the night?

I left Sturgis just about dark and drove back for one last night at Sheridan Lake. The next morning I moved my camp to the

Sylvan Lake campground in Custer State Park. That night I climbed a dark hillside and watched meteors rain from the sky. When I woke the next morning to a steady drizzle on the tent, I quickly dressed and drove up to the nearby lodge for breakfast. I found myself seated at a table next to a heavily tattooed lone biker. Seven o'clock in the morning in the dining room of a good resort surrounded by couples with children is as good a time as any for a woman alone to strike up a conversation with a man, so I took the plunge.

My opening gambit—"Going over to Sturgis today?"—was all that was needed to get Fred to talk about his bike, his job, his tattoos, and finally the dreaded "five percent." As it turned out, Fred was alone because his buddy had been in an accident and had flown back to Philadelphia to see an orthopedist. He seemed eager to talk, explaining that he worked in an oil refinery as a supervisor in charge of recovering sulfur dioxide before it enters the atmosphere and contributes to acid rain.

Fred told me about his tattoos, how long he'd had them, and what they cost. The most recent, only two days old and still painfully sensitive, had cost two hundred dollars. When I questioned him about the stigma that is still attached to people with tattoos, Fred shrugged. "They're like jewelry to me. I like them, and I don't want to take them off. But you're right. There is a stigma, so I wear long-sleeved shirts at work. And my mother hates them."

It was Fred who first mentioned motorcycle gangs. The Hell's Angels, he said, were here in force. I could recognize them by their tattoos—especially the skull with wings, and I learned this point of biker etiquette: "If a man who is not in the gang dares to wear such a tattoo, the Angels will tear him apart—usually break an arm and then rip it loose from the socket. It's just not done."

"A guy I met told me that about five percent of bikers are bad folks."

"Nah," Fred said. "Five percent is far too high. More like one percent." Then he explained that bikers know who the one percent are. They are members of one of several gangs—the Warlocks, the Banditos, the Outlaws, the Hell's Angels.

"One percent," Fred insisted. "Everyone knows it's not more than that. That guy who told you five percent was lying or crazy. But you really don't have to worry about the Angels or the other gangs here. Sturgis, you have to understand, is neutral ground. Violence is the gangs' work, but here they're on vacation like everybody else."

Fred and I exchanged addresses, talked a bit more about pollution control and acid rain, and planned to keep in touch. He left to begin a twenty-eight-hour straight pull for Philadelphia, and I went back to the campground.

I knew not to ask Fred "Why?" I suspect that his passion for biking, like that of tens of thousands of others here in these Black Hills, has something to do with being outside in breathtakingly beautiful places; with freedom, individuality, and "going wild." It may also be about friends, community, and belonging to something bigger than himself.

Black Elk

THE DAY AFTER the rally ended I woke early, determined to experience the Black Hills without crowds and noise. I
packed rain gear, breakfast, and a thermos of tea and headed up
the trail before any other campers were awake. I was the first on
the trail leading to Harney Peak in the Black Elk Wilderness, and
at last I enjoyed the solitude and quiet that designated wilderness
areas are intended to provide. I walked briskly, and in less than
two hours I was on the top, alone. But not for long. Soon there
were dozens of other hikers, laughing and talking.

One hiker—a slender, dark-haired boy—perched dangerously
close to a precipitous drop-off. Concerned, I carefully walked up
to him and asked if he was alone. "I ran all the way up. My mom
and dad are real slow. Besides, I wanted to be up here by myself."
I looked around at twenty-odd people and then back at the boy.
It was clear that from his point of view, he was alone. No parents
to bug him and tell him to come away from the edge of the cliff.
Yet he didn't seem to be a daredevil. For a few more minutes I
continued to stand protectively close by.

Harney Peak is at the center of the Black Hills, and it is the
highest point east of the Rockies. Black Elk, the Lakota medicine
man whose story is told in *Black Elk Speaks,* thought of this spot
as the center of the world. From where I stood with the boy, I
could turn around and see the whole sweep of the Black Hills.

"Indians used to come here," the boy said without taking his eyes off the landscape. "Lots of them. They hunted here. These were their hunting grounds."

After a few minutes of silence, he looked back at me and added, "I wish they were still here."

Before I went down the mountain, I convinced the boy to move back to a more secure spot, asked him how his parents were dressed, and told him I'd look for them and explain that he was safe and waiting for them on the summit. I'd been on the trail a good twenty minutes before I met people matching his description: a slender woman wearing a red tank top and a fat man in a plaid shirt. When I told them that I'd met Josh on top and he was fine, the boy's father growled, "I don't know what we're going to do with that boy. His coach tells us that he's Olympic material. He's only nine years old and he runs like the wind."

"You must have taught him a lot about Indians," I said.

"He's been talking to you about Indians?" his mother asked. "We don't know how he learned about them. Maybe from school. Joshua is adopted, and some of our friends think he might have Indian blood. We don't think so. His mother was blond and the social worker told us she didn't know who the father was. He wasn't from these parts. We're from over in Rapid City, but we don't know any Indians. They keep to themselves and hardly ever work. Just take government handouts and drink all the time."

This was not the first time since I'd been in South Dakota that I'd heard such derogatory comments about Indians, but I'd decided long ago not to argue with people who generalize about race. "I'm sorry to hear you say that" had become my standard reply. I thought of Joshua and was reminded of another child. Harney Peak is known as the site where the nine-year-old Black Elk had a powerful vision that directed him to lead the Lakotas, his people, back to the state of harmony, balance, and plenty they had once enjoyed there. I'd been reading *Black Elk Speaks,* and when I got back to camp, I turned to the part in which Black Elk tells of waking up after the vision to find his parents hovering over him: "I was sad because my mother and my father didn't seem to know I had been so far away."

The next morning I got up early again and took the Lost Cabin Trail into a different part of the wilderness. In less than a mile I came to a perfect spot for breakfast. I spread out my rain jacket, sat down, and took out an orange, a granola bar, and a thermos of tea. I peeled the orange slowly, eating it with deliberate enjoyment. I stored the peelings and paper in a plastic bag and returned them to my day pack. Then, sipping the tea, I looked around.

I was sitting on a large rock at the edge of the trail in a relatively narrow valley. On either side were hills. Except for the sounds of birds and the fussing of a little red squirrel, all was silent. There was no sound of Harleys, perhaps because the surrounding hills blocked any noise coming from nearby highways or maybe because the bikers were all on the way back to Houston, Cleveland, and Detroit. The valley floor was covered with foot-high grass, wildflowers, groves of aspen, and Ponderosa pines. Except for the trees and the scattered lupine and yarrow, I didn't know the names of any of the plants. There were so many, and most I didn't remember seeing before.

At that spot it was easy to imagine why many modern day Lakotas insist that the Black Hills are sacred and will settle for nothing less than the recovery of the lands ceded to them by the U.S. government in 1868. From the moment that miners accompanying Custer on a reconnaissance expedition into the hills discovered gold in 1874, the treaty became meaningless. Thousands of whites set out to find gold and the happiness they imagined it would bring.

The lengthy chain of events that followed Custer's illegal entry into Lakota lands eventually included a court decision in 1979 granting over a hundred million dollars in compensation for illegal seizure of the hills. Some Lakotas argued that they should take the money and be done with it. Others, who viewed the land as a mother, believed it should not be sold.

The struggle continues. The Black Elk Wilderness is contested land. To most Lakota Indians, I and all other white people who venture into these hills are trespassing, defiling the sacred lands that were once a source of food and fuel. In my travels I've often wondered about the experiences people call "spiritual" and the places they call "sacred." Both terms seem too ambiguous and imprecise to be of much use. What other than deeply felt responses to the beauty of a place could motivate those who claim such special qualities for one place rather than another?

Yet I could recall a few places on earth where I'd had experiences I would call spiritual if not mystical: the slopes of Kilauea Volcano in Hawaii, where I watched the sun set and a full moon rise at the same time; a cypress swamp in Florida; a grove of ancient firs in northern Norway; and the cotton fields and forests at the edge of my childhood home, where I went at the end of the day to watch the sun go down. Other people have surely felt that the slopes of the world's most active volcano and the space defined by an old-growth forest are charged with mystery, but few are likely to seek spiritual nourishment standing by a garbage can at the side of a dirt road at the edge of a small town in Georgia.

Yet if I could re-create one of those experiences, I would choose to be a five-year-old child again, taking from my mother's hands a sack of trash that I would carry out to the edge of the yard and deposit in the garbage can. Having performed this chore, I'd linger to watch the setting sun redden the cotton fields and the wild places beyond. Then I would rush back to my mother for approval. I suspect that the Lakotas' longing to once again "own" the Black Hills is not unlike my desire to recapture that world as it seemed my innocent eyes. Of course I can never go back to that time, never again know that pristine place I created in the light of the setting sun. Likewise the Lakotas can never go back to a time when bison, wolves, and grizzly bears competed for food with elk, coyotes, and beavers. But perhaps a part of these hills could be set aside for them to recover feelings of reverence and connectedness to the land. There is not and never will be enough wildlife in these hills to feed large numbers of people, but there is enough beauty and mystery and unpredictability to feed the soul. I wandered for some time down Lost Creek Trail, until I heard thunder in the distance and saw clouds gathering above. Only then did I turn back.

The turbocharged, raucous Sturgis folks were the polar opposite of the quiet campers and hikers in the Black Hills, but I suspected the two groups were driven by similar impulses. Maybe to break out of routines, lift languishing spirits, merge with something bigger than themselves—the wind, a thunderstorm, a forest, a meteor shower, the Black Hills themselves. I recognized the similarities to my own quest: by leaving my own community and spending day after day outdoors, I'd begun the process of sorting out, eliminating, simplifying, and choosing what seemed most important. It was in the Black Hills that I first recognized I was not so much abandoning community and society as I was clearing the mental space for what would come next in my life. While I had no intention of ever mounting a motorcycle and striking out across the country, I did long to join others with something like the energy and enthusiasm that the bikers brought to Sturgis.

I came down from Custer State Park on Sunday morning, August 14. A sign reading ORIANA'S BOOK CAFÉ flashed by my eyes as I headed north and west out of the Black Hills. The promise of those words didn't register at first; then, about two miles north of Hill City, I turned around. Book cafés have good coffee. Surely not in small towns in South Dakota, I thought. It didn't seem very likely. A few minutes later, as I peeked in the door of Oriana's, the smell of brewing espresso and baking bread pulled me in. Even John Muir would have abandoned asceticism if he had stumbled out of the wilderness into this place.

"A double skinny latte," I declared, expecting the young man behind the counter to tell me I was dreaming.

"Tall or grande?" he asked without looking up.

"Make it a grande, and I'll have one—no, make it two—of those honey-nut muffins."

On a table for all to peruse was a pile of magazines and newspapers with the all-too-common headlines: Health Care Plan Moribund, Whitewater Scandal, Devastation in Rwanda, Ethnic Cleansing and Genocide in Bosnia, Anti-Abortion Extremists, The West in Flames, HIV-Contaminated Blood. So much for *Time* magazine, I thought, as I reached for a tattered copy of the Sunday *New York Times*. Reading the editorials, I had a feeling of déjà vu. It was not until I turned to the front page that I realized I really had read the exact words before. The paper was four weeks old.

The patrons of Oriana's Book Café were gathered at crowded tables in small groups. I listened to them talk—about doings in the outside world, their children, books, a fund-raiser for the local school, upcoming elections, a funeral that afternoon. I had no way of knowing, but they seemed to like each other and to be concerned about the same things. They were part of a place and tied to each other by shared concerns. Creating community in a city seemed more difficult than in a small town like Hill City, South Dakota, or Dublin, Georgia, where I grew up. Many people I know in Atlanta don't even know each other. I felt a twinge of envy as I eavesdropped on the leisurely way these folks related to each other as if they were part of a loving family.

Before leaving Oriana's, I got out the atlas to study the map of Wyoming and consider my next step. A man at the adjoining table asked if I needed directions, and I explained that I was in search of a large wilderness area where there weren't many people. He was sympathetic.

"Be fewer people here in another week, once all the bikers are gone, but we still have the crowds that wander over from Mount Rushmore to climb Harney Peak. You may want to try the Bighorns." He pointed west and north of Buffalo, Wyoming, to a large green area extending all the way to the Montana border—the Bighorn National Forest, with more than a million acres and, inside that, the almost two-hundred-thousand-acre Cloud Peak Wilderness.

"Big mountains over there, some more than thirteen thousand feet high. That's rugged country. You can get away from people if you go in far enough."

I left the café focused on my intent to go to the Bighorns. It was past noon when I consulted the map and headed north on Highway 385 to Deadwood, an old mining town that had only recently closed its brothels, and to Spearfish, where I took Interstate 90 into Wyoming, driving straight into the afternoon sun. For the first few miles the signs indicating nearby communities were benign enough—Beulah, Aladdin, Sundance. After Gillette, a mining town, a sign announced that there would be no gas for the next sixty-eight miles. It failed to add that there were also no people on that desolate stretch. I saw only three more signs—"Dead Horse Road," "Dead Horse Creek," and "Crazy Woman Creek Road"—before coming to Buffalo, Wyoming, population 3,300, elevation 4,635.

The fourteen-dollar camping fee at Deer Park Campground outside Buffalo bought me the closest thing to luxury I'd experienced since crossing the Mississippi. As I turned into the long drive, I startled a doe with two fawns, and a hundred yards further, a family of wild turkeys. An hour after arriving, I was sitting in front of my tent in a deserted part of the campground at the edge of vast grasslands that stretched all the way to the Bighorns. As I gazed through the glow of the late afternoon sun at the scene in front of me, the golden light seemed to enter my body and warm my spirit even as the temperature was dropping with the sun. When darkness finally prevailed over the warmth of twilight, I washed clothes, showered, swam several laps in the campground pool, then soaked in the hot tub and watched the stars come out —first the evening star, then a scattering of others. By the time I crawled limp and sleepy from the hotter-than-hot water, the sky was glittering with stars.

Donna

〰〰〰 THE NEXT MORNING I woke to magic light, golden and rosy, and to seemingly clean air, though I could detect signs of smoke drifting eastward from the fires that were burning large parts of Montana, Idaho, Oregon, and Washington. After breakfast I broke camp and went to the Forest Service office in nearby Buffalo, Wyoming. I bought a topo map of the area and explained to the receptionist that I wanted to see the Cloud Peak Wilderness, the wildest part of the Bighorns. "You need to talk with Craig Cope," she said. "He's the wilderness coordinator for the Bighorns."

Craig and I talked in his office for an hour or so. "The hardest thing about this job," he told me, "is that I spend most of my life in this office. I hardly ever get out there. We only have five wilderness rangers, and they spend the warm weather months repairing trails, checking on backpackers, and cleaning up the litter people leave behind. They do a good job, but there's no way they can do it all."

When I asked what I would find in the interior, he pointed to the large map on the wall. "We've got 190,000 acres of wilderness with all kinds of terrain—large wooded areas, alpine meadows covered with grasses and flowers, streams lined with willows that moose eat, glacial moraines, and lakes. There are many acres of old burns with thousands of dead trees, some standing waiting to fall and even more lying on the ground, sometimes in tangled piles. Then above the timberline are the high peaks. Cloud Peak is the highest at 13,175 feet."

"Are there bears in there?"

"Very few, mostly been killed off. I've never seen one. We've got deer, elk, moose, bighorn sheep. Ranchers with permits graze stock there—cows and sheep. There are some parts of the wilderness that none of us working for the Forest Service has ever seen. Donna Wilson, one of our wilderness rangers, is going into one of them on her next tour."

Suddenly I saw my way into this wilderness, and before I could think about it, I asked Craig if I could go along as a volunteer.

He seemed dubious. "We're talking hiking all day in rugged terrain, digging drainage ditches, dismantling fire rings, repairing trails. Going up to 10,000 feet, maybe more. You up to that?"

"I can handle it," I said, implying that I'd spent all my weekends digging ditches, which of course I hadn't.

"Well, come back around noon to meet Donna, then. I bet she'll take you out."

Two hours later, Donna was waiting for me. Blond and tall, she was glowing with health and vitality. I learned that Donna has been married for twenty-six years to the same man, has two adult daughters and two grandchildren, and for many years had run a successful sporting-goods store that she sold in order to become a wilderness ranger. And she had done all this in only forty-three years. We liked each other instantly, and in a matter of minutes we had agreed to meet at the trailhead the next morning.

That afternoon I drove west on Highway 16 and from there turned north on a series of dirt roads, following signs to a primitive campground on the edge of the Cloud Peak Wilderness. Two campsites seemed to be occupied, but there was no sign of people. I chose a private site in an aspen grove and settled down to enjoy the rest of the day. I filled my solar shower bag with water and set it in the sun, then went off to hike for a few hours. As I was crossing a daisy-strewn meadow, the sky was mostly blue, but I noticed heavy clouds to the north. Then a bolt of lightning on the horizon was followed immediately by thunder. I picked up my pace and headed out. After weathering three violent thunderstorms in as many months, I had become skittish when I heard that all-too-familiar rumble.

When I returned to my campsite in the late afternoon, the water in the solar shower was hot and the clouds had blown over. I wasn't going to waste that water. Through trial and error, I'd developed a system for showering in the outdoors in relative safety: check the weather; collect soap, towel, and clean clothes; find a secluded spot; hang the shower bag; remove clothes; and soap, rinse, dry, and dress as quickly as possible. The air temperature was ideal, and for once I prolonged the shower until every drop of water was gone. It might be a week before I'd shower again. There's always the risk that someone will intrude on my shower, but so far that hasn't happened, and I've learned to love the feeling of having nothing but air between my body and the sky.

The next morning I broke camp and loaded my pack—tent, Thermarest pad, sleeping bag, a clean shirt, a Polartec jacket, thermal underwear, socks, rain gear, river sandals, a water bottle, a first-aid kit that I thought included iodine to purify water, and enough food for five days—instant oatmeal, minute rice, instant bean soups, protein powder, dried fruits, and energy bars. On the very top went a plastic bag with toothbrush and emergency medicines. In the pockets of my vest I carried a small notebook, a pen, a comb, lip gloss, and sunscreen. In one shirt pocket I carried toilet paper, in the other, a Ziploc bag to pack it out. There was no room for frills—no book, no camera, no bottle of wine.

When I met Donna at the trailhead, I was out of breath and rattled. When I apologized for being late, Donna smiled. "You're not late. For the next five days we're going on wilderness time. We'll hike to a Forest Service base camp on a ridge in part of the forest that burned in 1988. Our work in there will take as long as it takes."

Donna and I had been hiking for a couple of hours when we came to what at first seemed to me an insurmountable obstacle. Carrying a heavy pack, I felt unsteady enough as it was, and now I had to get across rushing water by clambering across on a wobbly log. Barely changing her pace, Donna quickly crossed to the other side. Ashamed to let Donna know how Oliver Creek had been transformed in my mind into the Colorado River, I stalled, looked down at the three feet between the log and the water, and almost panicked.

"Donna," I shouted. "I've got a problem. I can't make myself do this."

"That's not a problem. You're just afraid. Fear is normal out here. Here, let me help."

Donna took off her own pack and crossed back over to get mine. Once again on the other side, she looked back, expecting me to follow now that I'd shed the pack. Standing at the water's edge, I looked down. The distance between log and water had expanded, the water had become colder and deeper, the diameter of the log had shrunk, and the risk of falling seemed greater than ever.

Donna looked at me and smiled and suddenly I relaxed. Maybe, I thought, I could go across on my backside. Sitting on the log, I inched slowly across. Once on the other side, I remembered an experience I'd had in the Wind River Range with Ken Clanton the year before. I was not so strong then, my pack was much more unwieldy, and the rushing water we had to cross was deeper, faster, and colder. Ken managed to talk me across a series of log bridges, and once he took my pack. But I knew that in his mind my fear was a character flaw at least as serious as kleptomania or compulsive lying. Ken gave me advice about how to overcome my fear so that I too could bound across logs tossed by hunters or forest rangers across rushing rivers. Donna, on the other hand, encouraged me simply to acknowledge what I was actually feeling.

I confessed that confronting fear was a big part of what I was up to. Again and again I had found myself in situations that stimulated a rush of adrenalin, a pounding heart, or some other involuntary sensation. I didn't expect this to change.

"I think it's only men who think fear is something to be ashamed of," Donna offered. "Fear is nature's way of telling us to be careful, to look out, and to adjust our actions to a threat. If you'd tried to bound across that log, you might well have fallen, and you could have hurt yourself bad."

The rest of the hike was uneventful—no water to cross, no animals to avoid. Base camp consisted of an open, floorless and windowless canvas tent, probably World War II vintage. Inside the tent were two cots, useful for getting gear out of the dirt and away from critters but far too wobbly and mildewed for sleeping. The Wilderness Act prohibits permanent installations in designated wilderness, and this camp was clearly temporary. There was a Coleman stove, fuel, a shovel, and emergency food and medicines. Donna's own personal cache included a large sack of peanut M&Ms and a package of fat-free Fig Newtons. The whole camp would be removed at the end of the season. Downhill and only a few hundred yards away was Oliver Creek, where we would make frequent trips for water.

Nearby, between the many fallen trees and the still-standing, long-dead snags, we set up our tents. It was hard enough to find a level place with no large rocks but impossible to find one that was free from the risk of falling snags. Most had been dead so long they had no bark and no limbs left. Looming above my little tent, however, was a large tree, and in the crotch of its only remaining limb a fallen tree rested precariously. Donna tested it and concluded it was not likely to fall in the next few days.

Going into the wilderness always involves taking risks. Here on this ridge, the obvious risks were falling snags and lightning. The only animal that was likely to give us trouble was a female moose with a calf, and for that to happen, we'd have to get in her way. A female moose protecting her calf will charge her victims, knock them down, and then proceed to stomp them to death. Donna told me she'd been charged several times by a mother moose hell-bent on killing her.

"If a moose comes after us, run as fast as you can into a thicket of trees. Then get behind the biggest tree you can find so she can't get to you," she advised me.

I looked around a little nervously. "There are no thickets," I objected.

"Well, the moose are probably down below where the trees are alive and close together," Donna said, smiling to reassure me.

Moose, she said, mainly eat the willows down by Oliver Creek, and it was there that we later found the irrefutable evidence of their presence—fresh moose scat. In fact there was lots of scat—elk, deer, and moose. But there was no way to tell whether the moose scat was from a male or female. I preferred to think it was a bull.

With Donna I learned to observe and manage the various feelings called *fear.* I found that I could accept some risks with something like serenity while freezing with terror at others. I learned to tolerate moose as near-neighbors, even though I knew that many more people are hurt or killed by these large animals than by grizzly bears.

I had camped in moose and black-bear country, and I'd had both animals outside my tent in the night. I'd run into a big bull moose at fairly close range in Wyoming, and I'd watched a foraging grizzly at a safe distance. But it was grizzlies I feared. The summer before I'd taken day hikes in the backcountry of Yellowstone and once in Glacier, but I had no intention of camping overnight in the few remaining places where numerous grizzlies roam free. Humans, I rationalized, occupy most of the planet. I handled my fear of grizzlies with a determination to let them have their habitat, and I found comfort in the knowledge that a moose would never consider eating me for dinner, and unless I went snooping around in the willows where they often fed, I was not likely to have a problem.

Just after dark Donna and I settled into our tents. Our plan was to go directly to sleep and wake at dawn in order to have a full day to hike the trails and do what needed to be done. Although our tents were pitched more than fifteen feet apart, we somehow managed to talk well into the night, like teenage girls at a slumber party. We must have mentioned our husbands, children, and parents, but most of our talk was about wilderness. She told me about her adventures as the only woman wilderness ranger in this part of Wyoming—about being threatened by a man with an automatic weapon when she asked him to put his dog on a leash, about weathering violent thunderstorms high on a ridge while retrieving gear left there by a man who had tried and failed to kill himself, about saving an injured llama she sometimes uses as a pack animal by wrapping him in her sleeping bag while she endured a cold night with no cover. I told her about my terror just a month before in a thunderstorm in the Ellicott Rock Wilderness in North Carolina, about slogging up a trail alone in a Costa Rican rain forest, about watching the white ibis come in to roost on an island in the Everglades.

Before we finally fell asleep around midnight, Donna spoke lovingly of the quiet and solitude of the Cloud Peak Wilderness. Although we would be in the wilderness for five days, she told me she much preferred a ten-day tour. Only after about the third day does she begin to feel the rhythm of the wild.

"In the morning," Donna reminded me, "we'll wake up on wilderness time. There's no way to hurry or stay on a schedule out here. We'll do what we have to do, and it'll take the time it takes. We don't even know what we'll find tomorrow, let alone how much time we'll need to handle it."

That first night I slept so soundly that I was aware of nothing until I heard Donna unzip her tent and stumble off into the brush. She was amazed that I'd missed the night sounds: the alarm calls of a nearby moose, apparently disturbed when Donna turned over in her sleeping bag, and the high-pitched sounds that the female elks and their calves use as they call to each other in the night.

Whatever fear Donna had of being charged by a moose didn't restrict her efforts to see them. Early in the morning of our second day, she went down toward the stream where they feed on the willows. Moose are solitary creatures but will often respond to an elk's call. Using an elk caller, she tried to attract either of the large animals we knew were nearby, but we only succeeded in seeing deer and small mammals. I suspect the problem was our continual talk, which must have alerted moose and elks to move away from the trail.

Before we made breakfast, Donna taught me a new wilderness skill. I knew how to dig a six-inch privy hole and cover it without a trace. However, I hadn't imagined that there was a right way to urinate in the woods. If people relieve themselves on vegetation or in loose soil, there's a good chance that an animal will come by and feel compelled to take some action too. It might paw at the ground, dig up vegetation, and in the end leave its own mark. Deer will also eat plants for the salt in the urine. Urinating on the ground is a good way to start a process of degrading one part of the wilderness.

"So what should I do?" I asked.

"Easy. Piss on a rock," Donna said smiling. "If you do it right, there's no splattering, and you'll hardly leave a trace. No moose is going to come pawing at the rock. If a male coyote comes by, he'll put his mark even higher than yours. But no harm's done when a deer licks a rock." Then she showed me how to choose a large, comfortable rock with a gradual slope.

"The idea is to leave most of the piss on the rock and as little as possible on the ground."

After a breakfast of oatmeal mixed with protein powder, we hiked to the alpine lakes of Long and Ringbone and eventually worked our way back down to Sherd Lake. Donna carried a shovel and garbage bag; I carried lunch and emergency supplies in my pack. Working as we went, we dug small trenches, known as water bars, to prevent erosion on the trail; we piled rotting logs and tree parts onto areas that hikers were using to shortcut the trails; and we broke up innumerable fire rings and began the process that may someday lead to restored vegetation. Donna explained to me that a campfire that lasts only an hour sterilizes the ground for years. To hasten the process of restoration, rangers are continually breaking up the rings, scattering the ashes and other remains of the fire, and shoveling on leaves, duff, twigs, and other organic material.

"It could be ten years, or if others persist in building a fire here, it could be a century before this spot of the earth is restored to what it was before a campfire was first built here," Donna said sadly. "Yet, except in years of extreme fire danger like this one, the Forest Service continues to allow fires because of some silly idea that the public wants them."

"What do you say when someone tells you that they don't enjoy camping without a fire?" I asked.

"I tell them that a fire actually closes out the wilderness, that the light blinds them to the landscape around them and to the stars above. I tell them that fires should be reserved for emergencies, for the time when a person is wet and threatened with hypothermia. Everybody who goes into the wilderness should know how to build a fire, just as they should know how to do CPR. Both skills can save lives. People who use the woods need to change their attitudes about campfires. Sometimes they start forest fires, and they always sterilize the earth."

I rarely took the trouble to build a fire when I was camping alone, and after assisting in breaking up more than twenty fire rings, I promised Donna that except in an emergency, I would never build a fire again. The first time I'd heard that campfires are not a good idea was at the wilderness conference at Holden, but before that I didn't even think twice when I built fires with Ken Clanton in the Popo Agie Wilderness and with Jerome on the Olympic Peninsula. Although the Wilderness Act of 1964 was passed to keep some places "forever wild," I had helped to render small portions of these places "forever sterile." And I was only one of many thousands of people who camp in designated wilderness areas every year.

Whenever we encountered day hikers or backpackers, Donna stopped what she was doing to talk with them—to make sure they had registered when they entered the wilderness, to register on the spot those who had not, to remind them to respect the fire ban, to check for fishing licenses, and to make sure they understood to pack out everything they brought in, leaving no trace of their presence. We met one family with two children, probably five and seven. I noticed that the boy was carrying a juice can and asked if he would like me to take it out. Before handing me the can, he carefully placed it on the ground and flattened it. Donna was about to explain the seven "Leave No Trace" principles when his sister opened her tiny fanny pack and handed me an already crushed can that she was packing out.

Late that afternoon we were still picking up debris around

Sherd Lake. There were the usual beer cans, pieces of plastic, and scraps of aluminum foil. But one item we saw from a distance — something blue and bright lying at the edge of the water that turned out to be a pair of soiled bikini panties.

Donna shook her head, distressed that she finds such things all the time. On the other side of the lake, she showed me the scene of the most disturbing experience she had ever had in the wilderness. There near the shore was a flat area that had been degraded by campers. The Forest Service had roped it off, posted a sign prohibiting further camping in the site, and begun a revegetation project that would take several years to complete. One day when she was making her rounds in this area, Donna approached the spot and was horrified to find the ground strewn with empty liquor bottles and garbage. There were also several piles of putrid vomit. She counted more than a hundred spent cartridges that had been fired from a .357 magnum. The "No Camping" sign had been torn down and thrown in the middle of the mess. Lying on the sign was a dead gray jay, shot in the head.

Back at the base camp, Donna taught me how to take a one-cup shower. First, warm about a cup of water on the backpacking stove and put it in a small plastic squirt bottle. Then quickly strip off everything but river sandals, soap down with biodegradable soap, and "shower" with the remaining water, making sure to have enough for underarms and other relevant parts. Then quickly dry with a clean towel and pull on long thermal underwear. We took turns executing this procedure, and in less than five minutes we felt clean and warm in the Polartec jackets we'd pulled on over our underwear.

After a dinner of instant bean soup with added minute rice capped off by hot chocolate, Donna again heated water, this time to fill the water bottles, which we immediately carried to our tents and stuffed in our sleeping bags for insulation. We had both been too cool the night before, but the water bottles kept us warm all night. I didn't sleep as soundly as I had the night before, and several times I heard what sounded like large animals stumbling

BACK TO THE WILD

around in the dark as well as the high-pitched cow/calf talk of elk that seemed very near.

The next day we hiked out of the wilderness and caught a ride to a trailhead leading into a more remote part of the wilderness. Except for the first hundred yards or so there were no trails, no cairns, nothing to facilitate our progress. For three days we bushwhacked and boulder hopped through extremely rough terrain. Donna's job was to look for and, when possible, remove signs of illegal use of the wilderness—to locate any camps established by hunters or markers to direct them through this harsh landscape. While people with permits and licenses are allowed to hunt in this and many other national-forest wildernesses, they are not allowed to set up permanent camps or to mar the landscape with markers of any kind. We climbed continually, and from time to time we found cairns that had been carefully constructed to mark the way through to the meadows and high alpine lakes above. Donna thought that commercial outfitters, operating without permits and intending to bring elk hunters in for the fall hunt, had left these markers to indicate the way to some kind of camp. At first I worried that the people who had so carefully constructed the markers would get lost and perhaps die up there, and I resisted destroying the carefully piled stacks of rocks. But after a half mile or so, I was knocking down cairns with the pleasure I'd felt as a child knocking down a tower of blocks. So much for those guys.

The next violation of the Wilderness Act was a trail marked by bright orange tape tied around the trunks of snags so high up that we could barely reach them. Donna told me they had to have been placed there by people on horseback; again, probably outfitters without permits who would bring hunters in for the elk. We made a game out of spotting markers and scrambling up boulders to cut them loose.

It was late afternoon before we made it up to the ridge overlooking Magdalene Lake, where we set up camp. The lake was set in a glacial cirque some thousand feet below. The cirque's sides were strewn with large boulders, some as big as a small car. Among the boulders were fallen trees and a few standing snags left from a large fire years before. On the flat ridges at the top of the cirque were young ponderosa pines and other conifers struggling to take hold. Above were the rugged, jagged faces of the high peaks. On the ground a variety of small vegetation included bushes of plump, ripe raspberries and wild strawberries sweeter than I thought it was possible for berries to be.

There were very few places flat enough to pitch a tent, and I had difficulty choosing a site. Finally I found a spot of compressed grass that had been the bed of large animals a night or so before, and I enjoyed the idea of sleeping where elk and calves had so recently rested.

The altitude was ten thousand feet, considerably higher than our last base camp. A few feet down from the ridge was Duck Creek, our only source of water. The next day we would boulder hop and bushwhack up another two thousand feet to Paradise Lake. No one currently working for the Forest Service in the area had ever been there, and Donna, who had been a wilderness ranger for four years, was very curious about what we might find. By the time we chose a campsite, the temperature was dropping fast. We decided to forego the one-cup shower and eat before we became chilled. After yet another meal of instant bean soup, rice, and hot chocolate, we dressed in all our warm clothes, put hot-water bottles in our sleeping bags, and perched up on a large flat rock to watch the sunset and the nearly full moon rise over the mountains.

That night we talked about what our lives had been like when we were children. Donna told me that she was one-quarter American Indian. She didn't say Native American. Her father was born in Oklahoma, and her grandfather had been a full-blooded Cherokee. I told Donna about roaming the woods and swamps of rural south Georgia while pretending to be an Indian girl and about finding real arrowheads left there by the Creek Indians. She told me about growing up on a ranch in South Dakota and how she begged her father to let her ride out with him when he drove the cattle to market. When she was five years old, he agreed to let her come along, though at the state line—just before he entered

Wyoming—he insisted that she turn back. He knew that the horse she was riding would take her back to the ranch. Donna never had the slightest qualms about being alone for two or three hours on the open range, and she always returned home safely.

"My grandmother would have loved this place," I said. "Especially Lake Magdalene down below." I told Donna about her fishing expeditions, her love of swamps and other wild places.

"Maybe you learned to love the outdoors from her. I know I'm here in part because of my father's love of the land."

I looked at Donna's blond hair and Nordic features and saw no sign of her Native American heritage. But I watched her operate, and I knew she had something in her blood that I lacked. I saw her leap over creeks, climb steadily up boulder fields, and choose a direction without the help of map or compass. I felt her spirit respond to the landscape, and I noticed that every morning she gave thanks for the good fortune that allows her to roam the Cloud Peak Wilderness.

The next day we headed for Paradise Lake. After climbing some two thousand feet for more than five hours, mainly up boulders and over fallen snags, we still had not reached our destination. We stopped for lunch in a large meadow that Donna was sure was just short of the lake. It was already afternoon. Donna knew how much I wanted to go to Paradise Lake, but she easily convinced me that we should not try. It might take even longer to get down and then back up to the ridge where our tents were. She didn't want to take the chance of getting caught up here at twelve thousand feet as dark was coming on.

As we munched energy bars chased with water from Duck Creek, I mentioned that it was pretty unusual for two women to spend this much time together without ever talking about the men in their lives. Donna laughed and agreed, and then our talk turned to more personal matters. I told her that I loved my husband and that I wanted to stay married to him, but that I no longer intended to structure my days around the life he'd chosen to lead. Donna talked about her marriage, telling me that she felt lucky her husband had supported her decision to become a wilderness ranger, though it had meant selling her business. We agreed that for marriage to be successful for us, we had to be free to follow our passion.

Then we talked about the man-woman thing and discussed what we do when men hit on us. She said she thought a come-on could spoil a good friendship; I told her I hadn't figured that one out yet. We must have sat there for an hour or more, because when we looked up the light was softer and the golden meadow where we sat had begun to glow.

"Look around," Donna said quietly. "If this isn't paradise, I don't know what is." We came down the opposite side of the valley from the one we had come up, surprising ourselves by making it back to camp in less than three hours. We quickly warmed water for a shower and, stripping our clothes off in the last of the sunlight, soaped ourselves with Dr. Bronner's and cleaned up. Then Donna pointed down to Duck Creek below. In a matter of seconds we were scrambling down to the meadow, where we jumped into Duck Creek for a real dip. I'll never forget the joyful whoop Donna made as she rose from that icy water and ran up the bank toward her towel and clothes.

After our last dinner of instant beans and minute rice, Donna and I again sat on what we called Contemplation Rock. Donna talked about living lightly on the planet—of not taking more than our share of the earth's resources, of eating mainly a vegetarian diet. As the full moon rose over the large peak in the east, we could hear coyotes yelping and howling in preparation for the night's hunt.

The song of the coyotes put a cap on the day. Their work was beginning as ours was ending. Donna reached for the radio to call another ranger to meet us at the trailhead the next day at noon.

"Every time I really need this thing, the battery dies or I can't get a signal." And sure enough, the radio was dead. That meant we couldn't arrange a pickup or go out the way we'd come. Somehow, we'd have to find our way to a trail leading to the place where we'd left our vehicles.

"We have to go that way?" I asked, pointing to the north.

"I'm afraid so," Donna said.

My heart sank as I looked a thousand feet or so below at the lake, then at the boulder-strewn ridges beyond that. Donna pulled out a topo map and showed me where she thought we were. We would have a lot of up and down over boulders and fallen trees. Some of the ridges were quite steep. In the valleys and down by the lakes, we would have to cross wet, marshy areas with tall grass and intermittent streams. Neither of us had brought a compass.

We used the last of our fuel to heat water for our Nalgene bottles to warm our sleeping bags. Donna's water filter wasn't working very well, and it took twenty minutes to pump less than a quart. I'd also left mine in the van, and neither of us had brought iodine tablets. We would need to ration water, so we added tea bags to the hot-water bottles. In the morning the caffeine would help us get going.

When I settled into my tent and closed my eyes, I could still see the strangely illuminated landscape—the jagged peaks above, the moonlit lake below, and the pathless wilderness all around. Before I fell asleep, I took a hard look at my feelings—apprehension, anticipation, trepidation, and wonder about what would happen the next day. I couldn't afford to succumb to fear, but I was intensely aware that we had a challenging day ahead.

Donna and I woke with the sun, and in a matter of an hour we had broken camp and loaded our packs. The trek out of the wilderness was tough. For the first few miles, there was nothing even vaguely resembling a trail. Though Donna had never been in this part of the wilderness before, she knew the general direction and thought she knew the way to the nearest trail. She was more comfortable on the high boulder fields than down in the low places, where it was easy to step into deep holes. From time to time we would stop and negotiate, and when I had a choice I would slog through the mud, sinking sometimes to my knees, while Donna jumped from boulder to boulder, some of them six feet above the boggy ground.

Our rations were down to two energy bars and a small bag of dried fruit—not much to fuel such a strenuous trip. Step by step we made our way up and down the ridges, over the boulders, through the marshes, and across rushing streams. By noon the food was gone and water hard to come by. We still had miles to go. There were times when I literally crawled from one boulder to the next, using both hands and feet for balance.

It was early afternoon when we finally connected with the trail, and for a while we could walk at a normal pace. The last obstacle was a rushing creek about twenty feet across. I stopped at the edge and my heart sank. Donna reassured me. "The water is less than two feet deep. I don't think we'll fall, but if we do, we can get out before we get too cold. After that, we've only got a mile to go."

We stopped to take off our boots, put on river sandals, and roll our pants up to our knees. Then we waded out onto the slippery rocks. Donna crossed without incident, and I slipped and slid but somehow managed to remain upright. Once over on the other side, I looked down at what appeared to be clean, clear water. I was so thirsty that I almost gave in and drank, but I remembered Donna's warnings about *Giardia*—a tiny organism that contaminates much of the surface water even in remote and seemingly pristine backcountry and causes a severe form of dysentery.

When we finally reached the trailhead about half past four in the afternoon, Donna looked up at the clear sky and then back into the wilderness. "I'm so lucky," she said. Then she unbuckled her heavy pack and heaved it into the back of her truck. Clapping her hands together, she looked at me, smiled, and exclaimed, "I love my work!"

That night Donna and I met for dinner at the nearby Pine Lodge. Before we even looked at the menu, we ordered a couple of amber ales from a huge selection of microbrewery beers. As in most restaurants in Wyoming and Montana, the walls were decorated with the heads and skins of various wild animals, and the menu consisted of dishes from various parts of the cow. There were barbecued ribs, grilled liver with onions, hamburgers, various steaks, and of course prime rib. The only other item on the menu was a broiled trout. The waitress visibly winced when I explained that I wanted something low fat and ordered the fish. Then she leaned over and whispered in my ear, "I have to tell you that fish has been in the freezer as long as I've worked here. If you want something low fat, I suggest you take the prime rib. We don't put anything on it, and it's really good."

A few minutes later the food arrived—a huge slab of medium-rare beef and a large baked potato covered with sour cream. Donna raised her glass for a toast.

"It doesn't get any better than this," she said with a twinkle in her eye.

Paradise

〜〜〜〜 "FIRST FROST," I heard people say to each other when I stopped for breakfast at a local diner in Butte, Montana. It was August 23, 1994. The day before, I'd driven across Wyoming and most of Montana before stopping after dark in a campground on the edge of a horse pasture just outside Butte. I'd have many a frosty morning in the weeks to come.

That morning, I left the freeway at the Ninemile Road exit and from there drove a mile and a half to drop in on the National Wilderness Training Center, the only place in the country that teaches Forest and Park Service rangers to manage designated wilderness areas. At the nearby visitor's center I bought Rick Bass's *Ninemile Wolves* and went to the only restaurant/bar in the area, a large room predictably decorated with animal heads, antlers, and skins. I took a table under a large bearskin and next to a rabbit head with antelope antlers attached. I ordered a hamburger from the usual all-beef menu and settled down with my new book to discover that I had stumbled accidentally into the very valley where a pack of gray wolves roams. The Ninemile wolves, named for the Ninemile Valley just outside where I sat, may have been the only stable pack in the Lower 48 states except for those in Glacier National Park, Minnesota, and the Upper Peninsula of Michigan. Wolves would not be introduced to Yellowstone for another year, and no one was sure whether the effort to reintroduce red wolves in the Great Smoky Mountains would succeed.

Later that afternoon I drove up the valley, hoping to see these rare creatures but knowing that to be unlikely, as they were probably resting up for the evening hunt. Some eighteen months later I would see my first wolf in the wild, boldly hunting in an open snowfield in nearby Yellowstone, but that day, as I left the Nine-mile Valley, I was satisfied just to know the animals were nearby.

It was getting late when I realized that I had better find a place to camp before dark. I checked the Montana map and located Paradise, a town I'd wanted to visit when I passed that way a year before. There wasn't a soul on the street in Paradise, and most of the few storefronts had "Closed" signs hanging in a window. The only open establishment was the American Legion Bar. It was 5:30 P.M., and I realized that I was about to break at least one of the rules I'd set up to keep out of trouble:

1. Never go alone to a bar in the evening except in a hotel where you're staying.
2. Never smile at or exhibit any friendly signs to men after 5:00 P.M.
3. Never have a drink with strangers.
4. Be safely settled in a campsite before dark.
5. To find out what people really think, keep quiet about what you think.
6. Never accept invitations to go home with people you don't know.

That night in Paradise I broke all the rules, and never once did I feel I had taken a foolish risk. Paradise is not like any other place I've ever been.

A sign in the window of the American Legion Bar read "Thank You Firefighters." I thought this would be my excuse for breaking rule number one. After all, I wanted to learn more about the fires that were destroying large parts of the state's national forests and wilderness areas. I was dressed as usual in khaki slacks and a photographer's vest. I went back to the van, threw a camera over my shoulder, and grabbed a notebook. Thus armed, I opened the door of the bar and peered inside.

"Well, look-a-here. You just come and sit right by me, honey," a man's voice said. It took me a minute to adapt to the dim light. There must have been a dozen people in the small room. The man talking to me was at least seventy years old, and there were two seats between him and a middle-aged woman sitting at the end of the bar. I sat next to the woman, ignored the man, and prepared to order a Coke. No such luck.

"Roll 'em, honey," the man's voice said in a peremptory way. I looked down and saw a cup containing five dice.

The bartender, a benevolent-looking bearded man, glanced over at me and said, "It's okay, roll 'em. It's what we do here."

I took the dice cup, rolled 'em, and came up with three snake eyes and a pair of sixes. The man, the woman, and the bartender all shouted approval. "You're one lucky lady—you just won a free drink," the bartender told me. "Buddy here," he said pointing to the older man, "just staked you. What'll you have?" When I ordered a Coke, the whole bar groaned.

Debbie, the woman sitting next to me, asked if I was a reporter. I explained something about what I was doing, mentioned an interest in Montana wilderness areas, and asked about the recent spate of forest fires in the area.

"They're everywhere," she said. "Just a few miles down the road going west on 200 you'll see them from the road. We've had a terrible time here. Some of the people in this bar lost property." Debbie introduced me to Jill, who had been forced to evacuate her house without taking any of her belongings with her.

Debbie told me she was the only person in her family who'd gone to college but that her father, who made Smokey the Bear signs, was famous in these parts. She had just finished her master's degree in counseling, and now she had found a job in another small Montana town. There were virtually no jobs in Paradise and very little money for those who did find work there. Debbie had recently married a man from Paradise.

"When we got married," Debbie said, "we had our reception right here at this bar. The whole town came. We had a band in the back and everybody behaved. There was not a single fight, and not one DUI that night. It was a great honor to Miles and me that everybody, I mean *everybody*, behaved so well that night."

BACK TO THE WILD

I was still sipping a Coke when a hand reached across and put an open bottle of beer in front of me. Buddy was not giving up easily. I broke rule number two and smiled.

Dino, the bartender, came to my rescue over and over again that night; whenever Buddy became especially aggressive, there was Dino to bail me out. This time, however, it was Debbie who intervened. "One of the reasons I come to this bar rather than to the Mint Bar down the road in Plains is that Buddy drinks here. I love to hear him sing." In short order a guitar appeared, and for the next few minutes Debbie and Buddy sang a medley of Frank Sinatra/Joan Stafford duets, beginning with "I'll Never Smile Again" and ending with "Let's Get Away from It All." Afterwards Buddy passed the guitar back to Dino and reached across the still-empty stool between us to touch my hair, but Dino leaned across the bar between us and began to talk.

"Every year Buddy gives the best party we ever have here in Paradise—a grave-digging party. It's legal to bury folks in Montana without embalming or the help of an undertaker. Problem is, the ground's frozen in the winter, so you have to have your hole already dug just in case. Buddy here wants to make sure there's no slipup. He's got a nice place picked out up in the hills."

At that point Debbie chimed in, explaining how every year the whole town gathers for the party. "First we fill in last year's grave, and then we dig a new one. Then everybody gathers in the park for food and drink. It's our way of celebrating Buddy's living another year," she said.

"And the rest of us, too," Dino added.

Buddy raised the glass of spirits he was chasing with beer and said, "Let's all drink to another year." I broke rule number three and lifted the beer that had been warming in front of me for some time. When I lowered my bottle, Buddy grabbed my left hand. "Look here, Dino, I think that wedding ring's been on her hand a long time."

"Yeah, Buddy, I think you're right. Looks to me like she plans to keep it."

"Buddy," I said, "I've had this ring thirty years. I'd like to be wearing it thirty years from now."

Still holding my hand, he replied, "Then you better start having grave-diggin' parties. Works for me, and it'll probably work for you. Best way I know to keep from dying." I thought of all the ways I kept from dying. I didn't smoke, I exercised every day, and —except in Wyoming and Montana—I ate a low-fat diet. The grave-digging party might work even better. I looked out the door and realized it was getting dark. There went rule number four.

About that time Debbie's husband, Miles, her sister-in-law, Shirley, and Shirley's husband, Wayne, came in together. When Debbie introduced me as a writer there to learn about Montana's forests and wilderness, Wayne got interested and asked me three questions in a row.

The first—"You're not one of those tree-spikin' earth muffins, are you?"—I chose not to answer. The second—"Why come to a bar if you're not going to drink?"—I answered by picking up my second Bud. And the third—"Are you from Georgia?"—I rode all the way out. As it turned out, Wayne grew up in the country near Waycross, Georgia, about a hundred miles from my hometown. In no time I broke rule number five by letting Wayne know what I thought about his ideas. We locked horns on almost every topic that came up: designated wilderness, forest fires, clear-cutting, and the spotted-owl controversy. Both Wayne and Shirley were against the Wilderness Act and strongly opposed giving the wilderness designation to any more land in Montana.

"Look, I've lived here all my life," Shirley said. "This is my home. There are plenty of woods for everybody in Montana to hike in and hunt and do whatever we want to. There's no reason for us not to cut down these trees to make a living. You tell me why they have a right to set aside our woods so a bunch of rich folks from back east can come out here and walk around in fancy outdoor clothes."

Shirley knows that "our woods" are national forests, but—like ranchers I'd met in Wyoming—she and Wayne think federal lands in Montana should be for the use of native Montanans.

"North of here in the Kootenai National Forest there's lots of trees ready for cuttin'—thousands and thousands of acres," Wayne mentioned. "But some folks want to make it a wilderness. That's crazy. Trees mean jobs, food on the table, and wood in the stove."

I knew from reading Rick Bass that the Yaak Valley was located in the Kootenai, where there are still roadless areas populated with grizzlies, wolverines, mountain lions, moose, elks, hordes of deer, and an occasional wolf visiting from Canada. I also knew that there was no designated wilderness there, and that this amazing array of animals was sure to decline unless the clear-cutting is stopped and roadless habitat preserved. Understandably, Wayne's concerns were about trees and the jobs the trees could bring, and he never acknowledged that the economic needs of working people who earned their living in the timber industry were at odds with the health of the environment. His commitment to the immediate needs of communities that depend on timber was stronger than any concern about what to him was the distant future.

"Don't matter much anyway what happens to the Yaak now," he said. "It's been burning all summer. That fire'll keep on till the first snow. Ain't gonna be much left. And you know why? It's never been logged. Clear-cuts make firebreaks that stop the fire."

It was pointless to argue with Wayne. True, fires were raging and/or smoldering in parts of the Yaak Valley as they were all over the West, but it wasn't true that the Yaak had no clear-cuts. In fact there had been excessive clear-cutting, resulting in the inevitable erosion and silting of streams. One thing that's necessary for forest fires is enough trees to make a forest, but clear-cutting was hardly the way to prevent them.

Wayne and I never agreed on anything, but we were connected to each other by our mutual attachment to the coastal plains of Georgia. Relinquishing the argument about western forests, we found common ground by sharing childhood memories of our escapades in the woods. Though our memories were different, the details of the natural world we knew were the same: pine trees, live oaks, sandy soil, red clay, crickets, crawfish, rattlesnakes, and gopher turtles. Wayne's hometown of Waycross is the jumping-off point for the 438,000-acre Okefenokee Swamp, most of it designated wilderness. The swamp provides habitat for alligators, otters, herons, cranes, wood storks, and a myriad of other birds. Images of the Okefenokee's cypress forests and teeming animal life are indelibly burned in my memory—and in Wayne's.

Though I'd never been on a hunt, I could imagine Wayne raccoon hunting with kerosene lanterns on moonlit nights, and he would have no trouble picturing me fishing from a rowboat in a snake-infested pond with my grandmother. It must have been our talk of home that led Wayne to invite me to join him and Shirley for dinner at a nearby café, to camp out in my van in their front yard, and to go to breakfast with him early the next morning so he could arrange for me to meet some firefighters working a big fire down the road. I broke rule number six when I accepted his invitation.

While Wayne and I were talking, I realized that I was totally ignorant of local bar etiquette. Beer appeared in front of me, and I didn't know who to thank. I realized that I was probably expected to join in the treating, but I never figured out how to do it without being treated again in return. When I protested at the appearance of yet another beer, Wayne shrugged, "If you can't run with the big dogs, get off the porch."

When Wayne and Shirley and I got up to leave, Dino handed me a token they use for people who win a drink with a throw of the dice. "Maybe you'll come back some day and collect on that drink. Or you might just want it for a souvenir." Before I left, I thanked Buddy for the drinks and gave him my card. Buddy took out a scrap of paper and scribbled his address on it. But instead of Paradise, he wrote "Pair a dice." Handing me the paper, he explained, "That's the real name of this town. Railroad folks named it. They came in here to gamble. All you had to do in those days to make it in this town was to have a pair of dice."

"That's really all you need today," Dino said, and passed the dice cup down the bar.

I woke the next morning at six in Wayne's front yard, rolled out of the van, stepped over the dogs that were sleeping just outside the door, and slipped inside Wayne and Shirley's house to wash up. Wayne had insisted on buying my dinner the night before, but he did let me buy breakfast for the two of us. In the more sober light of day, we returned to the subject of the politics and economics of wilderness designation. Wayne pointed out that the big timber companies that mainly cut private land might well want large tracts of forests in Montana to be set aside as wilderness.

"A big wilderness designation raises the price of their timber. Maybe they figure that years from now, after they've cut all the private land, they'll move into Montana. Pay big bucks to somebody in Washington to change the law and free up this timber."

He told me that some people thought the spotted-owl controversy was fueled by the timber companies operating mainly in states other than Washington and Oregon. Close down the logging in the Northwest and raise the price of timber elsewhere. We both concluded that it was even possible environmentalists are unknowingly being used by the timber companies to tie up trees in wilderness, thus keeping prices high for trees the companies own. The spotted-owl controversy has allowed environmentalists to delay the destruction of old-growth forests in the extreme Northwest, and this has raised the price of timber in Idaho and Montana. I knew from my own experience that people who grow timber think in the long term and that the people who work to get laws passed know very well that laws can be repealed. Listening to Wayne helped me see how little I know about the hidden agendas that go into a piece of wilderness legislation. What might seem to be for the benefit of future generations may in fact be of immediate benefit to the large timber companies.

Wayne called a friend of his at the staging area for the firefighters and told him I would be coming to learn about forest fires. I said good-bye to him with a lot more respect than I'd had when we first met some twelve hours before. I headed northwest through Clark Fork River Valley. In a matter of minutes I had left Paradise and entered the fire zone, where dark smoke blackened the morning sky like threatening clouds preceding a thunderstorm. The staging area for the fire-fighting operation seemed more like a war zone than anything I'd seen before. Helicopters were taking off and landing, ambulances were standing by, dozens of folks were busy preparing food under large canvas shelters, and vehicles of all kinds were coming and going continually.

I hung around the sidelines for a while, listening to conversations and chatting with folks who were taking a break. Fire-management policies on public lands had sparked ongoing controversy since the fires of 1988 swept through Yellowstone, burning hundreds of thousands of acres, and every summer when parts of the West go up in flames, battle lines are drawn anew. That morning and in the years since, I've heard numerous contradictory ideas about fire prevention, control, and management, including the following:

1. Fire in the forests is terrible and should be avoided at all cost, versus fire is inevitable and necessary in many ecosystems.
2. Ninety years of fire suppression has created huge conflagrations, versus prohibiting logging in wilderness creates a tinderbox.
3. Prescribed burns are required to reduce fuel load in forests, versus prescribed burns are too risky.
4. Raging fires are the result of insufficient logging and road building, versus logging large, fire-resistant trees creates conditions for a hot burn.
5. Firefighters risk and sometimes lose their lives to save private homes that should never have been built in the forests, versus property owners have a right to fire protection, whatever the cost.

Some fires in wilderness are the result of a natural process, usually a lightning strike, but careless people who leave campfires burning in or near dry forests cause others. Deciding what to do when fires get out of control becomes more difficult with each new conflagration. The more I learn about fire, the more I see that there are no easy answers to the questions constantly raised about how to manage, prevent, and control it.

Before I left I met Wayne's friend, who was dispatching helicopters and monitoring a radio.

"So Wayne sent you," he said to me in greeting, and then urged me to stick around. After asking a few questions, I thanked him for his trouble and waved good-bye.

"Tell Wayne hello for me," he said, before going back to his job.

I realized I probably wouldn't see Wayne again and was surprised by a wave of sadness. Maybe I could come back to Buddy's grave-digging party next July 30th. I hoped he would have another year to celebrate. As it turned out, I did go back to Paradise two years later. Dino was still behind the bar, and Buddy was very much alive and just sober enough to be planning his next grave-digging party. I still receive a letter from Debbie at Christmas, but I've never heard from Wayne. But I may yet. I'm not finished with Paradise.

Anger and Alpenglow

〜〜〜 IT HAD BEEN exactly three weeks since I left home when I met Jerome at the Spokane airport. I'd spent the night before with our friends Ernie and Marilyn in Coeur d'Alene, Idaho. I'd had my hair colored, washed clothes, soaked in a hot bath, and slept in a bed for the first time in three weeks.

Waiting in the baggage area of the airport, I tried to imagine how he would be dressed. I knew he would have made a special effort to please me. I looked up and there he was dressed in black jeans, a deep blue outdoor shirt, cowboy boots, and a new black western-style hat cocked at an angle. I laughed, told him how much I liked the hat, and said, "You look mighty good to me."

As we stood waiting for baggage, I talked about the folks in Paradise. He caught me up on the latest news from children, parents, friends, and the dog. Richard and Monica were planning their delayed honeymoon in Europe; Laura was coming for a visit in November; Jerome had taken his mother to Cumberland Island for her birthday; one friend had had a heart attack, another had separated from his wife; and our dog Hugo's arthritis was responding well to steroids.

Then he told me he was planning a birthday party for himself in October at a country-and-western dance place. I felt a twinge of I'm not sure what. A number of possibilities went through my head: I should fly home to be there; he was trying to make me feel bad for being gone so long; he should wait a month until I returned. But then I knew I couldn't expect Jerome to put his life on hold because I was gone for three months. I couldn't have it both ways. Besides, he loved to dance, and it was his birthday. He would be joining me a few days after that in Utah, where we would celebrate our thirtieth anniversary. Still, I felt uneasy—jealous, perhaps, or maybe just left out.

As soon as we were in the car, I found that Jerome had brought the city's hurry sickness with him, and I was afraid of being infected with it. When we took the wrong turn leaving the airport, he reacted as if some major catastrophe were occurring.

"Damn it, that sign says we're heading east instead of west. Get out the map and see where we are," Jerome growled.

"I told you to look at the map before we started out."

"Look, I'll turn around at the next exit, but we've lost at least twenty minutes," he said with increasing annoyance.

"Twenty minutes is no big deal."

"It's a big deal if we don't make it to Mazama before 8:30. That's when the dining room closes."

"Like I say, it's no big deal. I've got bean soup, rice, fruit, and yogurt in the back. If we don't make it in time, we'll eat that."

I was suddenly more irritated than I'd been since I left home. Even after we got turned around and were going in the right direction, Jerome continued to watch the time. As we passed through the open hill country of eastern Washington, he drove a little too fast, and I continually checked my watch, studied the map, and estimated how long it would take to get to the inn where we had reserved a room and a table for dinner. All this hurry and concern with time spoiled our first several hours together for me. For Jerome, the headlong rush to make a dinner reservation was business as usual. I'd been away from the urban scene long enough to find his reaction intolerable.

"Jerome, I can't stand this rush," I finally barked.

"Look, get off my back. I'm doing the best I can, and I don't want to miss dinner."

Soon I was trying to calm him down, but nothing I said helped him relax. He remained in a tense posture and answered my questions in a detached way that suggested he would surely lose time if he gave me anything but the most cursory attention.

The feeling of urgency was far out of proportion to the circumstances. I was furious with Jerome. And I knew that living in the city, I often pushed myself in the same way.

It was 8:25 when we sat down in the dining room at the Mazama Country Inn on the eastern edge of the Cascades. Soon we were enjoying a bottle of wine and waiting for dinner. Jerome looked at his watch again and said, "That was close. I can't believe we made it."

"Well, we did make it, but it's not worth the rush. We could have taken our time, enjoyed the scenery, and made a picnic with some of the food I had in the van."

"Look, I made this dinner reservation a month ago, and I need a good meal."

"This makes no sense. You rush, rush, rush for four hours, poisoning yourself with adrenaline, even risking your life—and mine—driving too fast so you can have a plate of pasta and a salad."

"Well, I only have a week off, and I wanted this evening to be special," he countered.

"Jerome, I can't go on like this. At home we think nothing of jumping back in the car ten minutes after you get home from work, driving across town in the traffic, eating dinner in a hurry, and getting to a movie five minutes late. I'm not going to do that anymore, even if I never see another movie."

Jerome took a deep breath and looked puzzled. "Is it that bad?" he asked.

"Yes, it's that bad. And it's crazy. We don't enjoy anything living at that pace. It's even worse when we go to the symphony. Half the time you sleep through the concert, and when we get home, it's too late to even have a conversation."

"Look, I don't like rushing around any more than you do, but there's nothing we can do about that now, and I've had a lot to handle. I don't know what I can change right now."

"Okay, I'm sorry. But I don't agree that there's nothing we can do about it. Tell me what's been going on at work."

"Well, a hell of a lot has been going on," he said.

"You want to talk about that?" I asked.

"Yeah, I do. Things are changing in medicine so fast that sometimes it's hard to know where I'm heading. Not only that, but many of my patients have problems I can't fix."

"What do you mean?"

"I mean bad marriages, impossible job situations, kids on drugs, awful scars from childhood. It gets to me sometimes, listening to all this stuff and not being able to help."

"But you do help them with their medical problems," I said.

"Sure, but all this other stuff often makes their medical problems so much worse," he said. "People expect me to help them, and sometimes there's very little I can do."

"I'm sure you do help them some just by caring and listening. But you can only fix so much, and you can't make other people happy. That's up to them."

Jerome took a deep breath and let it out slowly, visibly relaxing for the first time.

"You're right. I do know I can't make these folks happy, but I wish I had more time."

"Well, let me tell you what I've learned in the wilderness. I've got the time I've got, and what I do takes the time it takes."

The sense of urgency that had plagued us since the airport slowly subsided, and by morning there was no longer any reason to hurry. For the next few days Jerome and I camped in a forest of large trees—hemlock, spruce, and fir. We took day hikes, beginning on trailheads accessible from the North Cascades Scenic Highway. The days were sunny, and the fires that were burning vast forests north of us were far enough away not to cause us any problems.

The hiking wasn't easy. The trails we took were all steep and led generally up and through talus (slopes of rock debris) to mountain passes with 360-degree views. I especially had difficulty keeping my balance on talus, though it was much easier than clambering over the huge boulders that covered large, trailless areas of the Bighorns.

The summer before, when I had spent two weeks exploring the Glacier Peak Wilderness in the North Cascades, I began to think of these mountains as more generous with their beauty than any mountain range I'd ever hiked. By that I mean that they give and give and give, and just when you think you've seen all the beauty that's possible to see in one day, they give again. The trails we took led from one awesome scene to another. One ranger we talked to described them as "half as high but twice as rugged as the Sierra Nevadas."

One day while we were hiking, we left the solar shower in the sun on top of the van to warm. Seven hours later we returned to hot water, which I insisted we use immediately before it got cold. It wasn't easy to get Jerome to take all his clothes off in the woods, but I succeeded in teaching him how to strip, soap with a loofah, shower, dry, and put on clean clothes—all in about five minutes. I couldn't help but laugh as he did all this while looking over his shoulder to see if anyone was coming, much as our dog Hugo does when he's relieving himself in a neighbor's yard.

On our fifth day in the Cascades we loaded our packs and traveled west and north to the Mount Baker Wilderness. We chose a popular trail that took us down into a valley and then gradually up to a moraine across from the enormous glacier that covers the western side of Mount Shuksan. Periodically along the trail, the completely snow-covered crown of Mount Baker would appear, only to be replaced a half mile or so later by the equally impressive spectacle of Mount Shuksan. When we reached Lake Anne, we set up camp on one of the few flat spots in the area. I had never slept so close to a large glacier, and the continuous low-pitched roar was a surprise. We oriented our tent so that the door opened out to Lake Anne. From there we followed a gradual path down to the lake for water.

That evening we perched on rocks, enjoying the sound and light show. First there was the setting sun, followed by the appearance of the evening star. As we prepared dinner small rodents visited us, and in the rocks beyond we could hear the shrill whistle of marmots calling out to each other. I never knew whether their call was one of alarm or passion, but either way it was relentless. Long after the sun dropped behind the mountain, there was ample light illuminating Shuksan. Clinging to the ice were two spots of color that I assumed were human figures climbing the glacier. When dark finally won out over the alpenglow, we saw flickering light at the very top of Shuksan. Someone was camping up there. Then turning back to the west, we saw shooting stars. A few minutes later we heard the crash of an avalanche.

We only saw one other person that night, a man from British Columbia who walked down our way around dark. He and Jerome chatted for a while in soft voices about the beauty of the place and about other trails we might take in the Mount Baker Wilderness. As he was leaving, our neighbor looked back over his shoulder and said, "You really should stay several days. There's so much to do right here. Walk up on the ridge across the lake tomorrow and you'll get a stupendous view of Mount Baker, and another day you might want to take the lower trail that winds back closer to the glacier."

Yes, there was a lot to do. There were stars and avalanches to watch, trails to follow, marmot whistles to hear, bears to avoid, water to filter, tea and oatmeal to make, and rocks to sit on. Before we climbed into our tent, we spent a few minutes longer watching the moonless star-filled night. We were finally on wilderness time.

Jerome and I made the mistake of getting into our tiny backpacking tent—appropriate for one person and a backpack or two people in love—at the same time. As we struggled to take off clothes, make pillows out of our rain gear and sweaters, and somehow get settled into our sleeping bags, we were soon laughing so hard we were afraid we might disturb our neighbor, even though he was half way around the lake. We felt like two people undressing in a phone booth. Finally, exhausted with laughter, we located our flashlights and other paraphernalia and settled down for nine hours of sleep lulled by the low-pitched sound of the slowly moving glacier.

We'd been told there might be bears in the area, and so we cooked a good hundred feet or so from our tent, carefully hanging all food items even further away from a limb of one of the few available trees. The next morning we found that our only visitors had been what locals call the little critters. I had hidden a Ziploc bag containing two apple cores under my pack. The next morning, when I moved the pack, there was the bag with a small hole in it, the shredded remains of the apples scattered about. Only the seeds were missing. I wondered what it would be like to be able to smell a mostly eaten apple carefully sealed inside a Ziploc baggy hidden under a large object.

There are bears in the North Cascades—a large number of black bears and a small population of grizzlies. Grizzlies are rarely seen since there are so few of them and they live so far in the backcountry, but because of the forest fires, some of the animals that live deep in the more remote areas had moved down to more heavily used areas. A woman I met in Mazama had told me about seeing several black bears, a mountain lion, and a large grizzly less than five miles from the inn just two weeks before. In early September both species of bears feed on the blueberries and huckleberries that cover much of the Cascades. As we entered the berry country coming down from Lake Anne, we passed a pair of hikers who told us there was a bear on the trail, and that if we didn't see it, we would surely smell it. In hopes of seeing the bear, Jerome suggested we keep quiet. With that I stopped and begged him to listen to three cardinal rules for hiking in bear country: do not surprise a bear or give it reason to feel threatened; hike with four or more people in bear country; and avoid attracting bears with the odor of food or toiletries.

We both laughed, realizing that if the said bear had stayed on the trail, we might very well surprise it by coming around a blind curve on the trail; there was no way to metamorphose into four people; and we were indeed carrying the remains of our food in our packs.

About a hundred yards down the trail, we walked through a strong, fetid odor. I had read enough about bears to know that the sighting of a bear accompanied by a strong odor may well mean that the bear is guarding the remains of an animal it has killed, eaten in part, and stashed until it can eat again. I immediately interpreted the stench in the air as carrion. Whether we were dealing with a smelly bear feasting on huckleberries or a bear guarding the rotting flesh of its next meal didn't matter. We were too tired and low on water to even consider turning around and going back up the trail. Besides, the bear might be going that way as well.

And so we sang, whistled, and carried on loud conversations, hoping to keep the bear at bay. After an hour or so, we relaxed. The last mile of the trail out of Lake Anne was a steep incline, and we had a hard time making that final pull. Our packs seemed heavier with every step. We were out of water, and I became increasingly thirsty. All I could think about were the cookies and the gallon of water I knew I'd left in the van. When we finally made it back to the trailhead, we both collapsed on the ground. First water and food, then the boots. There is nothing quite like the pleasure of pulling off hiking boots, peeling off damp socks, and exposing tired and bruised feet to the air.

Drawn to Alaska

~~~~~ As Jerome and I came out of the Mount Baker Wilderness, I suggested we go to Bellingham. When he asked me why I wanted to go there, I didn't really have an answer, and at that point Alaska was the last thing on my conscious mind. I'd heard there were ferries to the San Juan Islands from Bellingham, but I didn't know about the ferry to Alaska. Once in Bellingham, we wandered through the streets of Fairhaven, the town's artsy-craftsy section. We stopped for coffee, sat on the grass listening to a local jazz band, and eventually wandered down to the port. The day was Friday, the second of September. On one side of the terminal there was a sign for the Alaskan State Ferry, which leaves Bellingham every Friday and stops at various ports along the inside passage. The *Columbia* was in port and would leave in a few hours, and two and a half days later it would stop in Juneau.

Armed with brochures and schedules, we wandered back to Fairhaven for lunch. We both knew all the reasons "why not." I wouldn't be able to leave before September 9, a week later. It would be getting cold by then. Winter closes in during the last half of September, and the rains begin. All the staterooms on the boat were booked, so I'd have to sleep on the deck. Although people traveling on the deck were allowed to pitch small tents for shelter, there might be heavy winds and rain. I might get seasick. My tent might blow away. Many of the boats and some of the trains designed to take tourists around the state would discontinue service in the next few days. The most compelling reason why not was that Jerome would not be able to join me, as he'd planned to do three weeks later. If I were to go to Alaska the following week, it would be five weeks before we would see each other again. I was tempted to conclude that the reasons why not were overwhelming and that Alaska would have to wait for another day.

But what day? Next summer, perhaps, or the one after that. But I didn't want to go to Alaska as a tourist with everything planned out. I wanted to get on this ferry, stop at Ketchican, Sitka, Juneau, Haines, Skagway, or wherever I pleased. The door was open and I wanted to go through it.

Sitting in the sun at the Cobblestone Café, we studied schedules and read about the inside passage in the Lonely Planet Guide to Alaska. By the time we finished lunch, the decision was made. Jerome confessed to understandable envy, I confessed to feeling selfish, but we agreed that the five-week separation was not too high a price to pay for such an adventure. I knew I'd miss Jerome from time to time and that sometimes the missing would be painful. I love being with him, sharing the sight of a shooting star, the sound of an avalanche deep in the night, and a cup of tea in the morning. But I also love my solitude and the freedom it gives me, and I'm not sure I'd love one without the other.

The ticket agent had told me there was no need to book passage in advance since there was a lot of space on the deck of the ferry so late in the year, but I was ready to make a commitment. After lunch I bought a two-week ticket that would allow me to ride the *Columbia* and any other state ferry that traveled along the Inside Passage as often as I liked.

From Bellingham we drove to the town of Glacier and checked into the Snowline Lodge. That night we went to the Milano restaurant, where we had pasta and a couple of bottles of Full Sail Golden Ale. After dinner I was chatting with the cashier when the woman next to me interrupted, "It's so nice to hear a southern accent. Where are you from?"

I turned and saw a pretty forty-something woman who introduced herself to me as Leslie Golden from Tyron, North Carolina. In the South we speak of being from the place where we were born and grew up. I told her that I was from Dublin, Georgia, but that I'd lived most of my adult life in Atlanta. Leslie said she'd left the South some twenty years earlier and has lived in Alaska and Washington ever since. She told me that she missed the South terribly. When I asked her why, she didn't hesitate.

"I miss tradition, dinner parties with fine china, and nice clothes. I miss being able to wear my antique jewelry without apologizing. I miss manners and civility and children who say 'yes ma'am.' I miss it all. Tell me it still exists."

I hesitated. Leslie's need for the trappings of southern living was intense, but I had to tell her the truth—that I hardly ever give or go to formal dinner parties and that I meet my friends in restaurants; that my children have been known occasionally to say "yes ma'am" but only to their grandparents; that I still love what southerners call "good clothes" but wear them less and less; and that my few pieces of antique jewelry had long been locked in the safety-deposit box. Then I asked her if she also misses wearing white gloves and all that goes with them. She laughed and said that maybe she just missed home. Before she left we exchanged addresses and Leslie invited me to visit her at her home in the country near the tiny town of Maple Falls.

After driving Jerome back to the Spokane airport a few days later, I returned to the North Cascades. The next afternoon I drove down the country road where Leslie lived. After about a mile and a half, I came to a large lodgelike house set in an idyllic valley. Leslie was waiting for me outside. Something about the setting made me think of Africa. I imagined Leslie as a heroine in an early Doris Lessing story—a cultured woman living in an isolated place where no one appreciated the traditions or way of life of the place where she was born. She invited me in and showed me around her home, which was furnished with unusual antiques and oriental rugs. There were original paintings on the walls and fresh flowers in every room. There was also the pelt of a large wolf, complete with feet and head, on the back of a sofa in the library.

Leslie made tea, which she took out to the rocking chairs on her front porch. There were no houses visible from where we sat looking out at pastures and the mountains beyond. There was a

BACK TO THE WILD

warm, early-autumn glow to the waving grasses in the fields around the house and a peacefulness and quiet that I found very appealing.

We sat talking on the porch for some two hours. Leslie had moved to Alaska in her early twenties, working first as a buyer for Nordstrom's in Anchorage and later at various other jobs in smaller towns. Eventually she fell in love with and married Jeff Golden. After having two children, she moved to this place to have access to the schools and other conveniences she thought her children needed. Jeff spent five months each year at sea, fishing for salmon and halibut.

The conversation turned to Alaska, and I told Leslie I was planning to take the state ferry up the Inside Passage the next week. "The ferry is the only way to go," Leslie affirmed. "I always took the ferry, and I usually slept in one of the deck chairs rather than pitching a tent. But either way, that's the way for you to meet real Alaskans. Only tourists stay in the staterooms."

When I asked Leslie about hiking alone in Alaska, she gave me the by-now-standard advice: "You must take a gun." When I explained that I didn't have a gun, she suggested that perhaps I could rent one in Alaska. "There are so many bears up there," she added. I was well aware that there are bears in Alaska and that the brown bears, as the grizzlies are called, get much bigger than those in the Lower 48. I'd heard some of the biggest ones weigh up to fifteen hundred pounds. When I asked Leslie whether she'd ever encountered bears during her years in Alaska, she said, "oh, yes," and told me three stories.

Once she and her husband had been out fishing when their boat broke down. He fired a gun to summon a friend in a nearby cabin to come and get them. Since there was no room in the small boat for all their gear, they left some things at their campsite. The next morning when they came back, a grizzly had torn into the tent and shredded the sweater that Leslie had left there.

Another time she and Jeff were in a small fishing boat on a river. Assuming that she was safe from bears in a boat, Leslie was not particularly concerned about the large male grizzly they saw on one side of the river. Then the huge bear reared up, dived into the river, and swam to the other side, nearly upsetting their boat. Apparently the bear just wanted to cross the river, but Leslie told me she'd never felt particularly safe in a boat since then.

Most recently she was carrying one of her children in a backpack while hiking with Jeff and his mother. When they met a large grizzly on the trail, Jeff fired two shots to frighten it away. The bear, however, didn't budge. Leslie backed down the trail before turning around to escape, leaving her fearless husband and mother-in-law watching the bear.

"There are places in Alaska where there are more bears than people," Leslie said. "Don't just wander off in the woods without protection. A man with a powerful rifle who knows how to shoot is the best protection, but then men are dangerous, too, and they're going to be much more interested in you than the grizzlies will be."

Leslie went on to reiterate what I'd heard many times before: that a grizzly sow might attack you if she thinks you are threatening her cubs and a hungry bear might choose you for dinner. But this was the first time I'd been warned about the dangers of men. She stressed that men outnumber women everywhere in Alaska and that when they've been on a fishing boat or working on the pipeline, they may not have seen a woman for a long time.

"If a bush pilot takes you into the backcountry, he'll expect to stay with you. Some of the fishermen you meet might take you out to watch them work. In most cases you'd be fine, but a few men might take your request to go on the boat as 'consent,' and you might be raped."

I replied that I'd originally thought my age and wedding ring would be some protection, but that I'd learned not to count on that. Leslie agreed, noting that there were lots of older men in Alaska and some young ones who would think they'd have a better chance with an older woman. "Of course you'll have to talk to them if you're going to learn about Alaska. Be nice, but be cool. And don't let your soft, southern side show. They'll love it."

When I said good-bye to Leslie late in the afternoon, I wondered how her life would evolve. She was leaving the next day to take a photography course in France. She urged me to stay in touch and to come back for another visit when she returned, showing me guest quarters where I could stay and work on my writing.

I woke early on the morning of September 9 in a campground in Cascades National Park. There were heavy clouds in the west and rain seemed imminent, but with large areas of the northwestern forests still burning, I didn't dare wish for sun. A day of rain could save untold acres of forests.

I decided to take to Alaska only what would fit in my backpack. I crawled into the van and spread out those items that I thought I would need for the three weeks I'd spend there. I thought I had pared my belongings to a minimum when I packed the van five weeks before, but as I surveyed the clothes, camping gear, books, writing materials, and miscellaneous items, I realized that they would probably fill several backpacks. I set aside what seemed to be the essentials: a Thermarest pad, tent, and sleeping bag; Gore-Tex rain gear, long underwear, a sweater, two pairs of hiking pants, a vest, two shirts, a wool hat, gloves, hiking boots, underwear, a Polartec jacket, and yes—duct tape. My hair dryer, extra camera equipment, binoculars, and notebook computer would stay behind.

The Inside Passage

〰〰〰 IT WAS 10 P.M. before I fastened my pack and headed west along Highway 20 across the Cascades, through fog and light drizzle. By the time I reached Bellingham, the drizzle had turned to a driving rain. I found a bookstore with an espresso bar, where I bought two books to take on the boat—John McPhee's *Coming into the Country* and Larry Kaniut's *Bear Stories.* There I passed the time until departure, reading real-life stories of encounters with grizzlies in Alaska.

By boarding time the rain had stopped. Leslie, who has ridden these ferries many times, had told me how to find a place to sleep: "Go straight to the solarium on the top and at the back of the ship and claim a lounge chair with your pack. Then pitch a tent in case someone near you snores or harasses you." By the time I found the solarium, there was only one lounge chair left. I grabbed it, put my pack on one end, and sat on the other.

Only then did I look around. The first half of the solarium was covered, but it was open to wind and rain at the back. Under the roof were heaters and about fifty lounge chairs. Passengers were busy spreading sleeping bags and otherwise setting up camp. Those who came after the last lounge chair was gone quickly filled in the remaining floor space with camping gear. To my right was a woman about my age with her twenty-something daughter. To my left was a middle-aged man. Respecting some kind of invisible boundary, the solitary man and I never spoke even though his lounge was about eighteen inches away from mine.

Thinking that I might want privacy but not wanting to give up my space, I set up my tent in the open area. The wind was blowing hard, so I secured the tent to the deck with yards of duct tape. That way, I reasoned, I could have it both ways: the comfort of the lounge chair and warmth of the solarium and, when I needed it, the privacy of the tent. But things didn't quite work out that way.

The rain returned, the wind intensified, and in no time the tents were standing in water. Those people camping near the open end of the solarium were getting wet. I settled into my dry sleeping space well under the cover and never once used the tent. For the three nights on the boat I stayed dry and warm and relatively comfortable. I looked out at my tent and wondered how I would ever get all that wet nylon inside my pack, but the day before we docked in Juneau the sun came out long enough to dry it. Except for a few hours in Haines, that was the last I would see of the sun until the day I boarded the *Columbia* in Sitka to return to Bellingham. The sky did clear just enough one night for the northern lights to be visible for more than an hour off the port bow, and during the day the clouds and mist made one rainbow after another, several forming complete arches across our passage through the water. In addition to announcing the northern lights and rainbow spectacles, the captain of the ship would alert us when he sighted whales, both humpbacks and Orcas. Later I learned that *Orca* is the scientific and now politically correct name for the large mammals once known as killer whales.

Before the boat was underway, I'd met a number of the people who would be my companions for the next three days, and we soon fell into the easy rhythm of boat life. We had drinks at five in the bar and dinner at six at a window table in the dining room; we went to sleep at nine, when all the lights went out in the solarium, and got up with first light around six in the morning. To compensate for the discomfort of sleeping out on deck with strangers just barely protected from a driving rain, I regularly joined a group of folks for a hearty breakfast in the dining room.

The tourist season was winding down, and many of the passengers on the ferry were Alaskan residents or adventurers who had left jobs or spouses and were beginning something new.

Roger, recently divorced, was going to work as a cook for a fishing camp in the Yukon. Down below on the car deck was a converted school bus that he planned to live in. He hoped that eventually his two small children would come and live with him. Roger spent much of his time on the boat sleeping. When he was awake, he pored over Jane Brody's *Good Food Cook Book.*

David and Mary Beth had spent the last twenty years in Salt Lake City. He was an orthopedic surgeon, and Mary Beth had worked as the admissions officer of a private school. They had long thought that once their children were raised they would do something different—as they said, "break out of the linear progression" they'd been in for thirty years. David gave up his private practice and took a job with a branch of the Public Health Service that provides health care for native people in remote parts of Alaska. Mary Beth planned to run a bed-and-breakfast in their home. They were not the only people I met whose need to do something different led them to leave a good life and move to a place where they had no roots and knew practically no one. It was hard for me to imagine trading the sunshine, color, and beauty of Utah for the full-time winter darkness and cold of Anchorage and northern Alaska.

Rita, who was returning from visiting her parents in Philadelphia, had a different story. Strong, athletic, and good-looking, she had the confident air of someone about to step behind a dogsled to run the Iditerod endurance race. After graduating from the University of Virginia law school, she had taken a job with a small law firm in Juneau. For the last ten years she had specialized in the legal conflicts that develop among timber companies, the Forest Service, and local communities. Before moving to Alaska Rita had never been west of the Mississippi. Back east, her athletic activities had been limited to tennis, jogging, and swimming, and she'd never been backpacking. Now she drove a snowmobile, flew her own plane, went on extended treks in the backcountry with her boyfriend, and had her own repertoire of bear stories. She did not, however, carry a gun; she counted on the man in her life to handle any unpleasantness that might require firearms. "It's safer not to carry a gun unless you use it regularly. Besides, I never go out alone. Tom is really skilled with a gun, and he brings home most of our meat."

When I asked Rita if she had ever had a frightening bear encounter, she explained that encountering a grizzly in the wild is always terrifying, but that while she had seen grizzlies several times, none had ever threatened to attack her. She did, however, tell me the story of a woman who was not so lucky. Her friends Caroline and Don had a cabin in the woods by a riverbank. Late one night they heard an animal outside, and when they opened the door, a large grizzly pushed its way in; they escaped through the backdoor. Caroline managed to climb up on the roof and Don ran to the nearest cabin to get help and a gun. By the time Don returned, the bear had climbed on the roof and killed and eaten his wife. Only small pieces of her body were left. I had no reason to doubt Rita's story, which had many of the elements of the bear stories I would hear over and over again in the next three weeks. While I suspected some stories were fabricated to fit an Alaskan version of the tall tale, I generally believed what people told me about their own experiences.

Then there was Nathan. I was sitting just under the cover of the solarium alternately reading and staring at the sea when the stereotypical Alaskan outdoorsman approached me. "Excuse me, ma'am, but I heard you asking that forest ranger some questions she couldn't—or wouldn't—answer. I can tell you what you want to know." Earlier in the day a representative of the Forest Service had come on board when we docked in Ketchican. Her job was public relations, and her subject was the Tongass National Forest, which lined much of the shore of the Inside Passage that we were passing through. After her talk she agreed to answer questions people might have about the logging of the area. When I asked her which companies had cut much of the timber in the Tongass, she said vaguely, "Oh, we have lots of timber mills in southeastern Alaska. I can't keep up with all their names." This from a woman who worked for the Forest Service and had lived all her life in southeast Alaska, where the timber industry—along with fishing, mining, and tourism—has long been the mainstay of the economy.

Nathan spent about an hour explaining bits and pieces of the complex relationship between the Forest Service and two large timber companies: Ketchican Pulp Corporation (KPC), a subsidiary of Louisiana Pacific, and the Japanese-owned Alaskan Pulp Corporation (APC). Nathan had spent some twenty years in the timber industry, first as a logger and then as a foreman. As a union member he'd worked for the big companies, and he'd worked as an independent logger for small companies. It was from Nathan that I first learned about the fifty-year contracts that the Forest Service negotiated with KPC and APC.

After World War II the U.S. government wanted to secure a stable population in southeast Alaska by establishing a logging industry. Unprecedented contracts were negotiated guaranteeing KPC and APC a steady flow of timber in exchange for building mills and providing employment in the little towns along the Inside Passage. These contracts won't expire until early in the twenty-first century, but the consequences of four decades of logging the Tongass are just beginning to be understood. Approximately 80 percent of all the pulp from this forest has been shipped to Japan. The contracts require that logs must be processed in the United States, but smoothing a log on one side is all that is necessary for it to become an officially "processed" product called a "cant log." More than 90 percent of the cant logs from the Tongass have been shipped to Japan.

"Do you still work in the timber industry?" I asked Nathan.

"Not any more. Now I'm a hunting guide. Grizzlies and mountain goats."

"Are you afraid of the big bear?"

"Look, I don't even listen to bear stories. I can't afford to. My living depends on taking other people out to kill the suckers. If they can't kill 'em, I have to. I'm never out there without a .338. It's a powerful gun, good for big game: elk, moose, grizzly, cape buffalo. Hunters that pay me big money are there for the trophy. They go for the heart, and sometimes it's very hard to kill a bear that way. If I have to take over, the bear is already charging. I put the bullet right between the eyes. To hell with the trophy."

"That must be scary."

"Yeah," he said. "Sometimes I can't believe I've done it. You know, I was a flower child. I've had this ponytail since 1968. I lived in Haight Ashbury. We talked about making love, not war. I came to Alaska in search of freedom. I wanted to do my own thing and live in peace. And I've spent my whole adult life cutting down trees and killing animals. It doesn't make sense."

As the ferry was pulling up to the dock in Wrangle, Nathan extended his right hand as he produced his card with the other. "Nice talking to you. Let me know if you hear of anyone who wants to kill a bear. I can almost guarantee it."

On the boat and in every town I visited, I asked about bears and people were quick to tell me bear stories. A few ended with maulings, maimings, or death. More common, however, were stories of a near miss:

"I was fishing with my son when we saw a big sow coming straight for us. Just as I had given up on finding a tree to climb, she swerved off the path and disappeared in the woods."

"When I saw the bear she was already charging. I dropped to the ground in a fetal position. The bear sniffed around me and then left me cringing there."

Less common were the "wonderful things I've seen bears do" stories:

"Once in the Brooks Range I watched two half-grown bears climb up the side of a snowfield and then slide down on their backsides. When they got to the bottom, they started back up and did it over and over again."

"I once saw a huge male grizzly lying on its back on the banks of the McNeil River playing with a feather. Somehow it was able to hold the feather way up over its head and then watch it flutter down to its big belly. Then it would lift the feather and drop it again."

"A bear broke into the terminal building for the pipeline in Valdez, wandered through the offices taking M&Ms and other candy from desktops. Then it pushed its way into the ladies' room and couldn't get out."

"A sow with only one cub spends more time playing with it than does a mother with twins or triplets. I once watched a sow let her cub jump up and down on her belly like it was a trampoline. If the cub started to go off the side, she would swat it back to the middle."

By the time we docked in Juneau, I'd collected the names of about two dozen people. Mary Beth and David had invited me to visit them in Anchorage, and the ship's purser had urged me to come visit Gustavus, the tiny town across from Juneau where he lives. Those days among strangers on the waters of the Inside Passage marked a new phase of my journey. Everyone I met had something to teach me—about wilderness, about starting a new life, about living with uncertainty.

Juneau

〜〜〜〜 SET IN A crescent of land tucked into the side of Mount Juneau, the capital city of Alaska is surrounded by natural beauty rarely seen anywhere but in remote wilderness. The mountains that form the backdrop to the city are adorned with prodigious waterfalls that roar over the rocks and plunge into invisible canyons below. The morning I arrived in Juneau, clouds shrouded the peaks and a fine mist permeated the air. Still, I was able to make out the glacier-studded peaks to the east and the islands of the Inside Passage to the west. I checked into the Driftwood Lodge around eight in the morning and was told that I could come back and claim my room around eleven. I left my pack, put on a full suit of rain gear, and set out to explore this town of less than thirty thousand inhabitants. That morning there were no cruise ships in the harbor, the legislature was not in session, and the streets were almost empty.

I walked along the waterfront on Egan Drive and then seven blocks up a steep hill to the edge of Juneau, where I could look down at the town and up at breathtaking cliffs and waterfalls. From there I climbed another several hundred yards to the Gold Creek Bridge, which spans the rushing waters of the creek far below. Just crossing the bridge sent adrenaline rushing through my blood, and I started up the hill on the other side into the wildest forest I'd ever seen. Fog and clouds rested on the tops of hills and obscured the higher peaks. Rain fell steadily. I'd been told that bears cross the bridge and wander down to the houses just below to raid garbage cans. One house I'd passed toward the top of the hill had a "Bear Crossing" sign nailed to the mailbox. I thought of a coffee shop I'd passed some time ago and turned back toward town.

At the bottom of Franklin Street I found an espresso bar called the Yoga Den. I ordered a double latte and a bran muffin and took a seat where I could look out over the crowded room so that I could easily survey the clientele and indulge in a little eaves-dropping. The crowd was diverse: men in three-piece suits and women dressed for success, fishermen just off the water, men and women in hiking gear, and a variety of young people, some reading serious-looking books, others having solemn conversations.

That afternoon I wandered over to the public library, a striking building at the edge of the harbor. There I spent several hours reading Alaskan newspapers, skimming through books about forestry and mining, and looking out at the harbor and the islands beyond from the huge plate-glass windows that formed the front wall of the building. The next day, when a cruise boat arrived and docked directly in front of the library, blocking the spectacular view, I realized how lucky I was to have first experienced the city without the hordes who swarmed off the boat and crowded into the art galleries, souvenir shops, and bookstores. "On those days," one local woman told me later, "we just stay out of town. Now don't get me wrong, we're glad to have the tourists. They help keep us afloat, and without them the galleries couldn't survive. There's just not room for them and us at the same time. But the tourist season is over at the end of September, and then Juneau belongs to us for about three months—until the legislature arrives in January."

Except for other travelers I'd met on the boat, I didn't know a single soul in the state. Eager to learn about wilderness in south-east Alaska, I set out to find people who could teach me something. Early in the morning of my second day, I phoned the local office of the Sierra Club Legal Defense Fund and got the names of several people who might help me understand both the timber and mining issues in the region. By early afternoon I was sitting in the office of David Katz, the head of the Southeast Alaska Conservation Council (SEACC), from whom I learned that the most pressing concerns stemmed from the plans of a Canadian company called Echo Bay to reopen the Alaska-Juneau Mine, which had been closed since 1944. Later that day I talked with Darlene McCarthy, SEACC's authority on mines, who explained how reopening the mine would mean jobs, and for a while, an infusion of money into the local economy, but it would also mean the destruction of pristine wilderness areas very near town and possibly the poisoning of the water supply as well. After a long struggle, SEACC and other conservation groups eventually prevailed: the EPA denied Echo Bay the permit it needed to begin mining in 1995.

Once again I heard about the fifty-year contracts between the Forest Service and two large timber companies, and I also learned about the Native Claims Settlement Act of 1971, which resulted in the timbering of large areas by native people. Although one Forest Service employee denied that clear-cutting takes place, others explained that it has been common practice to level huge areas that were once prime habitat for wildlife. Excessive logging has resulted in declining populations of bears, deer, wolves, birds, and small animals, and it has caused serious silting in streams where salmon once spawned.

Congress passed the Alaskan National Interest Conservation Act (ANILCA) in 1980, which doubled the size of the National Park System and added tens of millions of acres to the National Wildlife Refuge System. With the passage of the act, Alaska had more designated wilderness than all the other states combined—more than fifty-eight million acres. But wilderness is never entirely safe. Extensive timber resources, minerals, and oil and natural-gas deposits will always be vulnerable to those who would rather profit from the wild than preserve it.

Much of my time in Juneau was spent in meetings with federal-agency officials and environmentalists, but not a day went by that I didn't put on rain gear and head up the hill into the wildlands that began just at the edge of the city. Not even the steady rains could keep me away from the overpowering beauty of the mist-shrouded forests, waterfalls, mountains, and rushing streams that surround Alaska's capital.

Haines

〰〰〰 By FRIDAY I was ready to move on, and around midday I boarded the ferry for Haines, a little fishing town some four and a half hours north. I checked into the Captain's Choice Motel just in time to clean up and make it to my appointment with Gershon Cohen, who ran the now defunct Alaska Clean Water Alliance (ACWA), then the only nonprofit organization in Alaska totally devoted to monitoring the ecological impact of fishing, timber, and mining on the waters in and around Alaska. At the time of my visit, mining was at the top of his agenda because of the plans to reopen the gold mine in Juneau. The state of Alaska has never developed the antidegradation regulations required by the Clean Water Act of 1977, which meant that industrial water pollution went unchecked. Cohen's goal was to force the state to set up appropriate clean-water regulations and to compel the mining industry to comply with them. Through his work with ACWA, Cohen played an important role in halting efforts to reopen the Juneau mine.

"People live simply here," he said. "As long as fish are plentiful, there will be enough money coming into the town to keep it going, but pollution from mines and overfishing could kill it."

After meeting with Cohen I went back to the motel, took a hot bath, opened a beer, and called Jerome. Despite four thousand miles and a four-hour time difference between us, we laughed and swapped funny stories to celebrate my fifty-third birthday. He told me that he'd been thinking about our conversation at the

Mazama Inn and had begun to notice how rushed he was most of the time. He didn't want to go on living that way. I told him change takes time and that I thought I'd broken through some barriers myself since I'd left for Alaska.

The next morning, after eating a stack of pancakes at a breakfast place implausibly called the Bamboo Lounge, I walked the mile and a half out of town to visit the people Gershon Cohen had referred to as "the grandparents of the environmental movement in southeast Alaska." Ray and Vivian Menaker had been in Haines long enough to have a street named for them: theirs was the last house on Menaker Road. As I left houses behind and walked in the steady rain through a heavily forested area, I began to fear that I'd missed a turn. But finally I saw Vivian standing by the side of her large, lush garden of broccoli, cabbage, onions, garlic, cauliflower, lettuce, and parsnips.

"I was afraid you'd gotten lost," she said, as she welcomed me into the cozy house where she and Ray had lived for almost forty years. There was a crackling blaze in the sitting-room fireplace. We gathered around the fire, and for the next two hours Ray and Vivian told me stories about their struggles to set guidelines for logging the state and national forests in the area, to prevent logging practices that destroy critical areas around streams and rivers, and to preserve sufficient forest habitat for the abundant wildlife in the area. They were especially proud of the work they had done to establish the fifty-thousand-acre Alaska Chilkat Bald Eagle Preserve, which was set aside in 1982 as a refuge and feeding ground for the thousands of eagles that come there every fall to feed on the chum salmon run in the Chilkat River. The fishing and tourist industries are essential to the economy of Haines, and many tourists come just to see the eagles.

While Vivian spread out maps showing the plans for future logging in the area, Ray showed me photographs, including one of a moose that a few days before had been just outside the house. When I asked if they had grizzlies nearby, Vivian exclaimed, "Oh my, yes. They're everywhere. Why, just a few weeks ago I had a little cub out there in my strawberry patch. I knew its mother had to be nearby, so I didn't dare go chase it away. It ate every berry in no time. And speaking of eating, let me get us some lunch."

In a matter of minutes Vivian had spread out cold chicken, a bowl of raw vegetables from the garden, homemade bread, and jam. Ray proudly announced that he had killed the chicken the day before and that Vivian had grown the vegetables, made the jam, and baked the bread. When I offered to help clean up, Vivian explained that there would not be any hot water until night, when she fired up the woodstove to cook dinner. While we ate they told me about coming to Haines in 1954, expecting to stay a year. Instead they built this house two years later, raised four children, and worked for years as public-school teachers. Then they retired early, Ray to concentrate on the *Chilkat Valley News,* a newspaper he had founded, and Vivian to do environmental work.

When I noticed the spinning wheel at the edge of the fireplace, Vivian offered, "Ray spins; I weave and sew." Like many people in Alaska, Ray and Vivian are largely self-sufficient. They grow most of their fruits and vegetables, raise chickens for meat, and make their clothes from scratch.

Ray had to go to the local radio station where he reads stories on the air every Saturday afternoon, and he took me along to show me the highlights of the local arts center—a 250-seat theater, a prized Steinway, dance studios, and the radio station. Then he introduced me to the afternoon volunteer disk jockey, a woman about his age who had just finished a rock-and-roll program. Not everyone in Haines has telephone service, and the radio station serves as a communication center as well as a source of news and entertainment. Several times a day the station broadcasts messages, both public and private. When I was there, Ray called in an announcement to a friend of his that he wanted me to meet. "Ray Menaker would like Dan Henry to drive over to meet a visitor from Atlanta." Many people in Haines listen to the personal messages just to keep up with what's going on in town.

After saying good-bye to Ray, I walked back to town to find a copy of the local newspaper. There on the front page were two bear stories: The headline was "Bear Grabs Chilkoot Camper," the other, "Bears, People Drawn to River." Bears were always making news in this part of the world, but an attack in the state-park campground and the appearance night after night of a dozen or so large animals that came to feed on the salmon at the river was front-page news. The second story reported that people not only were gathering at the river to watch the bears but were shining large spotlights on them. The spotlighted bears, becoming irritable and aggressive, were attacking each other.

The more humans invade the bears' feeding grounds, the more habituated the animals become to people and the more danger there is to both species. But the bears have the most to lose. I knew from childhood visits to the Great Smoky Mountains that habituated bears are less likely to be startled or frightened by humans and less likely to run, even from hunters. They are therefore more likely to be killed.

Here was a dilemma. I could have gone with locals who had offered to take me to watch the bears. With the safety of a vehicle nearby, I would not have taken much of a chance. But somehow watching bears that way was not a very attractive prospect. By not going and by speaking out against the practice, I could add my voice to those of the people who feel that wild animals should be left alone. So what did I do? Easy. I took the high moral ground and stayed away from the bears—which is to say that, car or no car, I was afraid of grizzlies, especially those that had been annoyed by gawking crowds with spotlights.

The next day I was sitting in the Mountain Market, a combination health-food store and coffee shop, when I overheard a woman talking at the next table. "Well, I heard something outside my tent. At first I thought it was a person, and I was really scared. Then I thought, no—it's only a bear. I was thinking that if I made a noise I might piss it off. So I lay there very still and quiet, waiting for it to sniff around and go away. Then I remembered that a guy I knew told me when he comes on a bear, he faces it straight on and tightens his stomach muscles. I tried to tighten mine and nothing happened. About that time I felt teeth sink into my leg. I screamed, and it let go. Then I started making all kinds of noise. You know, I yelled, banged things together, and eventually found my keys and ran to my car."

The woman paused for a minute to let the details sink in while the others at the table peppered her with questions. Then she continued her story, explaining how she drove herself to the police station, where the woman dispatcher was very sympathetic but a state trooper asked her if maybe she had been swatted rather than bitten.

"I knew that what I felt was strong jaws and teeth, but this man made me feel like a squeaky little girl crying wolf rather than bear," she said indignantly. "I didn't want to make too much of a deal about it, because I didn't want this guy to go out and kill the bear. I knew I'd been bitten, but by the time I left the police station other people had their own versions of what had happened."

I waited until she came to a stopping point and then went over to the table and introduced myself to the three young women: Megan, the bear-bite survivor; Dayna, who lives alone in a cabin in the woods; and Ellen, who had just come into town. All three women had traveled to Alaska alone, and while I wanted to find out about the others, I mostly had questions for Megan. How traumatic was the experience? Did she have nightmares about bears? Would she camp again? When I asked her these questions, she played down the whole experience.

"Look, it was my fault. I should never have been camping in a tent at Chilkoot Lake. I knew there were bears there, but I didn't think they would bother me. That's what happens when people and bears get used to each other. People forget that bears are predators and that humans can be prey. And, yeah—I'll camp out again, but not where I know there are bears."

When I asked Megan why she thought the bear had attacked, she shrugged. "Who knows? I'd been working in a restaurant and hadn't taken a bath. Maybe it smelled the steak teriyaki and was looking for a meal. Maybe it was just curious."

"It's an amazing thing that happened to you and amazing that you survived," I offered.

Megan smiled and with a twinkle in her eye said, "Yeah, how many people can say they've been touched but not seriously wounded by a grizzly?"

She showed me her injured leg, and it was quite a bit more

than a "touch." She had a bad bruise, complete with puncture marks from the teeth. The doctor who finally looked at the wound confirmed that the deep bruise and tissue damage were caused by a bear's powerful jaws.

For almost three hours Megan, Dayna, Ellen, and I sat at the Mountain Market and talked about our experiences traveling alone. Dayna and Megan were twenty-three, Ellen thirty-one. Our talk meandered. Ellen told us about her spiritual quest, her exploration of her past lives, and her recent adventures in the Yukon. I asked Dayna if she felt she had knowledge of past lives, and she answered without hesitation, "Oh, yes—I have a very old soul." Megan, on the other hand, confessed to being of two minds on the subject. "I'm intrigued by the idea, but when I begin to think about it, my rational mind steps in and tells me I'm full of shit."

The subject of reincarnation, along with astrological explanations for what happens to people, recurred in Ellen's conversation. I was in the minority in having no particular interest or belief in past lives, and my attention had begun to wander. Then the talk shifted acutely when Ellen said thoughtfully, "Sometimes I think this journey I'm on is about fear—about getting in touch with fear and learning how fear works in my life. I hear bear stories and feel the fear creeping in. The other day I saw a pile of fresh bear scat in the woods when I was hiking alone. At first I thought that if the bear just took a shit here, it must have gone on somewhere else. But as I walked on, I got really scared and decided to get out of there."

When I began to talk about my own fear of bears, though, Ellen shifted gears. "Well, it sounds to me like you're obsessed with grizzlies. You may have been mauled by one in a former life. And maybe you're not interested in your past lives because terrible things happened to you that you don't want to look at."

I didn't bite, but Ellen persisted. "I may be turned around by fear sometimes, but I really know that if I meet a bear in the wilderness, the best thing to do is sit down quietly, stay calm, and send the bear good energy."

Perhaps to defuse the tension she sensed growing between

me and Ellen, Megan chimed in with a story about an archaeologist friend of hers who studied ancient cultures. She chatted on about this man's research and then out of the blue announced, "And you know what? This guy has a friend who actually took the rectal temperature of a polar bear." I resisted saying that I was sure this procedure required the use of powerful drugs, not just calming "good energy."

At this point Dayna's friend Aaron joined us and invited us to go out to a place in the forest where he was camping for the summer. He'd never seen any bears out there, he said, but there certainly could be some. Along the trail there was a good crop of wild cranberries (which grizzlies like to eat). In a matter of minutes we'd gathered up sweaters and rain gear, piled in Dayna's truck, and headed out of town and into the woods.

A thirty-minute hike uphill into the forest brought us to Aaron's camp. Decorating the site were the loose bones of two moose and several assorted smaller animals. Both Ellen and Dayna had dogs, who immediately set to fighting over the bones. Aaron and his friend had cut hemlock boughs and stripped the bark off trees to build an elaborate sweat house, which Aaron confessed they had never used.

There were, however, two huge, well-used fire rings. I thought of Donna and how effectively she had convinced me to give up campfires. I tried to explain to Aaron about campfires sterilizing the soil, but he was unmoved by my arguments, saying emphatically, "I'll tell you one thing, I'll always have a campfire when I camp out, and nothing you say is going to change my mind."

Ellen quickly sided with Aaron, "He's right. Fires, after all, are sacred elements in many rituals. I mean, fire is *spiritual,* don't you think?"

"I think fire is fire, and, yes—some people use it in their rituals. But that doesn't excuse using it carelessly or making a horrible scar on the earth like this."

Aaron finally fell silent, but Ellen continued to keep the argument alive by instructing me in the sacred rituals of "primitive" people. Just before we gathered up our belongings to leave, Ellen announced that she needed to pee, but when I began to tell her how to urinate on a rock the way Donna had taught me, she changed her mind. "I forgot, this is my moon time. I might leave blood, and blood attracts bears."

Shit, I thought, here I am in bear country with a menstruating woman. Though Ellen insisted that we walk out of the forest in meditative silence in order to feel the spirits, I continued to talk to Dayna and Aaron so that any nearby animals would know we were there and get out of the way. I was not prepared to sit quietly in front of a big grizzly and send it whatever good energy I could muster.

When we arrived at the trailhead, Dayna invited us to have dinner at her cabin in the woods, but Megan and Aaron had to work and Ellen had an unspecified prior commitment. At first I accepted, but when Dayna began to give me directions through the woods I had second thoughts. Something about the bear stories and thoughts of returning to town alone through the unfamiliar woods after dark gave me the now-familiar cold shivers. I countered by inviting her to join me for dinner in town, but she begged off, explaining that she really wanted to get home before dark.

By the time I boarded the ferry two days later, I felt at home in Haines. I'd gotten to know the woman who runs the bookstore and learned about her husband's plans to build a strong cage for people to get in to watch bears safely and enjoy what he calls "the rush without the risk." (She explained that he was afraid someone would steal his idea before he could get a patent and so was very secretive about his project.) After I'd paid a few visits to the Bamboo Lounge, the grocery store, and the library, people recognized me and asked me how things were going. Before I left, locals were greeting me on the street, calling me by my first name. "Hey, Melissa, meet us at the Mountain Market for a coffee," or "Want to go with us to watch bears tonight?"

I could imagine living in Haines. As at Holden Village, the isolation and proximity to wilderness required simple living and concern for elemental things. Like Paradise, Montana, it was a real place—a community where people knew and took care of each other.

When I left Haines, I took the ferry to the tiny gold-rush town of Skagway, just 14 miles away up the Lynn Canal but 370 miles by the highway that goes through the Yukon. There were only a few tourists in town, and I enjoyed wandering through the empty streets of the old town in the rain. There was a full moon over Skagway, but all I could see of it was a slight glow under the clouds. The next day I took a three-and-a-half-hour trip on the White Pass and Yukon Route, a narrow-gage railroad that carries tourists through the old gold-rush route to the Yukon. The trip I took was the last one of the season, as the railroad closes down the middle of September, not to reopen until mid-May. After another night in the now almost empty old town, I caught the ferry back to Juneau.

Living outdoors as I was doing before I came to Alaska, I was always conscious of the phases of the moon, but I never saw the moon in Alaska. The only clear night on the ferry coming up had been during the dark of the moon; there had been a heavy cloud cover every night since. As it turned out, I didn't see the moon again until I came to Utah, where I saw a thin crescent setting over the Wasatch Mountains. That moon would see me all the way home.

BACK TO THE WILD

Socked In, Stood Up, and Stranded

〰〰〰 I WOKE EARLY on the morning of September 22 in the Driftwood Lodge in Juneau. It was raining even harder than usual. Outside the window, fog obscured half the mountains that form the backdrop to the town and sat defiantly on top of the few buildings that are more than three stories high. The waterfalls that cascade down from the top of Mount Juneau were barely visible through the thick air.

I had returned to Juneau for two reasons—to look into a timber company's alleged tampering with its books and to learn about the toxic waste produced by gold mining. Dave Katz of SEACC had agreed to talk to me about the Forest Service's deals with timber companies to cut the Tongass, and Darlene McCarthy had invited me to hike up to a pristine place called Sheep Creek that had been proposed as a holding area for the toxic wastes the reopened gold mine would produce. I called the SEACC office and found out Dave Katz was stranded in Ketchikan. All commercial flights into Juneau had been canceled indefinitely because of the weather. Then I called Darlene. Her son had a sore throat, and she had to take him to the doctor. There was no way she could go with me to Sheep Creek. "Besides," she said, "in this weather we probably couldn't have gotten up there anyway."

My heart sank. I'd given up an opportunity to go to Prince of Wales Island to meet Doug Person, who was studying wolves there and tracking their activities. The last boat heading that way had already left Juneau. I'd come to Alaska expecting to be able to camp out, only to find a world so wet that I would have had to pitch my tent in standing water. To lighten my pack I mailed my tent and sleeping bag to general delivery in Bellingham.

Here I was stranded in Juneau, more than four thousand miles from home. My spirits sank even further. I longed to be almost anywhere other than this waterlogged place where I knew no one and didn't really know who to trust. I thought of how beautiful the weather is in Atlanta in late September, how much I'd like to be sitting in the garden early in the morning drinking coffee and reading the *New York Times.*

I was tempted to give up trying to understand the many threats to the vast wilderness known as the Tongass. After a few days of talking to lawyers, Forest Service folks, Fish and Wildlife employees, and professional environmentalists, I'd gathered a mass of generally accepted facts and some totally contradictory information. I'd seen large clear-cuts on national-forest land, with every hemlock and spruce removed—nothing left but bare, eroding rock and soil—no underbrush, no sign of life. I'd seen the narrow little bands of trees left on the shorelines to prevent tourists from seeing the devastation beyond. Yet when I asked a Forest Service information officer about logging practices in the Tongass —without ever mentioning clear-cutting—she snapped, "Any clear-cutting you've seen was done by the native corporations up here. Indians don't care about the land. They cut down every twig. You won't see that on Forest Service land."

By the time I heard this dubious pronouncement, I'd learned a lot about what has happened to the Forest Service lands in the Tongass. I'd seen aerial photographs of the clear-cuts on both national-forest land and native-corporation land. I knew that clear-cutting is the norm, not the exception. Two companies, Ketchican Pulp Corporation (KPC) and Alaska Pulp Corporation (APC), had harvested much of the high-quality timber, and the vast majority had been shipped to Japan. Repeatedly, I'd heard that APC had long claimed it was losing money on the sale of Tongass trees and that the Forest Service was compensating the company for its losses so that Alaskans would continue to have the jobs the company provided. Several people told me that APC was selling at a loss to its own parent company, which in turn was selling at a considerable profit.

Most people I talked to seemed to accept these "facts," but what happens behind the closed doors where the deals are made between the Forest Service and the timber companies and on the remote islands where much of the timbering takes place is not so clear. I'd been told on the one hand that forests are a renewable resource and on the other that logging practices in much of southeast Alaska are destroying the ability of the forest to regenerate.

One sawmill owner I met in Haines told me he'd been put out of business by Weyerhauser, which had reneged on a promise to provide him with timber.

"I used to have a good business, but they ruined me," he said. "I don't understand why everybody can't get together. If we could agree to a 250-year cycle and cut the trees so they could come back again, then we'd always have trees to cut."

I wondered whether cutting the Tongass at a sustainable rate would mean converting wild forests with abundant wildlife to tree farms. If this happened, would there be enough forage for deer or prey for wolves? Would the continual silting of streams destroy the spawning ground for salmon? Would the bears have enough to eat? And finally, would independent Alaskans be able to work cooperatively to find ways to exploit the forest resources without destroying them? I doubted it.

Dispirited, I picked up the phone and called Alaska Airlines, only to find that there would be no flights out until the weather lifted and all flights were booked for the next two days. A one-way ticket to Seattle cost $450. My car was in Bellingham, a bus ride and probably another $50 away from Seattle. In order to leave in forty-eight hours—if the weather cleared—I would have to sacrifice the ferry ticket I'd already paid for and spend at least $500. Wasting money was not something I liked to do, but my spirits were so low that I was tempted.

I'd been staring out the window for some time before it dawned on me that the rain was no longer blowing sideways and there was more light penetrating the clouds. I reconsidered my options. I could fly out in two days, retrieve my car, and head south for the sun; or I could take the ferry to Sitka the next day and spend another week trying to make some sense of Alaska's muddled wilderness issues. The ferry wouldn't leave until the next afternoon, and I'd have to sleep out on the deck, possibly in a downpour. I looked one more time at the now lightening sky, pulled on rain gear and boots, walked out into the streets of Juneau, and headed uphill to the trails that lead into the forests above. At the top end of the town—the beginning of the wild—I looked up at the raging waterfalls, down at the harbor, and out at the snow-covered peaks beyond. Entering the forest of spruce, hemlock, and cedar, I picked up my pace, knowing I would stay another week in Alaska.

You Have to Ask

~~~~~ WALKING THROUGH the forest of giant spruce at the edge of Sitka, I was drawn first by the sounds of seabirds. Thousands of them circled the mouth of the Indian River, making enough racket to muffle a normal human conversation. My brain processed only one sense at a time. After the sound I noticed the smell—the strong, penetrating stench of dead and dying salmon. It drew me to the mouth of the river, where I saw thousands of silver carcasses.

The heavy rains had washed down legions of fish that had spawned and died upstream. The mouth of the river was jammed with their bodies, which blocked the way of those fish just beginning their spawning run. As the waters receded, many corpses lined the banks. I watched the birds swoop down and grab bits of decaying flesh and fish eggs from the top of the water. I wandered along the riverbanks and noticed that the eye sockets had been pecked clean from all the carcasses lying there. I looked across the river at the grassy meadow on the other side: perfect grizzly habitat. I'd been told that they occasionally came down this far to feed on the salmon, especially after heavy rains.

As the wind began to blow rain in my face, I turned to walk upstream along a path paralleling the river. There the fish were so vigorous and determined that it was hard to imagine they too would shortly be food for the ravenous birds. But not before they had done everything possible to insure the survival of their species. Further up in the shallows, a female hovered over the sand and gravel of the river bottom, carefully inching her body into the streambed to excavate a cavity for the eggs. Floating above and around her were two males, each driven to have his sperm fertilize the eggs. Pushing each other aside, they took turns riding the water above her. Then suddenly the water became milky white. Eggs laid and fertilized. The deed was done, and the genetic heritage of at least one of the males would have a chance of survival—unless the eggs broke loose to be eaten by the birds waiting downstream or some manmade contaminant interfered with this primal rite.

A few hours later I was climbing the stairs to Larry Edwards's kayak shop over the bookstore and espresso shop in downtown Sitka. Larry was the kayak man in Sitka and was also Greenpeace's man in that part of Alaska. I'd come to see him because he was the named plaintiff in a class-action suit—*Larry Edwards* v. *Alaska Pulp Corporation.* APC owned the pulp mill that Larry claimed had polluted the waters around Sitka. Larry confirmed much that I'd already heard about the timber industry's relationship with the Forest Service and stressed the damage clear-cutting had wrought on wildlife habitat. Not particularly optimistic, he insisted on the importance of looking at the big picture. "What's needed," he told me, "is to force the Forest Service to obey the law and make sure that Congress acts to prevent the collapse of the ecosystem." The ecosystem of a waterway where salmon spawn is easily destroyed simply by clear-cutting upstream and silting the streambed. Salmon need loose gravel for spawning, not a thick layer of silt and sand.

Larry gave me the names and telephone numbers of several people in Sitka, but when I called the president of the Sitka Conservation Society, I had the following brief conversation:

"Hello, my name is Melissa Walker. I'm a writer interested in wilderness and people who work to save it. Larry Edwards suggested I call you."

"Yeah."

"Larry told me that you know a lot about how the Forest Service is helping the timber industry destroy the wilderness, and I'd like to talk to you about it."

"Well, I don't want to do that."

"Okay. But could you tell me what made you say that?"

"No, I won't."

"Is it because you don't think I'm who I say I am?"

"Yes, that's right. Good-bye."

With a lawsuit pending, he probably had good reason to be suspicious. What was really surprising was that so many people trusted me. Larry Edwards, Gershon Cohen, Dave Katz, and others had all rummaged through their files and made copies of various documents for me. When I asked Larry why he trusted me, he said, "I don't have anything to hide."

Later that day I phoned Larry Edward's friend, the writer Richard Nelson, who talked openly and at length about both his writing and his commitment to "using the land appropriately while nurturing its wildness." He was working on a book about deer and was very interested in hunters who kill animals for food but do so with respect and humility. *Heart and Blood: Living with Deer in America,* published in 1997, helped me understand that hunting for some people is a way of coming to terms with themselves as predators.

During my time in Sitka I talked to local people, browsed in the bookstore, and hung out in the espresso shop. Sitting by a window overlooking the sea, I read through piles of *Alaska Magazine* in the local library. Every morning and every afternoon, I hiked out to the edge of town and wandered through the Sitka spruce forest to the mouth of the Indian River to watch yet again the spectacle of life and death staged by salmon struggling to keep their species alive.

One afternoon at the nearby visitor's center of the Sitka National Historical Park, I began talking with a pretty redheaded woman who was also alone. I offered to walk through the forest with her to the Tlinkit totems that are placed throughout the trees. We walked and talked for some time before we introduced ourselves. When I told her my name, she looked at me with a half smile and said, "My name is Pandora." Thinking that she was teasing me, I asked whether her mother knew what she had done to her. "I don't think she did," Pandora answered seriously. Before we left the forest, we agreed to meet for dinner that night.

Pandora was an anthropologist and had spent the last four months or so in Anchorage working as a consultant for Exxon in the trial over damages from the Valdez oil spill. Her job was to assess the damage to native populations. Much of what had happened was privileged information, though, and so we talked about books—Pandora was reading a biography of John Muir; I was reading Richard Nelson's *The Island Within.* She told me about the wild places she'd been and eventually spoke of more personal matters. Since she had long been an academic anthropologist, I asked her if people gave her a hard time for serving as a consultant for Exxon.

"Some people can't get beyond thinking of Exxon as the Darth Vader of the corporate world, so, yes—they give me a hard time. But I tell them even Darth Vader needs good advice."

We talked about what was publicly known about the trial and whether the six-billion-dollar settlement would stick. She thought it would be reduced. I steered away from asking questions that I assumed Pandora was bound not to answer. I was glad to learn that she would be taking the ferry back to Bellingham in two days. We would have more time to talk then.

The trip from Sitka to Bellingham was a visual wonder. We moved from rainbow to rainbow and watched whales spouting and diving. Schools of dolphins regularly played in our wake, and elephant seals occasionally surfaced near the boat. One night, however, the fog was so thick that the captain had to drop anchor in the middle of the channel, where we waited more than fifteen hours for the fog to lift.

Pandora and I agreed to meet on the last night for a "real drink." Standing at the bar, we each ordered a martini. The bartender got out two lowball glasses and filled them with ice. Then he took a bottle of Gordon's gin, poured about a shot in each glass, and pushed them over to us.

"That'll be eight dollars," he said.

"What about the vermouth?" Pandora asked.

"Well, you have to ask for that," he said without moving.

"Okay. Could we have vermouth?"

Searching around, the bartender finally came up with a bottle of Gallo vermouth, which he poured over the top without stirring.

"How about an olive?" Pandora persisted.

"You have to ask for that, too," he said while threading three olives on a toothpick and dropping them into Pandora's drink. "Look, lady," he said with rising annoyance, "this is the Alaskan State Ferry. Don't be so particular. You're lucky to have a bar at all."

The drink helped break down some of the constraint I felt talking about the oil spill, but even so we only skirted the subject. Since I had left Bellingham almost three weeks before, I'd heard different points of view about how long it would be before Prince William Sound returned to what it had been—if ever. Pandora thought it had already recovered remarkably, as evidenced by the rebounding populations of sea otters and birds. A developer I met on the ferry insisted that the oil spill had actually improved conditions in the sound by killing off the excess mammals that were eating too many fish. A photographer from Anchorage told me that he'd spent the first four days after the spill traveling the sound in a boat taking pictures and that he had not seen anything so terrible since Vietnam.

Rebound, recovery, healing, revival, convalescence. I had originally left home to learn about wilderness. Along the way I had recovered from the stress of an overscheduled life and I had revived the simple, focused life I'd enjoyed as a nineteen-year-old girl in the Colorado Rockies. I'd wanted to find out what Thoreau meant when he said, "In wildness is the preservation of the world," but the more I looked for ways that the wild could heal and foster human life, the more concerned I became with the reverse: how humans could preserve wildness by beginning to undo some of the damage we've done. From my experience, the transforming power of the natural world is activated as we extend love and nurture to the earth and its many forms of life. In caring for nature, we care for ourselves. We are, after all, wild, and part of the whole.

Reprieve

~~~~~ WHEN WE DOCKED in Bellingham at about nine in the morning, Pandora ran for a taxi to get to the airport and I walked over to the parking lot and opened up the van. My belongings seemed safe. The overcast sky looked as if it might clear. I stopped for gas, pulled onto Interstate 5, and headed south, determined not to stop until I found sunshine.

As I traveled south from Bellingham, I was hoping for a reprieve from gray skies and continuous rain. Just past Seattle the sun broke through, and in a matter of minutes the sky cleared. Never had clear skies looked so bright and blue. By midafternoon I saw a sign pointing to Mount St. Helens, and I remembered watching on TV the eruptions that blew its top off in 1980. I turned east on Highway 504, wound around Coldwater Ridge, parked in the visitors' center, and hiked the trail to Coldwater Lake.

Since that devastating eruption, the land, which had been reduced to a wasteland of volcanic ash, had been slowly recovering—in a decade and a half, life had returned in abundance—birds, small plants, deer, elk, and even trees. Even so, as I climbed up the trail just before dark I was overwhelmed by the devastation. When I reached the top, I sat on the edge of the ridge looking out at what not so long ago was a forest of towering hemlock and Douglas fir. In the distance the volcano was barely visible in the deepening twilight. I closed my eyes to shut out what was left of the light.

Fourteen years—a nanosecond in geologic time but an eternity in a single lifetime. I remember watching the evening news reports of the cataclysmic events following the eruption: an earthquake, mud slides, toppled logs surging down flooding rivers, smoke and ash projected many miles into the air, masses of animals burned alive. When Mount St. Helens blew, I was thirty-eight years old and unconcerned with aging. Most people I knew were healthy. My children were still children, and the turbulence of their adolescence hadn't begun. My mother was sixty-five years old, active, and strong.

The Coldwater Ridge Visitor's Center was closed when I emerged from the trail, and there were no cars left in the parking lot. I stopped to call home from the pay phone out front, but instead of Jerome's voice, I heard my own: "If you want to leave a message, leave it at the beep." I stood there in the gathering darkness and felt a wave of anxiety roll over me, and for reasons I can't explain, I punched in the code for remote messages and waited.

"Jerome, this is your mother-in-law, darling. Just thinking about you."

"Jerome, this is Nancy. I need to talk to you about a patient."

"Dr. Walker, this is the answering service. You have a message."

"Jerome, this is Mike. Just want you to know we'll be there for your birthday party. It sounds like fun."

"Dad, Monica's cooking a nice low-fat dinner tonight. Why don't you come over to eat around seven?"

As I hung up the phone, I breathed a sigh of relief. Things were going on pretty much as they had before I left. There were no messages from strange women, and when I called Richard's house, Jerome was there. I told him I was looking out on a mist-shrouded volcano, feeling sad and lonely, that Alaska had been a real stretch, and that there was a lot I didn't understand about the places I'd seen. He told me that he'd missed me before, but that he was really missing me now. He reminded me that in eight days he would meet me in the Salt Lake airport. He promised me sunshine and a bottle of champagne.

I climbed into my van and headed down the ridge, found a

campsite in a state park, and pitched my tent under a giant Douglas fir. I prepared a light supper and sat cross-legged on the ground, watching the stars appear. Owls called to each other high in the trees. It was good to be back in familiar territory, and I looked forward to sleeping on the ground again.

The next morning the sky was overcast. After making breakfast, I headed west toward the Oregon coast. As I was traveling along the south side of the Columbia River Valley, the clouds scattered, and by the time I reached the little town of Astoria, the skies were again a flawless, cloudless blue appropriate for the first day in October.

I was starving when I finally took a table at a restaurant overlooking the Columbia River. While waiting for a plate of seafood salad to arrive, I listened to the talk around me.

"What's that animal out there?" a woman at the next table asked the waitress.

"Oh, they're the nastiest animals. Slimy. There're too many of them. They eat all the fish. That's why we don't have any fish in the river anymore. I hate to say it, but sooner or later we're gonna have to kill 'em. I mean, the environmentalists won't like it. They think they know everything, but they don't know nothing."

"So what are they?"

"Sea lions. They're not good for anything. They just eat and sleep and then they die of old age. Nothing eats them. They live forever, and they don't do nothing."

"Well, I guess they do something. I mean they catch their own food."

"Not really. They just eat what comes along. And they steal. Trust me, they're nasty animals. Pigs. Just like pigs. I hate 'em."

The waitress continued this tirade with other customers. After lunch, as I explored this pleasing little town, I heard other conversations about this animal that to many locals is the nemesis of the Oregon coast.

"If it were legal to kill sea lions," a man in the coffee shop told me, "they'd be extinct. They take fish right out of nets and off hooks."

"So what's the solution?"

"You've heard of tree huggers? Well, none of 'em better take up hugging sea lions. Those animals have got to go. People here have had enough."

"How long has there been a problem?"

"Not long here. Just a few years, but down in California they've been following fishermen for at least fifteen years."

The same number of years that the fish population has been dropping, I thought, probably because of overfishing, pollution, and silting of spawning streams. Maybe there's a connection, or maybe the animals have just figured out that it's easier to take fish from fishermen. I kept my mouth shut. What did I know about sea lions? No point in getting labeled a tree hugger in this part of the world, I thought, expecting to camp out nearby. "Well, you folks sure do have a problem," I said.

That afternoon I set up my tent at Fort Stevens State Park, at the mouth of the Columbia River, in time to explore nearby Fort Clatsop, reconstructed by the National Park Service on the spot where Lewis and Clark wintered over in 1805–6. Then I took a long walk along the broad, sandy beach where Meriwether Lewis and his men foraged for food and boiled seawater for salt that cold, wet, hungry winter. On the beach just south of there, Clark and a party of men butchered a whale that had washed ashore. Sacagawea successfully pleaded with the men to take her along, arguing that she had come a long way to see the great waters and that she should be allowed to see the monstrous fish as well.

The beach was deserted except for the remains of an old wreck. I walked south for about an hour, mesmerized by the stark stretch of sea and sand stretching in front of me. To the east were tall grasses, a few trees, and scruffy-looking ground plants. A few gulls sailed idly over the water. Looking out to sea, I almost stumbled on a large dead bird with a long neck, dingy whitish-brown feathers, and a pinkish bill—an immature tundra swan, perhaps dead from eating contaminated fish or from the exhaustion of the long migration. Maybe it, too, had come from Alaska in search of sun and warmth.

By the time I made it back to the wreck, the sun was low on the horizon. I zipped up my jacket, sat cross-legged in the sand,

and watched as wisps of clouds caught the light and the sky became a kaleidoscope of moving color, gold, yellow, mauve, and orange replacing the blue and white of the afternoon sky. The last time I had watched a sunset was sitting with Jerome at the base of the Mount Shuksan glacier a month before. Seeing this sunset was like having good sex after a period of abstinence, as I was surprised all over again by the familiar miracle. Remembering the sunset ceremony on the dock at Key West, where hundreds of people gather every afternoon to applaud the setting sun as it slips yet again into the sea, I clapped my hands in solitary pleasure.

There was still enough light for a walk through the dunes and down the road to my campsite and for making a simple meal before darkness fell. There would be no moonlight until the new moon appeared five days later, but I resisted using a flashlight. Inside the tent there was no light at all, and the darkness was strangely comforting.

The next morning, as I was about to make breakfast, a woman from a nearby campsite called to me. "Hey, you're a real pioneer camping out by yourself. Come have a cup of coffee with us." I saw no way to say no to this warm invitation, so I agreed to bring my own tea and come over to her campsite. Expecting to find a couple, I was surprised to find three women instead: Joni, her thirty-something daughter Lisa, and their friend Ramona. Joni confessed that she'd felt sorry for me and had asked me over because she thought I was lonely. I explained that what I was up to required traveling alone.

"I wish I could travel alone," Joni said, "but my children won't let me. They say I'm too crazy, that I'll get myself in trouble. I've been divorced eighteen years, and I love to get out, but I always take Ramona or Lisa or some other woman friend with me."

"Why do you want to travel alone?" I asked Joni.

"I don't know," she responded, "but I do. I want to be more independent. I also want to strip down my life. I have too much stuff and too many complications. I'd love to do what you're doing."

I looked around at Joni's huge RV, complete with kitchen and sleeping space for six. "Do you think you'd be satisfied with a minivan like mine?"

"Well, maybe something a little bigger than that, you know, for the times when I would want to bring a friend along."

"I could," Ramona said. "I can do without so much stuff. Since I found out I have cancer, I've learned that things aren't so important. All I ever want now is to feel good enough to enjoy the day."

For a while we talked about how Ramona's illness has changed what is important to her, how she no longer puts off doing what she wants, and how she avoids at all costs being with what she called "toxic people." I told her that one of the benefits of my leaving home was separating from people whose negative ways drained me dry. Chemotherapy, Ramona told me, is poison enough. Then I changed the subject and explained that Jerome would join me in about a week and that I hoped he wouldn't bring too much stuff.

"Excuse me for getting personal, but you must have a very strong marriage to be able to do what you do. I mean, a man has to be pretty secure to let his wife go off on her own. I've never had a man who would let me do what you're doing."

"You're right. We do have a strong marriage. It's never been easy or uncomplicated, but it's better now than ever. And there are things Jerome likes about my being gone. He likes having evenings to himself to read, or listen to music, or do whatever he wants to do. Since I've been gone, he's figured out some of the changes he wants to make in his own life. I'm not sure he knows it, but I think he likes me much better when I'm living my own life."

"Has your husband always let you do what you want to do?"

There was the phrase—LET ME—I'd heard women of my mother's generation use when they declined to do something that in some cases they really didn't want to do anyway. I knew a few women of my generation who allowed themselves to be chained to a man's whims and expectations, and I felt really sad for those who had abdicated their freedom to the men in their lives.

"I haven't always done what I wanted to do. This is something new for me. I think women have a hard time claiming their own lives. When I've denied my own wishes, it wasn't because my husband stopped me. I stopped myself."

"What did you do that you wish you hadn't done?" she persisted.

"Well, I stayed in a job and in some friendships much longer than was good for me, and I really regret having been frantically busy. I wish I'd only chosen activities—work or play—that I could do with passion and at a comfortable pace. It's not so much that I haven't done what I wanted to do, but that I thought I could do it all."

Joni looked me straight in the eye and returned to what really interested her. "Aren't you worried about other women?"

"Once in a while. Last night, for example, I called home and Jerome wasn't there. I checked the messages on the answering machine just to see if there was anything suspicious, but there wasn't. I don't really believe I have anything to worry about."

"Don't you get lonely?" she pressed.

"Most of the time I'm too busy, too absorbed with what's going on around me to feel lonely. But sometimes I do. Eventually those feelings pass, though, and I'm always glad that I didn't give in to them."

"I guess I give in to feelings much earlier in the game," Joni admitted. "Maybe I ought to do what I want to do no matter what my children or friends think. Maybe I'll just sell this monster, get something small, and go on an adventure by myself."

Ramona chimed in at this point. "I say do what you want to do while you can. The day will come when you won't be able to."

Almost two hours passed before I went back to my campsite to get ready for the day. A few minutes later Joni pulled out in her huge RV, waved good-bye, and shouted across the campground, "Sisters of the road unite!"

That night I had a dream that I couldn't ignore. I was walking along the beach. In the distance I saw a grizzly bear walking toward me in what seemed like slow motion. As the bear got closer, it metamorphosed into a woman who looked like my younger self. She walked directly toward me, handed me her card, and then continued down the beach. Stunned, I looked down at the card, which read:

Melissa Grizzly
"It's Her Call"

Everyone I had talked to about a serious encounter with a grizzly spoke of knowing immediately that whatever happened was up to the bear. Except for experienced hunters with powerful weapons who are lucky enough to see a bear in time to get a good aim, no human can control how a grizzly encounter will go. "It's the bear's call," Leslie Golden had told me before I left for Alaska. "Nobody can do bear think," Ken had warned.

Ever since I'd watched the grizzly intently foraging for food in Yellowstone, I'd assumed that my attraction to the big bear had to do with wanting to live my own life with the same immediacy that a foraging grizzly enjoys, to do only what I could do with that kind of concentration. And yes, I wanted to make my own calls.

Like grizzlies, humans are biological opportunists. Grizzlies can spend the afternoon picking huckleberries, catching and eating hundreds of pounds of fish, attacking and tearing the entrails from a thousand-pound moose, lying on their backs in the sun swatting at a feather, or rising up on their hind legs to confront anyone who dares to threaten their right to take a particular path through the woods. Humans have similar choices, yet we often succumb to real or imagined obstacles and settle for what is familiar and near at hand.

I broke camp after only two days on the Oregon coast. Clouds were gathering in the north. Time to move on. That afternoon I headed east through the Columbia River Gorge on Interstate 84. For the first time in two months, I was driving east with the setting sun behind me.

The next day, I turned north in a light rain to visit the bizarre volcanic landscape called Craters of the Moon. At six thousand feet, the rain changed first to sleet and then to snow. In no time the already-peculiar landscape became stranger still as the snow filled in some of the shallow depressions in the black rock, giving an eerie glow to this unearthly place. Eventually, I emerged from the craters in the little town of Arco. There I headed south and followed a string of volcanoes almost the whole way to

Pocatello, Idaho. The next day I would head for the blue skies, colorful rocks, and clear, dry air of southern Utah.

I met Jerome at the Salt Lake airport, and we spent the next eight days in Zion National Park. We set up camp next to the Virgin River, where that first evening we talked into the night and kept each other warm as the first winter storm blew in and sprinkled snow on the canyon rim. Jerome was more relaxed than the last time we'd been together. Something had shifted. We camped in one place for the whole week and spent our days hiking and exploring the many side canyons in Zion. At night we sat by the river and talked about the changes we wanted to make when I came home. The last night we celebrated our thirtieth anniversary with champagne and a nice dinner at Flanigan's Inn. Like the year before, I had a carnivorous feast—elk, quail, and buffalo. This time Jerome joined me.

As in the past, Jerome's departure required that I settle back into solitude. Winter was approaching, the temperature at night was around thirty degrees, and snow had dusted the peaks above the valley. Anticipating freezing temperatures, most of the other campers had packed up and left, but I had learned how to keep warm most of the time. Without the benefit of Jerome's body warmth, I settled down in my winter sleeping bag warmed in advance by two Nalgene bottles of hot water.

The Man-Woman Thing

〰〰〰 MY FRIEND Carol had been adamant in warning me about men before I left home the first time. When I told her I didn't expect to be bothered by men at my age, she laughed. "Don't be naive. There are men who'll come on to anybody under the right conditions. You don't have to look like Jane Fonda. You don't have to have big boobs, and you don't have to be young. Trust me—if you bathe, don't look half-bad, and seem available, there will be men who consider you fair game. Even if you let your hair go gray, gained twenty pounds, and wore ugly clothes, some man would come after you. He would just be fatter and older than the ones who'll go for you now."

I confess that I'm still aware of the moment a man's attention to me moves beyond that required for the job we are doing or the subject we are discussing. Like most women I know who want it to be clear that they are unavailable, I have learned to behave in my everyday life in ways that hardly ever bring unwanted attention. I've rarely had to confront "the man-woman thing."

Being on the road was another matter. For the seven months I was away from home, I met and talked with many men, and occasionally I did perceive a seductive glance, tone of voice, or gesture. At Holden Village I introduced myself to the man who gave the opening speech at the wilderness conference. I asked him a few questions, complimented his speech, and told him I'd read one of his books, only to find that he thought I'd issued an invitation. For the rest of the conference, he saved me a seat and motioned for me to join him, asked me to sit with him for meals, and on the last evening invited me to share a bottle of wine. I walked a fine line between learning what I could from this man, who was an expert on wilderness and public lands, and holding myself sufficiently aloof to discourage an unwelcome move. Beyond that, I didn't know what to do. Somehow I managed to get through the three days without his crossing over the boundaries I had drawn, only to have him invite me to join him for a weekend on Vancouver Island as he was leaving. All the references I'd made to my husband and children were to no avail. Still trying to avoid letting him know I'd even noticed his intentions, I responded coolly that I couldn't possibly fit Canada into my plans.

When a man was only marginally interesting and not attractive, I knew exactly what to do. One evening in the Everglades, I met a man I'll call B. J. Late each afternoon, people gather on an observation deck suspended over Eco Pond to watch the birds assemble for their evening rituals. I think of it as an alternative cocktail hour; all that's missing is the tinkling of ice and the sparkle of wine glasses catching the light from the setting sun. But the folks that congregate there come for a different kind of high, the kind that comes from seeing a wild species for the first time —a least bittern climbing up a cattail, a sora rail creeping on the ground among the reeds, a pair of roseate spoonbills soaring in with a flock of white ibises.

That evening there were people from around the U.S., a couple from Australia, four young people from Germany, and a single man from Japan. Hanging from necks and perched on tripods was an impressive array of expensive optical equipment—binoculars, spotting scopes, and cameras with telephoto lenses. There was the usual comparison of equipment and talk about who had the brightest and sharpest scope or the longest lens. The small Japanese man outdid even the Germans, with a 500-millimeter lens on his camera. The Australian man had impressed the crowd with his 10 × 40 Zeiss binoculars. When I tried unsuccessfully to frame a yellow-crowned night heron with my 85-millimeter lens, I began to experience lens envy. B. J. was the only one on the deck who had no optical equipment at all, but that did not stop him from periodically pointing to a barely visible bird across the pond and asking repeatedly, "Is that a heron or an egret?"

As the light began to fade the party dispersed, people wandering back to the campground to cook supper or to the nearby Flamingo, the only restaurant within fifty miles. I had planned to treat myself to dinner at the Flamingo, and I'd reserved a table overlooking the bay. B. J. followed along and asked if he could join me. I agreed, since I'd spent much of the day alone and was not sorry to have a little conversation.

B. J. had plenty of that. He made sure I understood that he was a well-known academic in Canada, telling me about the books he had written and the one he was currently writing. Let's just say the topics were esoteric and theoretical. After an earnest attempt to explain a pet theory, B. J. asked me what I thought of his ideas. I told him they were probably very important, but that I just didn't have a theoretical mind.

It had been years, if not decades, since I'd fallen into the trap of feeling sorry for a man I really wanted to get rid of. After dinner B. J. suggested we sit on a bench at the edge of Florida Bay and enjoy the sea breeze blowing in from the south. He sat in the middle of the bench, and I perched tentatively at the very end, trying to leave as much room as possible between us. I'd made it clear that I was married, and that I planned to call Jerome later in the evening. I was beginning to feel uncomfortable, but I didn't want to go back to the campground until B. J. had left for Miami. He had not asked where I was staying, but since the only possibilities were the Flamingo Lodge and the campground, he wouldn't have much trouble finding me. He knew I was driving a white minivan. If I were to leave first, then he could follow me back to the isolated spot where my tent was pitched. Ignoring his suggestive remark that our time together (all of two hours) had been like a one-act play, I talked about the beauty of the place and waited for him to leave. Then came the hit.

"Why," he demanded, "are you sitting so far away?"

Glancing at the eighteen inches or so between us, I heard the perfect words fly from my mouth. "Because we're not going to do the man-woman thing." The silence that followed let me know that I wouldn't need to talk about my happy marriage or hold forth on the virtues of monogamy. In a matter of minutes, B. J. was talking about driving back to Miami. I walked out into the parking lot with him and watched him get in his car and turn north on the only road out of Flamingo.

Since what I wanted to do was get rid of this fellow, my spontaneous comeback was exactly the right thing to say, but there were times when I met men in out-of-the-way places that I did want to know—scientists, photographers, adventurers, rangers, hunters, ranchers, environmental activists, writers, even one publisher. Encounters with such men were much easier if they were accompanied by female companions. I had thought when I first left home that at the age of fifty-one I was no longer vulnerable to the casual come-on, and I assumed that men on the make would certainly be looking for younger women. Most of the time that seemed to be true, but not always.

Mind you, I'm not referring to the threat of assault or rape but to the threat of a compliment, a seductive glance, or a suggestive remark—what my daughter Laura calls the "hit." In the case of the self-important academic I met at Eco Pond, there was no problem. I learned all I wanted to learn from and about him over dinner. It was easy to put down B. J., but I didn't know what to do when I sensed the man-woman thing coming from a man I wanted to know better, one who might have been a valuable contact if not a friend. I'd long assumed that friendship with a man was extremely difficult to establish unless it grew out of some larger context such as shared professional interests or mutual friends. I didn't know how to handle the getting-to-know-you business with a man I met outside my home territory, especially on the rare occasions when I felt attracted to him. Only once on my travels did I experience what felt like a mutual attraction with a man I would have liked to know.

The day after Jerome left Utah I met John, a nature and wildlife photographer, in what passed for a health-food restaurant in the little town of Springdale at the south end of Zion Canyon. He was a compelling man, and after talking to him only a few minutes I knew I wanted to get to know him better. I was sitting at the table where I plugged in my computer and worked during off-hours when John came in, ordered a plate of beans and rice, and asked me what I was writing. We chatted, and I soon learned that he was based in Alaska but spent half the year in the Lower 48 photographing wildlife. In a matter of minutes he was talking about what was really important to him—wildlife, wilderness, and the souls of animals. He talked about photographing grizzly bears, polar bears, and whooping cranes. He told me amazing stories about encounters with animals and talked about the spiritual aspect of wilderness and his belief that being in wilderness helps people make the shift from conventional religion to an understanding that God is not manmade.

John and I talked for almost three hours before we said goodbye and departed for different campgrounds in Zion National Park. Two nights later his van was again outside Oscar's Deli when I went there for dinner, and again we fell into easy talk about life on the road, the necessity for solitude, and the wonders of southern Utah. He spoke of his wife, and I talked about Jerome's visit. Again night had fallen, and I was beginning to feel uneasy, not because I expected a "hit," but because I would like to have talked on into the night and I didn't know a suitable way to go about it. John had made no inappropriate remarks, nothing about having a drink back at his campground, nothing about a hike up the canyon in the moonlight. Nor did he make any move to go. So eventually I said goodnight and made up a story about having some work to do. By the time I drove back down the canyon to my campsite on the banks of the Virgin River, the full moon had climbed over the canyon walls, revealing their rosy undertones and bringing enough light into the valley for me to see the golden glow of the cottonwoods.

John had told me he would be photographing in Zion for another two weeks. Then he would be heading for the Arctic to photograph polar bears. I would be leaving in four more days. Twice I saw his van parked on the side of the road. I didn't stop and I didn't go back to Oscar's, but I haven't given up thinking about John and the exciting work he does. I would have liked to be his friend.

Tom was a different story. One morning I was writing at a corner table in the dining room at the Zion Lodge. I enjoyed working there, and the staff was very helpful, allowing me to stay long after breakfast was over. Tom came over to my table to chat with me, explaining that he was an aviation engineer but that he really wanted to be a writer. He'd written several stories and wanted to know how to go about publishing them. He wondered if at thirty-two he was too old to change careers and become a writer. Would I have dinner with him that night? It never occurred to me that with his youth and movie-star good looks he would go for a woman twenty years older than he, so I agreed to meet him at a Mexican restaurant just outside the canyon.

From the moment I walked into the Bit and Spur restaurant and bar, it was clear that Tom and I had different agendas. I was meeting a young man to talk about his writing; Tom, on the other hand, had a date. What to do? I made a few references to my family and mentioned that I would need to get back to the campground early enough to call my husband. Sitting at the bar, we drank a pitcher of weak Utah beer; then we moved from the bar to a table and ate mounds of Mexican food. Tom told me about his failed marriage and his two small children. When he talked about his plans for his own future, he was upbeat, perhaps even a little manic. But underneath his pose of confidence, I sensed despair. When he turned from his personal hopes to what he called the "big picture," the optimism dissipated. "You know, we've cut down all the trees, eaten all the fish, polluted all the water, and dirtied up the air. There's not much left. It's hard to imagine any kind of future in the long run." Then he shifted his attention from the big picture to me, and I knew it was time for me to go.

I insisted on paying the bill and gathered up my belongings, hoping to escape without a direct confrontation. Then he told me that a friend had dropped him off and he would appreciate a ride back to the lodge. There were no taxis in Springdale, and I couldn't quite bring myself to leave Tom stranded, since no one at the Bit and Spur seemed sober enough to walk across the parking lot, let alone drive safely up the canyon.

There was nothing subtle about Tom's hit. On the ride back up the canyon, he mentioned the nice bottle of chardonnay he had chilled in his room and wondered how after so many nights in a tent I could turn down the chance to stay in a comfortable bed.

"Look, Tom," I said, resisting the I'm-old-enough-to-be-your-mother routine. "You're much younger than I am, and besides, I'm married. It never crossed my mind that you were interested in me in the man-woman way. I'm sorry about the misunderstanding."

"Yeah," he responded. "You should have told me you were married. I don't care how old you are."

I looked down at the wide gold band in plain view on my left hand. What did I have to do? My marital state was really not the issue, and I was tired of defending myself by parading out my marriage, my age, or the ages of my children. I was especially tired of closing off all that men had to offer me just to avoid scenes like this one. And I was tired of hearing myself take the blame for misunderstandings. Finally, I said, "Look, if I were twenty-five, single, and looking for a man, I wouldn't come to your room for a one-night stand. Why the hell do you assume that agreeing to meet you for dinner is an invitation to seduction?" I ended this outburst without really knowing how I might act if I had been born in 1969 instead of 1941. And what if I didn't have a man waiting for me at home? Maybe I would be carrying condoms in my purse. Maybe I would drink the wine.

When I let Tom out in front of the lodge, I suppressed an urge to apologize for misleading him and said instead, "I suggest that if what you want is a relationship, you don't start with wine chilling in your room. Get to know a person first."

"That's what I was trying to do. I'd like to see you again," he said sheepishly.

"Goodnight, Tom," I said rather sternly, and drove away without telling him that the evening was not altogether unpleasant for me. There was, after all, something nice about having an attractive young man interested in me. I hadn't expected that would ever happen to me again. Back at my campsite I felt a little ashamed; maybe I'd led him on just to find out if I was attractive to a handsome man his age. Still, I'd like to figure out how to get to know men like John better without leading them to think I'm the one going for the man-woman thing. After all, I didn't want to limit my contacts to women and to men with children and the family dog in tow.

And if an interesting and attractive man should ask me to dinner? I guess I could play it almost all the way—and bail out just before the chardonnay. Or I could look him straight in the eye and say, "I assume it's not necessary to mention that I'm a happily married, middle-aged mother of two adult children. I could be a grandmother soon. We are just talking about dinner, aren't we?"

Can't Be Sure

~~~~~ EARLY THE next morning I was wakened by the yapping noise of coyotes calling out to each other as they do at dusk and dawn. I groped for a flashlight and looked at my watch. Six o'clock. I slipped out of my sleeping bag, pulled on a sweater, gloves, and hat, and made tea. This would be my last day in Zion, and I wanted to make the most of it.

As the sun came over the cliffs, warming the rocks and dispelling the frost, I felt my spirits lift. Carrying my second cup of tea, I walked down to sit by the banks of the Virgin River. Across the flowing water was a solitary doe looking my way. I had disturbed her grazing, and in a moment she stiffened and bolted away. An hour later, along the trail to Angel's Landing, I came upon a porcupine stretched out on the limb of a tree, munching on a leaf. This solitary, usually nocturnal animal seemed as oblivious to my presence as to the rising sun. It would be a day full of wonders. Sinking down into the grass at a comfortable distance from the still-feeding porcupine, I looked up at the canyon walls, whitened in places with a dusting of snow. As I gazed up, the streaks of white began to fade, exposing the reds, oranges, and golds of Zion. In a matter of minutes the rocks took on a fiery glow.

There is a trail along the Virgin River that ends at what is called the Narrows, where only a few feet separate the quarter-mile-high sides of the canyon. By midmorning there would be crowds of people on this easy trail, but I managed to get there early. I never tired of the daily ritual of watching the darkened rocks glow and then brighten in the full light of day. That last morning of my first of many trips to Zion, I watched a pair of dippers dive and disappear under the water, searching the river bottom for the aquatic insects and larvae that make up their diet.

Sitting on a rock jutting out into the river, I was acutely aware of the chasm that separates modern humans from most other creatures. While we have the advantage of being able to enter their habitats, they cannot enter ours without risking their lives. In the almost seven months that I'd been living mostly outdoors, I'd never once been in a situation when I thought my presence was welcomed or desired by wild animals. Yet, like other people I knew, I was attracted to the idea of communing with nature. It was tempting to imagine that nature responds in some way to us, that there is some kind of interchange between humans and elements of the natural scene—the river, bird, snake, or doe. But I know it's not true. With the exception of domestic animals and those wild critters that have learned that we might provide them with food, I knew of no animals that could possibly be better off because of my presence. I could, however, think of several attitudes that creatures in the wild might have toward us—that we are predators, that we are prey, that we might have food they want, that we are curiosities and worth a little investigation, that we are nuisances to be avoided. Most animals seemed to lean toward the last attitude and prefer to be left alone.

The rocks that formed the canyon where I sat were formed in geologic time by the invasive habits of water, wind, and ice. Millennium after millennium of hard freezes and quick thaws, storms, blizzards, and endlessly flowing water had carved out this canyon and hundreds of others in southern Utah and northern Arizona. Humans have had next to no impact on these ancient processes. Animals, however, are immediately affected by the ways of humans. We disturb their young, their habitats, their breeding; we kill them for food, sport, and perversity; we destroy their food and poison their water; we cut highways across their migration paths and pollute the air they breathe. Even if we could communicate meaning to wild creatures, I would have trouble knowing what to say that would improve their lives except to warn them that humans can be dangerous. But they seem to know this already.

Earlier that summer, Jerome and I were hiking in the Smokies when a newborn fawn appeared out of the brush and began following along behind Jerome. It was tempting to think that the fawn was following some primal instinct to connect with a two-legged creature, but I suspect that it was just confused. Having been in the world little more than a day, it had not developed the discrimination necessary for survival. Even as a child, I somehow knew that wild animals have no real connection with humans. The frogs that I caught, the flying squirrel that I raised, the rattlesnake that coiled and raised its head to frighten me, and the lightning bugs that I kept in jars—none would have sought me out. Deer and their young, whales and dolphins, wolves and grizzly bears would all be much better off without people; but people is what they've got—people and the consequences of our careless ways.

Once when I was breaking camp early one morning, a lone raven walked out of the nearby trees dragging one wing as if it were injured. At first I thought the bird was faking to lure me away from its nest, but then I remembered that no bird would produce a clutch of eggs with winter coming on. Circling my campsite, cocking its head and croaking loudly from time to time, the bird was surely begging, having learned that people who are breaking up camp are more likely to throw it scraps than those who are just settling in. Dragging its wing must have worked before, but not with me. Pulling away, I looked back just in time to see the raven spread both wings and fly up into a nearby pine, croaking loudly as it went.

There is really nothing inspiring about the occasional bird, coyote, squirrel, chipmunk, gray jay, raven, deer, or bear that has learned to associate people with food. These animals, like the fawn, are confused. They don't know that the same creatures that dispense bread crumbs, sugar, or carrots might also distribute arrows, bullets, or poison. Nor do they know that a steady diet of human food is sometimes fatal.

How can I be sure that wild animals aren't capable of making spiritual connections with the human world? I can't be sure, but something about the way they scurry off the path into bushes and under rocks suggests to me that, more than anything, wild animals want to be left alone. I could be wrong. Maybe for the bear, the bird, the snake, or the rabbit, the exquisite moment when a human being looks it straight in the eye is worth the farm. But I don't think so.

I left Zion early in the morning. By 10:00 A.M. I had crossed into Arizona and picked up State Highway 89 through the Navajo Nation. Just south of the little town of Cameron, I turned west again toward the Grand Canyon. A year before I had sat alone under an overcast sky on Bright Angel Point on the north rim, but when I arrived at the south rim on October 23, 1994, the sky was blue, the air clear, and the canyon was, indeed, grand. I walked along the rim far enough to lose the crowds and found a spot where I could actually see the Colorado River a mile below. I've been in many landscapes that seemed to beckon me, but not this one. As I watched the afternoon light fade over the canyon, I felt small and insignificant. Instead of calling me down into its depths, the canyon seemed to say, "Step back. You are nothing in this place where you could so easily die. Your death might not even be noticed."

I claimed a campsite in a nearly empty campground. Night temperatures were dropping into the twenties, and few people seemed to want to endure the cold. I pitched a tent among ponderosa pines, put on a sweater and jacket, and then wandered back to the El Tovar Hotel for dinner. Even though I was dressed in hiking clothes, I was taken to a window table large enough for two, where I sipped a glass of wine and watched the sun set over the canyon. "What good luck," I said to the waiter, referring to the window table. What incredible good fortune, I said to myself, thinking of this place and my life. A couple of hours later, full and sleepy, I paid the bill, tipped generously, and handed the waiter my Nalgene bottle, asking him to fill it with boiling water.

Sunrise at the canyon is not so well attended as sunset. The temperature the next morning was in the mid-twenties, but the sky was clear. I arrived at the rim in near darkness a little before 6:30 A.M., about fifteen minutes before sunrise. There was only one other person nearby, an elderly man from England. We stood silently in the darkness several yards apart. A few minutes later the first rays of the sun began to illuminate the walls, and as the spectacle of light and color progressed, he looked over at me and said, "I've wanted to see this since I was a little boy." Tears welled up in his eyes. "It's like being present at the dawn of time."

Back in the El Tovar dining room, I took seriously the Park Service's advice that people who plan to hike in the canyon should eat a hearty breakfast and carry as much water as possible. After fresh orange juice, good coffee, and something called a Navajo taco served with piles of scrambled eggs and black beans, I was ready for the day.

By 9:00 A.M. I was cautiously descending into the canyon on the South Kaibab Trail and hiked to Cedar Ridge, the place where I—like most hikers—turned around. The trail was wide, steep, and crowded. Here families, groups of young people, older couples, groups of friends, and solitary hikers like me were out on a long-anticipated adventure into the inner canyon. Leaving behind the ponderosa pine and Gambel oak at the top, I soon found myself in the Upper Sonoran zone of piñon pine, juniper, and sagebrush. Below was the Desert Riparian zone along the Colorado River, surrounded by the Lower Sonoran desert world of cacti—ocotillo, barrel cactus, and cholla. On the trail I met rim-to-rim hikers who repeatedly test themselves against the rigors of the canyon, descending from the north rim and coming up on the south side, always trying to break their previous record. Others had come from halfway around the world for the once-in-a-lifetime experience they'd dreamed of for years. I emerged from the canyon in time to see the sunset from the top. Sitting on a rock close to the edge as the sun began to sink and the rocks to glow, I vowed to come back again.

Two years later Jerome and I did come back together, and we were lucky enough to get the last two reservations in bunkrooms at Phantom Ranch at the bottom of the canyon. We started our first day in freezing temperatures in the campground on the south rim, ate our lunch in warm sunshine at Cedar Ridge, and drank the recommended gallon of water each in the eight hours it took us to get to the hot desert at the bottom. That night around the dinner table at Phantom Ranch, we ate huge quantities of food and talked to the hikers who were there from all over the world — Australia, Sweden, Holland, and the U.S.

As I write this in the summer of 2001, I'm about to leave for what will be my fifth trip to the canyon, and fortunately I'll be more than content to descend into the canyon on foot. But if I were an expert rafter with a sturdy boat and reliable crew, I would not be able to launch it on the Colorado. Instead, I would be allowed to get on a waiting list that promises to save me a place twenty years out.

Since I first sat shivering and alone on the north rim in 1993, I've learned something about the controversies that surround efforts to preserve the wildness of the canyon, which to this day does not have any designated wilderness. The National Park Service, however, has proposed about a million acres for wilderness, the first step toward inclusion in the National Wilderness System. The agency has not yet taken the steps needed to protect the canyon and the river that created it.

Why not? No one knows for sure, but as with any wilderness designation, there are many interest groups pushing for policies that will allow them to use the canyon as they please. The most vocal of these are commercial outfitters who take people down the river in giant motorized pontoon rafts that carry up to thirty people. In the season — late spring through early fall — there may be as many as eight rafts launched on the river at a time. With trips lasting at least seven days, there could easily be fifty boats carrying over a thousand people: that's a noisy craft for every four miles of the two-hundred-mile trip.

So much for a wilderness experience. Ninety percent of all permits issued during the high season go to commercial groups who have a big financial stake in keeping more than a lion's share of the limited permits. Wilderness designation that includes the river could put them out of business. It could also allow ordinary folks with nonmotorized rafts to get the permits for which they now have to wait two decades or more.

Talking to the Thunder Gods

〰〰〰 AFTER LEAVING the Grand Canyon, I drove all the way across the Navajo Nation and spent the night camped near Canyon de Chelly. The temperature dropped into the low twenties, and a strong wind made for a cold night. Wrapped in a winter sleeping bag, hugging my Nalgene bottle full of hot water, I dreamed of home. Hugo, golden and bursting with canine vitality, bounding out the door to meet me as I returned. Jerome, bringing up a breakfast tray and the *New York Times* for us to share in bed on a rainy Sunday morning. The whole family gathered around a dinner table swapping stories. Blooming peach trees, cypress swamps, the smell of honeysuckle lying on the air. A red clay road winding through kudzu, cotton fields, and endless acres of pines. Images of my mother, young again, flickered through the dreams. When I woke the next morning, it seemed I'd dreamed all night. Dreams of home.

Several days later, I joined a group of assorted folk for a three-day environmental workshop near Santa Fe organized by Michael Last, an environmental lawyer from Boston. We spent part of the time in gatherings discussing sustainable living and the rest hiking in the mountains, tracking animals, and in an unexpected storm, confronting the thunder gods. The outdoor part of the workshop was led by John Stokes, a man who seems to leave a lasting impression on everyone who meets him. John exudes generative energy, and women and men, young and old, are attracted to his vitality. One woman I know talks of how he spreads magic dust wherever he goes. Maybe he does. For sure, John Stokes is a sexy guy, even though there was nothing about his behavior to suggest that he was about to make a pass at me or anyone else. He let us know that he was committed to the woman in his life and that he was crazy about his little girl, Jade.

A storyteller, musician, and master tracker, John Stokes fills a niche on the planet that I didn't know existed before I met him. After attending Princeton, John went off to Australia to learn tracking from aboriginal peoples; after returning, he founded the Tracking Project, a nonprofit organization serving young people and adults. His students participate in ceremonies of spiritual healing and appreciation of earth, fire, water, wind, plants, and creatures. As a professional tracker and wilderness guide, he collaborates with Native American men from various tribes to teach people to track animals and to recognize and interpret the signs they leave on the earth. With the help of the thunder gods, John can also scare you almost to death.

On one of our outdoor outings, when a violent thunderstorm came up suddenly, he urged ten other people and me to take cover in a cave. We were hiking up to the ruins of an Anasazi pueblo at the top of a mesa high in the Jemez Mountains west of Santa Fe. Just as we came out above the trees, I heard the first thunder roll. John and the others acted as if nothing was happening, but all I could think of were the many rules that we were defying by continuing up that exposed ridge with a storm brewing. I called to John and suggested we go back down until it was over.

"Not to worry, Melissa," he said in a comforting tone. "I'll talk to the thunder gods."

I had no confidence in the thunder gods, but somehow John succeeded in keeping me moving in an upward direction. As soon as I saw a lightning bolt, I began to count—one, one thousand; two, one thousand; three, one thousand . . . ten, one thousand. Then came the thunder. Oh, well, I thought, it's two miles away. Besides, John must know something I don't know about the direction of the winds. Though I wanted to believe that the storm was blowing away from us, I could clearly see the clouds thickening and the sky getting dark. We were still climbing the ridge and were maybe two hundred feet from the top of the mesa when the rain and hail began to fall. John pointed to an overhang and led the group into what looked like a shallow cave. All I could hear was Ken Clanton's voice saying, "Lightning travels through the ground, so you should never go into a cave. Some people don't know that, but I'm the guy who takes them out in body bags."

Some people don't know that, I thought. "John, I don't think it's safe to go in that cave. I'm heading back down," I shouted. I recalled more advice that Ken had given me the year before. "If you can't get all the way down, look around for the highest spot—a hill, mountaintop or ridge—and move at least halfway down it. Get away from the tallest tree by at least half its height. Balance on the rubber soles of your boots. Squat, don't sit, and don't put your hands on the ground. Take anything metal off your body— keys, belt buckles, cameras—and leave them some distance away.

One, one thousand; two, one thousand . . .

"Melissa," I heard John shout one last time, "Come on up here. The hail is more likely to kill you than the lightning. It gets to be the size of baseballs up here."

I sat out that storm some five hundred feet down the side of the mountain. Looming behind me was the sheer wall of rock soaring up to the flat-top mesa. Extending outward on either side but maybe a mile or more away were the arms of other massive red rock formations, and from where I was perched, I could see the lightning repeatedly striking the high ridges on either side. Crouched there, balancing on the bottoms of my feet, I felt a strange calm with an edge of exhilaration. Once I heard thunder crashing directly behind me, and I thought I felt something like a wave of energy pass by and through my body. Probably lightning had hit the mesa where we were heading. I thought of John and the others in the cave below the mesa. For the next few minutes I felt more intensely alive than I could remember ever having felt before. Then I heard Ken's voice again. "The human body is an excellent lightning rod, mostly water." Maybe I'd die, but if so, it wouldn't be because I didn't do everything I knew to do in order to stay alive.

I had never been one to court near-death experiences, and weathering this storm felt like an opportunity for life. But I had recently experienced other storms that felt much more like death. A few months earlier I was on a commercial flight from south Florida to Atlanta when the pilot announced that we would be in a holding pattern for some time in order to avoid heavy thunderstorms over the Atlanta area. For two hours we circled. There was a lot of turbulence, and the passengers were unusually quiet. Finally we began the approach into the Atlanta area in what was still a very stormy sky. The flight crew never announced what was happening, but the descent, which seemed to go on forever, was rough. I noticed a grown man in a yarmulke praying, and the woman sitting next to me took my hand while reassuring me—or herself—that she was a Catholic and she knew everything would be all right. Then the lightning hit, and a ball of fire rolled down each side of the plane. I later learned that commercial planes are built to sustain a lightning strike and that what we'd seen is called *ball lightning*, which usually dissipates without causing harm. When the plane landed, we all filed out in silence. No one thanked us for flying Delta.

A few weeks after that storm, Jerome and I backpacked into the Ellicott Rock Wilderness and made camp on the banks of the Chattooga River at the spot where Georgia, North Carolina, and South Carolina converge. As we dropped down into the river gorge, there were signs of a storm brewing, but we kept going, thinking we would have time to set up camp before the rains came and not thinking at all about the thunder and lightning that almost invariably accompany rain in the spring and summer in those parts. Several hundred yards short of our destination, the thunder began to roll, and by the time we reached the bottom, the storm was so violent that there was no way to stretch a tarp, let alone pitch a tent. We stashed our packs in the shelter of a rock and looked around for cover. We were surrounded by giant old-growth hemlock and hardwoods fanning out in all directions. There was no way to get more than a few feet from a very tall tree. Okay, Ken, what do I do now? I conjured up his response:

"You're already down in a gorge, and the lightning is hitting high above on the ridge. Just calm down, try to keep your pack dry, and wait it out." The lightning may have been hitting high on the ridge, but judging by the simultaneous thunder, it was directly overhead. I couldn't calm down. In fact, with every strike I cringed and clung to Jerome and tried to crouch even lower to the earth as bursts of light illuminated the sky and thunder roared through the gorge. There was no way to choose life. Life would have to choose us.

The storm that I weathered perched on the side of that mountain in New Mexico subsided after about thirty minutes. Soaked to the skin, I struggled back up to the path to join the others just as they emerged dry and comfortable from under the rocks.

"Melissa, it's okay to do it your way. You go by the rules," John said with a twinkle in his eye. "I just talk to the thunder gods. Remember, they bring the water that renews." And the fire that kills, I thought.

When the group disbanded early in the afternoon of our third day together, I packed up, drove almost two hundred miles south, and set up camp outside the Bosque del Apache National Wildlife Refuge. About thirty thousand of the refuge's fifty-seven thousand acres are designated wilderness. I woke early the next morning and entered the refuge just as thousands of newly arrived scarlet-crowned greater sandhill cranes rose into the sky, filling the air with their haunting cries, soon to be joined by squadrons of snow geese. On one side of the sky were the four-foot-long cranes, their wings spreading out to six, maybe seven feet. Beyond were the blindingly white snow geese, drowning out the crane music with their loud nasal honks.

About fifteen thousand sandhill cranes and forty-eight thousand geese spend some time in Bosque del Apache each winter.

A few whooping cranes join the sandhills in the annual migration to this place, and I searched the skies hoping to see the five-foot-tall white birds I'd looked for the year before in Aransas. Once again they eluded me, and at the visitors' center I learned that the efforts of the wildlife biologists to save the whoopers in this area have failed. Only five arrived in 1993; three plus one hybrid came in 1994. The repopulation project had been abandoned. In the fall of 2000 one lone whooper came to Bosque del Apache.

That evening I sat quietly at the edge of a large meadow. Eyes closed, ears alert, I opened my spirit to darkness, flight, sound, and life. The combined energy of birds in flight washed through me with a force like that of the thunderstorm I'd braved a few days before. When I opened my eyes, the light of the setting sun had turned white plumage to gold, and as darkness fell, thousands of birds sank to the ground to sleep.

More dreams of home. Still I resisted. I was hungry for one more journey in the wilderness. Driving south from Bosque del Apache on Interstate 25, I turned west toward Silver City, then north again, and drove forty-four miles up a narrow, steep road to the Gila Wilderness. In 1924, under the leadership of Aldo Leopold, more than half a million acres of the Gila National Forest became the first legally protected wilderness in the world. This eventually led to the passage of the Wilderness Act in 1964.

A few miles into this remote place, I lost all signals on the radio. The road dead-ended at the edge of the wilderness where a primitive Forest Service campground faced the broad flats of the Gila River Valley. There was no charge for staying there and, in fact, no sign of an official presence, no bulletin board with notices warning of mountain lions or bears, no list of rules indicating the number of campers allowed in a site or the beginning and end of quiet time.

The only other campers were two women who seemed to have settled in for a while. They had pitched a fair-sized tent, strung a clothesline, and set up easels. It turned out both were artists, and when I first arrived they merely nodded and went on painting, as if it was the most natural thing in the world for two women to be capturing this wild place on canvas. I assumed they didn't want to be disturbed, which was fine with me. I'd come here for one last dose of solitude before going home.

I chose a site about a hundred feet away from the women and set up my tent in shirtsleeves, relishing the warm sun on my skin. Then I set off for a short hike to explore the valley and nearby cave dwellings. When I returned to camp in the late afternoon, the temperature began to drop. Before sunset I put on a sweater, then a jacket. Finally I added a Gore-Tex parka. With gloves and a wool hat I was almost comfortable when darkness fell.

Since the women were packing up their outdoor studio for the night, I called over and asked if they'd like to join me for a cup of tea. They did, and later that night, after cooking my own dinner, I joined them around their campfire for hot chocolate and talk. The temperature was dropping rapidly, the fire was in an existing fire ring, and I decided this was not the time for a lecture on the damaging effects of fire. They told me how they'd saved enough money to live on the road for a year and then quit their jobs—Joy was a teacher and Faye a police officer—in order to paint full-time. As long as they lived in free national-forest campgrounds like this one, they had plenty of money for art supplies, gas, and food. They needed little else. Just before we said good night, a large black panel van pulled up and parked on the edge of the camping area. No one got out, and we couldn't see who was inside.

By dawn the temperature had dropped well below freezing. I boiled water for tea and ate a granola bar before setting off for my first foray into the Gila Wilderness. With a day pack filled with emergency supplies and enough food and water to last until late afternoon, I walked up the river valley toward the wilderness entrance. Since I was alone and there were no other signs of morning hikers, I decided to stay on established trails and go in only as far as I felt comfortable. That turned out not to be very far. Shortly after I passed the sign—"GILA WILDERNESS"—marking the boundary of the vast wild lands beyond, I began to notice evidence of extensive grazing. There were cow droppings everywhere and in places the land had been grazed bare. Then I heard the first shot. I froze. Why hadn't I remembered that hunting season had begun? The Gila was, after all, an ideal hunting ground. I looked down at my clothes—olive-green pants and sweater and a sand-colored vest. More gunfire. I didn't know whether these hunters were after deer or elk or something else, but I was determined not to be mistaken for whatever it was. There was nothing to do but turn around and retrace my steps as fast as I could.

On the way out I met a ranger who told me about some places where I could hike safely out of the range of hunters. There are always hunters in the wilderness during the season, she told me, but most of them are careful and obey the rules. "That's a lot more than can be said about ranchers who have permits to graze cows in the wilderness," she added, explaining that they bring in more animals than permits allow and overgraze the land, causing a lot of damage. I emerged from the wilderness to another round of gunfire, then silence. I spent the afternoon hiking in areas near enough to the road to be safe from hunters.

That night the lone occupant of the black van joined Joy, Faye, and me at our campfire. Carlos told us that he was a photographer and that he was here to take pictures of the Gila. He, too, had forgotten about hunting season. Carlos told us nothing else about himself and evaded all the direct questions. He seemed anxious and worried that someone might be pursuing him.

"Anybody driving an unmarked van with Texas plates is suspect in this part of the world," he said. "They think I'm running drugs in from Mexico. I'm here taking pictures, but I don't want people to know about that either. I have to be very careful."

Except for one beat-up Nikon, I never saw any camera equipment. He left early and came back late, presumably after storing lenses and camera bodies in the windowless part of the van. A nervous man, Carlos chain-smoked and avoided eye contact. I had no reason to believe or not to believe his story, but I never felt threatened. More than likely, Carlos was there to take pictures of the Gila. For whom and what I'll never know for sure. Probably he just wanted to be left alone to do his work, and he was surprised to find three women in this remote spot at the end of the road.

Early the next day I hiked up to the nearby Gila Cliff Dwellings, a national monument. To avoid day visitors who might make it to this remote spot, I started early to ensure solitude. The trail leads up a narrow canyon cut over millions of years by the small creek that still flows there. High on one side of the canyon are six caves, where some forty or fifty Pueblo people of the Mogollon culture lived in homes built with stones and mortar more than seven hundred years ago.

In the cold morning air I sat near the edge of one of the rooms and looked across at the sand, yellow, and gold colors of the canyon wall and down some three hundred feet. I tried to imagine how the men and women who lived in these rooms had protected their children from falling, how they had entered the tiny doors to their dwellings burdened with a deer they had killed or corn and squash they had grown in the nearby wide valley of the Gila River.

I was still sitting in that spot when the morning sun warmed the cave enough for me to peel off my jacket and soak up the penetrating rays. It would be another flawless day—cloudless, no sign of the thunder gods. I closed my eyes and thought back into the more recent past—to bears snuffling outside my tent in Wyoming, the cry of a mountain lion in the Olympic Peninsula, whales breaching the gray waters of the Inside Passage, a lone grizzly intently foraging for food in Yellowstone. Then I saw a rowboat crossing the Rio Grande into Mexico in total darkness, heard the roar of an avalanche high in the Cascades, felt my skin prickle all over in the wilds of Oregon, and tasted fear in my mouth as I inched across a slickrock ledge high above Lost Canyon in Utah. I opened my eyes in the golden light of a room where the ancients had lived.

I had not really planned to hike deep into the Gila Wilderness, hunting season or not. It's far too dangerous to go into such a place alone, mainly because something as simple as a broken leg could be curtains. In order to tear myself away, I made a promise to return with a backpack filled with supplies enough for several days and at least one companion who knows the wilderness. There were no grizzlies in the Gila, but there were and probably always will be people with guns. Risk in such places, as in our own backyards, is unavoidable. I could minimize that risk by staying out of the woods during hunting season, but in the woods, as in the city, there was no way to ensure safety.

Exactly ninety days had passed since I'd left home in early August, and in less than a week I'd be back at home again. I'd spent seven of the last fifteen months on the road or in wild places. I'd separated myself from all the old pulls, and I'd learned to go where I felt drawn to go. I realized that it was time to go home and stay put—for a while.

I knew that the first few weeks after I returned would be busy with friends and family—a visit from Laura, a party for my father's eighty-fifth birthday, family dinners for all, and visits with a few friends. Jerome and I, I hoped, would begin to create a new life— slower paced and more focused on what really matters to us. For me, that would involve finding my place in the world of wilderness preservation. I was ready to do my part.

I also knew that after the first few weeks, the hard part would begin as I worked to integrate what I'd learned in the wilderness into the messiness and unpredictability of everyday life: to live more simply and to spend time with people whose interests overlapped with mine and who fed rather than drained my energy. For work, I wanted only what I could do well at a leisurely pace and with passion; for friends, no more than I could enjoy in mutually rewarding ways; for love, husband, family, and the few friends who cared for my welfare as much and in the same way as I cared for theirs. For community, all the people that I joined in common undertakings. For home, all the places that I love and want to protect.

When I went away for the first time, home was Georgia. It was the mountains, the swamps, and the woods where I roamed; the house where I grew up and the one where Jerome and I raised our children; it was a cotton field, a pine forest, and the garden where I drink my coffee on spring mornings. As I prepared to return, I realized that in the months that I'd been away, home had expanded to encompass a glacial moraine high in the Cloud Peak

Wilderness in Wyoming, a river clogged with spawning salmon in Alaska, and this sun-drenched cave dwelling on the edge of the Gila Wilderness.

Sitting quietly, I understood how loving a place is the first step to making it home. A person, I thought, looking out at the morning glow on the canyon walls, could fall in love with far less. But just as I had to limit the number of people I truly loved, I also had to draw boundaries around the places that I would love. Loving is meaningless until it turns into action, and that morning I knew that in the time I had left on this earth, there was only so much I could do, only so much I could love. It was time to choose with care.